The Nature of Asian Politics

The Nature of Asian Politics is a broad and thematic treatment of the fundamental factors that characterize politics in the fourteen key countries of Southeast and Northeast Asia. Bruce Gilley begins with an overview of state-society relations, then moves on to the fundamental questions of development and democracy, and finally shifts to an exploration of governance and public policy in the region. This book proposes an Asian Governance Model that is useful for understanding politics from Japan to Indonesia. By reviving an earlier paradigm known as "Oriental despotism" and applying it to political theories about the Asian region, this book is likely to attract wide debate among students of Asian politics and among Western policy makers seeking to engage the region.

Bruce Gilley is a leading international scholar on the comparative and international politics of Asia and China and an expert on questions of democracy, state building, and political legitimacy. He is an associate professor of political science and the director of the doctoral program in public affairs and policy in the Mark O. Hatfield School of Government at Portland State University. His books include *The Right to Rule* and *China's Democratic Future*. His research articles have appeared in journals such as *Comparative Political Studies*, *Environmental Politics*, and *Political Science Quarterly*. He serves on the editorial boards of the *Journal of Democracy* and the *Journal of Contemporary China*.

The Nature of Asian Politics

BRUCE GILLEY

Portland State University, Oregon

CAMBRIDGE
UNIVERSITY PRESS

32 Avenue of the Americas, New York, NY 10013-2473, USA

Cambridge University Press is part of the University of Cambridge.

It furthers the University's mission by disseminating knowledge in the pursuit of education, learning, and research at the highest international levels of excellence.

www.cambridge.org
Information on this title: www.cambridge.org/9780521152396

© Bruce Gilley 2014

First published 2014

A catalog record for this publication is available from the British Library.

Library of Congress Cataloging in Publication data
Gilley, Bruce, 1966–
The nature of Asian politics / Bruce Gilley.
pages   cm
Includes bibliographical references and index.
ISBN 978-0-521-76171-0 (hardback) – ISBN 978-0-521-15239-6 (paperback)
1. Asia – Politics and government – 21st century. 2. Democracy –
Asia. 3. Democratization – Asia. 4. Political culture – Asia. I. Title.
JQ36.G55   2014
320.95–dc23   2014009739

ISBN 978-0-521-76171-0 Hardback
ISBN 978-0-521-15239-6 Paperback

For my children, Julia and Jasper, who will write their own stories

Contents

Figures

Tables

Preface

While visiting Indonesia in 2011, the premier of China proclaimed: "We are witnessing the all-round rise of Asia and a great rejuvenation of Oriental Civilization."[1] The claim was notable but not because of the first part. The "rise," or "awakening," of Asia has been anticipated or announced with regularity since Japan defeated Russian forces in a series of skirmishes on land and sea in 1904 and 1905. That event ushered in a period in which both Asians and non-Asians alike argued that the region was in the ascendance.[2] The rise of Asia is an old story, and it is a reasonably accurate one as well.

Rather, it was the second part of the declaration that was interesting: the definition of an "Oriental Civilization" that spans the eastern half of Asia from Beijing to Jakarta. In the early 1900s, this region was considered the core of Asia. China's premier seemed to be saying that whatever divergences it witnessed during the twentieth century, it was again converging on a common Asiatic heritage. It was a claim that the region, which is often referred to as Northeast Asia and Southeast Asia, or just East Asia, is both internally coherent and globally distinctive. Peking Man and Java Man, those ancient human ancestors whose lineages begat the peoples of the East Asia, were making common cause.

What is Asia and what, if anything, makes it distinctive? There are cultural, social, economic, and political dimensions to this question. My focus here is on the political dimension, broadly defined. The aim of this book is twofold: to describe and explain the essential facts of politics in Asia; and to use these findings to inform contemporary debates about politics in general. While a better understanding of Asian politics is inherently worthwhile, there is no reason why the experiences of one-third of humanity should be confined to the region itself.

Two great intellectual debts are important to note. Substantively, Lucian Pye's *Asian Power and Politics* of 1985 remains unsurpassed as an interpretation of the political sociology of Asia. It is the sort of book that has withstood the test of time. In the decades since its publication, the study of Asian politics has exploded. As a result, it has become more difficult to integrate findings. One key aspiration of this book is to make a claim about what we have learned about Asian politics as a whole since Pye. This task is different for different chapters. The literature on economic development (Chapter 3) and democracy (Chapter 4) on Asia is vast, and the challenge here is to beat a pathway through a very thick jungle. By contrast, the literature on state-society relations (Chapter 2), governance (Chapter 5), and public policy (Chapter 6) is remarkably sparse, and the challenge here is to create and integrate these subjects into the understanding of Asian politics.

In pursuing a broad interpretation of Asian politics, I have found myself moving freely between grand narratives and comparative statistics on the one hand and often very fine-grained stories on the other hand – the Malacca Sultanate; the rise of Taiwan's Shinkong Group; Indonesia's democratic transition; the Narita Airport protest movement in Japan. Sometimes long excursions on the ground can illuminate the landscape better than can broad surveys from the mountaintop. Throughout, I have extensively footnoted the text to highlight what I believe are the major works on various subjects.

More prosaically, this book owes its inspiration to Goran Hyden's magnificent synthesis and meditation on African politics, entitled *African Politics in Comparative Perspective*, first published by Cambridge University Press in 2006. Hyden's work strikes me as a rare treat in our hyperspecialized world. It is both accessible and far-reaching, as well as solidly social scientific and comparative. While using it in the classroom, I wondered what a similar book on Asian politics would look like. Cambridge University Press was equally curious. My answer is in your hands.

I owe special thanks to Benjamin Reilly of Murdoch University and Andrew MacIntyre of Australian National University, kingpins of Australia's unrivaled Asian politics assemblage, for encouraging this ridiculous enterprise in its early days. I also want to acknowledge the faculty, students, and staff at my cozy home institution, Portland State University, which manages to achieve so much despite its modest resources, mainly because of a remarkable will to excel.

I

Introduction

Around the year 1400,[1] a dispossessed Sumatran prince fled his home at the tip of the Malay Peninsula to establish a new kingdom farther north along the narrow strait that connects the South China Sea to the Indian Ocean.[2] The new settlement was named after the melaka trees that grew abundantly along the estuarial rivers of the region. The calm and fine port, with its favorable winds, moderate temperatures, a well-protected harbor, and expansive flat land, soon attracted traders. Within a decade of its founding, Malacca contained 6,000 people.

Malacca stood at the confluence of several great and enlightened kingdoms of early modern Asia. On the western periphery was the resplendent and enlightened new Mughal empire of India. To the south was the declining but still impressive Javanese Majapahit kingdom. To the northwest was the powerful new Ayutthaya, or Siam, kingdom of the Thais. And looming over the northeast was the culturally confident new Ming dynasty of China, which would lead a resurgence of Asia's cosmopolitan and oceanic traditions.

Every year from October onward, Chinese junks arrived at Malacca on the northeast monsoon winds carrying brocades, silks, satins, porcelain, and copper for transshipment to India and Europe. Ships also came from the Ryukyu Islands (the string of islands that link Japan and Taiwan) carrying silver and porcelain. After they set sail for home with the coming of the westerly monsoon in April, other ships would arrive from India and Europe bringing iron, textiles, glassware, opium, vermilion, and quicksilver. "Gold was so plentiful that children played with it," noted one contemporary observer.[3] The Chinese were expected to bring gifts, while the Indians paid a 6 percent tax on the value of their shipments. From elsewhere in the region, merchants arrived hoping to tap into this East–West trade. The Acehnese, for example, brought nutmeg, pepper, mace, cloves, camphor, and sandalwood. Because of the changing winds, goods had to be off-loaded and stored at Malacca, which happily took its cut. Local merchants sold fruits, meats, sugar, honey, beans, fish, and vegetables to the sailors, and guarded their stores. Taxes were low and trade was easy.

By the end of the 1400s, Malacca was Southeast Asia's largest city, with 50,000 to 100,000 residents.[4] The Lisbon doctor Tomé Pires, who visited from 1512 to 1515, counted eighty-four languages spoken in the city. Even the Malaccan sultan himself and his chief minister, the Bendahara, traded for their own accounts but only in competition with others. China's attempt to keep all foreign trade in the hands of the region's states – the Ming dynasty's Bureau of Maritime Trade had been established for this purpose in 1403 – was slowly undermined by Malacca's free-trading ethos and abandoned in 1435. In a letter of 1468 proposing trade relations to the ruler of the Ryukyu Islands, the Malaccan sultan wrote that "to master the blue oceans, people must engage in commerce and trade."[5] The notion that national security came not from owning guns but from trading butter was not uniquely Asian. But it came to be practiced more successfully and widely in Asia than anywhere else.[6] As Pires wrote: "Malacca is a city that was made for merchandise, fitter than any other in the world.... Whoever is the lord of Malacca has his hand on the throat of Venice."[7]

The authority of the Malaccan sultans was built on several sources: their lineages, which could be traced back to sultanates in Sumatra; their embrace of Islam in the middle of the century, at which point they became "God's shadow on Earth"; and the traditional Malay concept of *daulat*, roughly translated as "sovereignty." Despite their authority, the Malaccan sultans were not despots. An explicit pact of consent, a *bersumpah-sumpahan*, or "solemn oath," was formed with a representative of the people under each sultan. A section of the Laws of Malacca written between 1422 and 1444 outlined the duty of a ruler to his people and his relationship to his ministers.

The Malacca Sultanate had bureaucracies managing trade and taxation; detailed maritime, property, contract, criminal, and marriage laws ("A man who recovers a sampan carrying goods must be paid either one-third or one-half of the value of the goods in it, depending on whether the sampan was visible from the shore at the time of recovery"[8]); protocols for royal audiences; and institutionalized complaint and court systems. Malacca's laws were copied widely by other kingdoms in the Malay-Indonesian archipelago.

Besides the Bendahara, there were three other chief ministers and an exact structure of eight ministers, sixteen deputy ministers, and thirty-two district chiefs. Specialized officials called *Syahbandars* were appointed to deal with the shipping and warehousing concerns of each major ethnic group trading in the port, and they were usually drawn from the ethnic group itself. They also looked after orphaned children. A Committee of Ten determined the value of each ship's cargo in the presence of the Bendahara for the purposes of taxation. Periodic raids were launched against pirates operating from nearby Singapura in order to keep sea lanes open and safe. "The King of Malacca deals kindly and reasonably with [sea-traders], which is a thing that greatly attracts merchants, especially foreigners," wrote Pires.[9]

Malacca also ran a shrewd foreign policy. The international relations of Asia in the 1400s looked remarkably similar to those of ancient Greece. Malacca's founder had been hounded out of Singapura by an alliance of vassal states of Siam, and he had in turn allied with others for protection. But, as with the ancient Greek world, putting too conflictual a gloss on this world overlooks its remarkable peacefulness, especially under the dominating presence of the Ming. The Malaccan court paid lip service to Chinese greatness by hosting the official fleets of the Ming court under the Chinese Muslim Zheng He and by sending embassies to Nanjing and then to the new Ming capital at Beijing. It also promised to keep the straits free of pirates. In return, ships that transited at Malacca were given preference when they arrived in China.[10] China also promised protection against Thai and Vietnamese aggression. The Ming emperors decreed Malacca to be a "kingdom" (*guo*) and its ruler a "king" (*wang*), integrating both into its expansive universal system of order, in which there were no boundaries (*wu wai*). Malacca was given an inscribed stone tablet to set atop a mountain recognizing its special status as an ally of China (an honor given only to Malacca, Japan, Brunei, and Cochin, the last of which is in today's southern India). In private, however, the Malaccan sultans considered themselves the moral equals of China's emperors. One local myth told of a Ming emperor who contracted a terrible rash after mistreating the sultan. He was cured by bathing in water that had been used to wash the sultan's feet.

At the same time, Malaccan sultans sent regular tribute as well as Indian textiles to Ayudhya, the Siamese kingdom on which its rice supply depended, unbeknownst to the Chinese. (Meanwhile, the Chinese were also stopping off in Siam on their way to Malacca to engage in similar hedging diplomacy). Indeed, the Siamese also listed Malacca as one of their dependencies. The Malaccans happily prospered from their status as friends of both. Closer to home, the Malaccan sultans maintained their own subregional tributary system, providing honors and support to allies in smaller trading ports up and down the strait. The emphasis of the Malaccan sultans was on ensuring domestic peace, governing well, promoting prosperity, and avoiding conflict.

Malacca was the most famous and influential of a series of "port polities" that emerged in Asia, beginning with Srivijaya on the southeastern coast of modern-day Sumatra, which had become a flourishing port around 670 AD. The key to state building in those that succeeded, argues Hall, was not massive, centralized power but "networked linkages" among different ethnic communities, trade routes, religious traditions, and regional allies.[11] Even after European colonization, the port-based model of political organization continued to dominate the region. "Imperial capitals-cum-emporia" arose in an arc that covered the modern-day cities of Shenyang, Nagasaki, Shanghai, Xiamen, Manila, Hoi An, Bangkok, Saigon, Singapore, and Rangoon.[12] They became cosmopolitan regions that bridged India and China, as well as the inland agrarian and coastal trading communities. Local governments emerged here on the basis of the trading economy and were instrumental to it. The intensive trade relations created an "Asian Mediterranean" of Northeast and Southeast Asia.[13] "Southeast Asia and southern China, linked by the seas, become part of the same canvas of interaction as well as of a cohesive trade network that also came to include southern Japan and the Ryukyu Islands," wrote Lockard.[14]

The Malacca Sultanate lasted for slightly more than a century. In 1511, the Portuguese overthrew the Sultanate with the help of Tamil textile merchants and the crew of five Chinese junks anchored in the harbor. This city of "much profit and great honor," as Pires described it, was seen by the Portuguese as a place of commerce, mission, and empire. The captain of the newly built Malacca Fort was appointed directly by the Portuguese king, but for the most part the Portuguese allowed the governance of the "non-Christian" population to carry on much as before. A local Bendahara continued to act as chief minister, a local chief Syahbandar continued to manage the port, and a local Temenggung continued to govern the Malay population. Technical positions were filled by Flemish, German, Italian, and Dutch specialists, giving rise to an enduring Eurasian population in Malacca. One Portuguese official commented disapprovingly that his miscegenating colleagues "have more relatives in Gujarat than in Tras-os-Montes."[15] The city was at its most swashbuckling in this era, thriving by day and dangerous by night (visiting merchants always slept on their ships for safety). St. Francis Xavier, who visited Malacca three times while on his way to China and Japan, wrote scathingly of the laxity of the Portuguese administrators.[16]

The Portuguese were evicted from Malacca in 1641 by the Dutch after a brutal five-month siege that reduced the population through death and flight from 20,000 to just 2,000.[17] The young Dutch jurist Hugo Grotius's justification of Dutch tactics in the war for Malacca formed the founding principles of international law.[18] The Dutch considered Malacca to be a strategic as well as economic site. But as the Chinese had done, they wanted to monopolize its trade under their government, in this case through the Dutch East India Company. Locals were subject to an array of taxes, directives, and prohibitions on their economic activities. Fishermen were forbidden to sell their catch directly to ships anchored in the harbor and were forced to bring it to the central "market," where the best catch had to be sold to Company staff at a fixed price. Company authorities limited the number of junks from China to one or two per year, hoping to steer more trade to their headquarters in Batavia. As a result, trade increasingly left Malacca for other ports – Aceh, Johor, Kedah, and then later Penang and Singapore. By 1698, the Dutch governor would refer to Malacca as "more a place of necessary residence and garrison than of trade."[19] The population had recovered to only 5,000 by 1700, and a large proportion of it was now Chinese, whom the Dutch saw as more industrious and obedient than the Malays or Indonesians. Bugis pirates from Celebes (in present-day Indonesia) cut off access to the straits and laid siege to the city in 1756. One Company official concluded: "We are deadly hated by all nations."[20]

In 1795, the British, whose ships had come to dominate the straits, took control of Malacca from the demoralized Dutch as part of a diplomatic deal between the two countries.[21] Reflecting their primarily commercial interest in Malacca (their military base was at Penang), the British in 1807 blew up the 300-year-old fort built by the Portuguese, lest it fall into rival hands. "The gunpowder exploded with a noise like thunder and pieces of the fort as large as elephants were blown into the air and cascaded into the sea," recalled one Malay observer.[22] The British commercial focus served the port well, and the population swelled to 68,000 by 1860. As in other parts of Asia, European colonialism was developmental in Asia (and extractive or minimalist in Africa) because the precolonial political structures and norms made it so.[23] Rubber, coconut, tapioca, and rice became the source of its new prosperity. The Dunlop Rubber Company was founded here, and it went on to become synonymous with tires and tennis balls. The resident British councilor described Malacca in 1895 as "a favorable example of a prosperous agricultural district where crime is almost unknown and the people are happy and contented."[24] By 1921, Malacca's population had climbed to 153,000.

British rule and local prosperity gave rise to a class of local notables, including one of Malaya's most important constitutional reformers, Tan Cheng Lock (1883–1960), who was known as "the Sage of Malacca."[25] A successful businessman, Tan was a member of the appointed legislature of the British Straits Settlement from 1923 to 1934. There he argued for an inclusive and democratic Malayan state that would be distinguished by its education, industry, and enlightenment. He founded the Malayan Chinese Association in 1949 as the Chinese arm of the broader independence movement. A fervent anticommunist, he believed that property ownership was the key to democracy. His son would become minister of finance in the new Malaysia.

Prior to independence, however, Malacca was overrun by the Japanese, who occupied the port from 1942 to 1945.[26] They began by executing hundreds of Chinese teachers and shopkeepers suspected of sympathies with the anti-Japan movement in China (Tan Cheng Lock fled to Bangalore). Thereafter, the occupation was administered by a moderate and competent Japanese governor, Tsurumi Ken, who spoke fluent English. The city was said to be the best place in Malaya to lay low during the occupation. The bridge across the Malacca River that had been destroyed by retreating Australian soldiers was rebuilt, and schools, mosques, temples, and churches were reopened. Tsurumi organized several academic conferences on Islam and Malay traditions. The Japanese ideal of discipline and a new Japanese-led Asian order appealed to many Malaccans, who hastened to enroll their children in the local Japanese cadet school. The local consultative committee was composed of seven Malays, five Chinese, two Indians, and one Eurasian. Tsurumi was given a rousing local send-off when he had to flee the return of European colonialists in 1944.

In 1948, Malacca, now with 239,000 people, was absorbed into a new British Malayan Federation that included all of the Malay states except Singapore. It was in Malacca in 1956, on a field in front of the British Colonial Club, where the nationalist leader and first prime minister, Tunku Abdul Rahman (who had a succession of Chinese, English, and Malayan wives), announced an agreement with London for an independent Malaya. The official car used by Rahman in the 1957 independence ceremony is still on display in Malacca.

As one of thirteen states in the newly independent Federation of Malaysia after 1963, the broadly delineated State of Malacca enjoyed a genteel existence. Government-built free trade zones and industrial estates, along with schemes for agricultural land expansion and a new focus on tourism, helped growth. State-led development in Malaysia – especially the opening up of inland agricultural areas and the creation of infrastructure along the coastal corridor from Penang to Singapore – benefited Malacca. State politics was always boisterous, owing to the opposition's long-time strength there.

Today, tourism, retirement, and medical services (especially for wealthy Indonesians) are growing industries, along with higher education, computer parts, oil and gas refining, and food processing. The Malaccan government launched an initiative in 2011 to develop "extreme aviation sports for youth" to "help mould the young to have a strong personality, mentally and physically."[27] Malacca was declared a world heritage site by the United Nations, which called it a testament to "a living multi-cultural heritage and tradition of Asia, where the many religions and cultures met and coexisted."[28] The government held celebrations of "500 years of Portuguese culture" in 2011.

The ideals and institutions of the "aristocratic-administrative class" created during the Malacca Sultanate have exerted a profound influence on Malaysian and Asian history. The notion of powerful administrative states led by competent and benevolent rulers is a template for Asian political culture. In the 1980s, Malaysia's rulers explicitly invoked the Malacca Sultanate as a model for political harmony and legitimacy, suitably updated to incorporate state-led development.[29] As Malaysia's postwar ruling coalition broke down, it sought to revive the country's sultans as "protectors" of the nation.[30] An Institute for History and Patriotism Research was established by the Malaccan government in 1999 to promote the Sultanate's achievements. The Sultanate, wrote one anthropologist, "is represented as prosperous, dominating the trade routes of the region, respected by outside powers notably China and Siam, and internally harmonious despite its widely diverse population."[31] Some see the Malacca Sultanate as the origin of Asian regionalism.[32]

Today, Malaysia remains as close to a "typical" country in Asia as there is. It is middle-income, semi-democratic, developmental, and cosmopolitan, and it marches to a mixture of indigenous cultural values and Chinese business interests. A trip to Kuala Lumpur is the best one-stop visit to Asia. Moreover, the Straits of Malacca have returned as the central focal point for regional politics and trade. A resurgent Chinese empire seeks an accommodation of its interests alongside the current representative of European civilization, the United States. Both are striving to be the protective suzerains to which Asian rulers pay tribute. Meanwhile, the countries of the region play them off one another and continue to profit handsomely.

RECLAIMING THE FAR EAST

What is Asia? In common parlance, Asia is the region formed by the roughly north–south axis that joins what were the ancient kingdoms of Southeast Asia, especially those of Siam and Java, with the celestial empires of Northeast Asia, especially those of China and Japan. This is what geographers call East Asia, or what used to be called the Far East. It is a region centered on seas, as shown by the coastal locations of virtually all its major cities, as well as the wide dispersion of its major ports. This means that its societies and politics have long been trade-oriented and cosmopolitan. To be more specific, Asia includes fourteen major countries divided into three clusters (see Table 1.1): the *northeast cluster* of China, Japan, North Korea, South Korea, and Taiwan was most directly influenced by successive Chinese empires; the *Indochina cluster* of Thailand, Cambodia, Vietnam, Laos, and Myanmar arose within the competing sphere of Thai kingdoms; and the *littoral southeast cluster* of Malaysia, Singapore, the Philippines, and Indonesia emerged within the Malay-Indonesian cultural sphere. (The region also includes the micro-states of Brunei and East Timor, and the China-controlled cities of Hong Kong and Macau). Vietnam is the most *geographically* central country of Asia, and it looks the part with its dour Confucian northern capital of Hanoi and its vibrant southern trading city of Ho Chi Minh (Saigon).

Asia thus defined makes up one-third of the world's population, with 2.2 billion people. Even without China (1.4 billion people), the other thirteen countries hold 800 million people, more than Latin America or the Middle East, and roughly the same as sub-Saharan Africa and the West. Unremarkable for their populations in the Asian context, Indonesia, Japan, the Philippines, and Vietnam would be gigantic presences in any other region. The region now accounts for one-third of the

TABLE 1.1. *Countries of Asia by Population and Income*

Country	Capital	Population (m)	GDP Per Capita (US$)
Northeast Cluster			
China	Beijing	1,361	9,055
Japan	Tokyo	128	35,855
South Korea	Seoul	50	31,949
North Korea	Pyongyang	25	1,900
Taiwan	Taipei	23	38,357
Indochina Cluster			
Vietnam	Hanoi	89	3,788
Thailand	Bangkok	68	9,503
Myanmar	Nay Pyi Taw	64	1,612
Cambodia	Phnom Penh	15	2,395
Laos	Vientiane	7	2,847
Southeast Littoral Cluster			
Indonesia	Jakarta	245	4,923
Philippines	Manila	96	4,380
Malaysia	Kuala Lumpur	30	16,794
Singapore	–	5	60,799

Note: Figures for 2012.
Source: International Monetary Fund.

global economy; half of that comes from China, which holds a larger share than any other region except for the West. Defense spending in Asia now exceeds that of Europe, and the region is a key locus of global economic and political power.

Asia is wildly diverse as a region. A simple survey of comparative levels of economic, political, and cultural indicators shows that compared to five other regions, Asia is the most varied in terms of its regime types, development levels, and state capacity, and also has a more diverse mixture of both culturally homogenous and culturally heterogeneous populations (see Figure 1.1). By contrast, the West is made up of very homogenous states, which is perhaps one reason it has been so hospitable to grand theorizing.

Asia has been variable across time as well as place. The common patterns of liberal Western, autocratic Middle Eastern, revolutionary Latin American, and predatory African politics of the post–World War II era have arguably changed less than the uncommon patterns of Asia have.

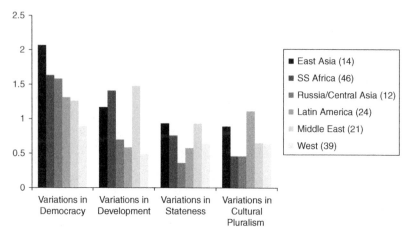

FIGURE 1.1. Diversity by region.

Notes: Democracy: Combined Average Rating, 2009, Freedom House; Development: GNI per capita, 2009, US$ PPP, World Development Indicators; Stateness: Average of Government Effectiveness and Political Stability, 2009, World Bank Governance Indicators; Cultural Pluralism: Cultural Fractionalization Index. Standard deviations for the two interval variables (democracy and stateness), coefficients of variation for two ratio variables (development and cultural diversity). Countries with populations above 500,000 only.

Asia has witnessed above-average development in ten out of fourteen countries (the exceptions being the Philippines, North Korea, Cambodia, and Myanmar) compared to developing countries as a whole, as well as dramatic changes in regime types or constitutions in ten out of fourteen countries (the exceptions being Singapore, Malaysia, North Korea, and Japan). Liberal, autocratic, revolutionary, and predatory waves have come and gone throughout the region.

Given this diversity, it is no surprise that Asia has been the source of many of the most enduring social theories that stress difference, uniqueness, and fine detail. Anthropologist Clifford Geertz developed the concepts of "thick interpretation" and "local knowledge" of social phenomena while pondering the cultural and social nuances of things such as cockfighting and funeral rites in Indonesia.[33] Political scientist James Scott originated the idea of "hidden transcripts" behind public claims to power in his studies of Malaysian paddy farmers.[34] The study of China and Japan, meanwhile, has been dominated by a belief in their unique civilizational features, traits that political scientist Samuel Huntington endorsed in his "clash of civilizations" thesis.[35]

The argument for the coherence of any region rests on three foundations: the existence of a shared geography and history; the intensity of contemporary interactions; and the existence of a shared identity. In all three respects, the fourteen countries of Asia form a relatively coherent whole despite their empirical diversity. The story of Malacca highlights the long historical linkages within the region, of which Chinese populations, Eastern Buddhism, and an open trading ethos remain vivid reminders. Since the early 1980s, Asia has caught up to Europe on many measures of trade integration.[36] In services, Asia exceeds other regions in its inward integration.[37] Financial holdings and broader economic integration indicators, such as the synchronization of economic growth, show a surge in closeness, as well.[38] Tourist arrivals within the fourteen states, meanwhile, now account for more than half of all tourist arrivals, converging closely on levels in other regions like Europe and Latin America.[39]

Unlike Europe, however, where integration resulted from political decisions, in Asia integration has happened on its own. The politicians have scrambled to catch up. The "ASEAN Plus Three" grouping that brings together the members of the Association of Southeast Asian Nations with Japan, China, and South Korea reflects attempts to formalize what is already a coherent whole. ASEAN Plus Three is the successor to Japan's World War II–era Greater East Asia Co-Prosperity Sphere and earlier to the Chinese tributary system of 1368 to 1841 that united Northeast and Southeast Asia.

Asia is, like any other region, a "myth,"[40] if the term "region" is meant to imply a coherent, integrated whole. It is a diverse stew of people but one that by virtue of a shared geography has developed several shared cultural and political features over time, which, when reinforced by contemporary economic integration, have given rise to a distinctive regional identity.

In particular, one cannot escape the centrality of China to Asia as a region. China calls itself the "central state," and this centrality has three dimensions. One is the Sinic heritage that pervades the region's culture, society, history, and ethnicities, standing always as the universal, civilized, authoritative, and timeless alternative to indigenous "barbarian" alternatives, as well as to the West. Another is the brute geographic and economic centrality of China to the region. China is the only country other than Japan with intense interactions in all three clusters of Northeast Asia, Indochina, and Southeast Asia. Its economic, demographic, and geographic size makes it the behemoth of the region. Moreover, a rising

China has been the key factor in reigniting the search for a regional view-point about appropriate models, norms, and ideas of political conduct that was begun by Japan. The "China model" is better seen as an articulation of a latent "Asian model," to which China is now contributing.

Within this model, Asia proper excludes the peripheral areas of South Asia, Central Asia, Pacific Island Asia, and Australasia. No matter how much the political elites of India, Mongolia, Fiji, or Australia wish to be seen as "Asian," they are so only in a bureaucratic sense. In the sense that matters – their histories, cultures, societies, and domestic and international politics – they are on the periphery of the contemporary Asian core. Asia proper is centered on the maritime axis that we today call the East and South China Seas.

By excluding India in particular, I do not underestimate the historical connections between India and the Far East. Indian religions and political culture were profound influences that shaped the early development of the region. However, the "Indianization" thesis of Southeast Asia has been the subject of much revision in recent decades, as evidence of pre-Indian polities has emerged. Malacca itself was deeply imbricated in trade with and cultural influences from India, but its identity was no mere fragment of Indian culture. Moreover, Indian influence declined in the region from about the mid-1300s onward due to the rise of powerful new kingdoms in present-day Myanmar, Thailand, Indonesia, and Vietnam; the spread of Islam; and most importantly, the rise of a new Chinese empire under the Ming, which reoriented the region around the Chinese cultural sphere.

More to the point, the Asian core never developed anything like the caste-based social structures or the cellular local political systems of India that made centralized rule so fraught there. Brahmins in India, as Weber noted,[41] did not owe their status to the state or to external conditions that the state could control, and they were thus more akin to the hereditary lords of Europe than to the Confucian literati of Northeast Asia or the religious courtiers of Southeast Asia. India has often been described as a country with "dual systems of power" – the central state on the one hand, and the competing local power holders (*zamindari* landlords, *talukdar* village chiefs, Brahmin and other caste leaders, princely *maharajahs*, and provincial politicians) on the other hand. The joke is often heard that India's national slogan is: "Divided we stand." In Southeast and Northeast Asia, the absence of such caste traditions meant that sacred and secular authority remained one and the same.

Southeast Asia was surely influenced by the Indic tradition through the god-king traditions of Hinduism. But the social, economic, and political affinities of Southeast Asia are today closer to those of Northeast Asia than to those of India. The unified cultural hierarchy, developmental ethos, centralizing and majoritarian impulses, and state-preserving views of rights that, as we shall see, are some of the features of Asian politics put Southeast Asia squarely within the Asian, not Indic, tradition. The "authoritarian leviathans" of Asia are unthinkable in India with its weak state tradition.[42] The rich and enduring traditions of state-challenging social mobilization and activism in India have no equals in Asia. Northeast Asia, meanwhile, not only reshaped Buddhism profoundly, but it also had its own indigenous traditions, in particular Confucianism, which limited the Indic influence.

Asia, thus defined, is both a puzzle and a challenge. While it is easy enough to identify the economic and cultural traditions that make up the region, thinking about the political dynamics within the region is trickier. Given its diversity, it is no surprise that Asia has been particularly inhospitable to grand theorizing. There is a long Western tradition of making sweeping generalizations about the politics of everything lying east of the Danube or the Bosporus – a tradition known as "Orientalism." But as for attempts to make general claims about the actors, institutions, processes, and outcomes of public decision making in the fourteen countries that make up the Far East, there has been a notable absence of material.

Ever since the first generation of books on the region after World War II – in particular Kahin and Hinton's 1958 *Major Governments of Asia* and Macridis and Ward's 1963 *Modern Political Systems: Asia*[43] – the tendency has been to think of the region as impossibly complex and best treated on a country-by-country basis. About once a decade, a major work on the politics of Asia appears.[44] But none attempts a systematic theory about how politics in Asia works. Scholars drawn to Asia are almost always lured by its richness and variety, and they shy away from applying singular theories to explain countries as diverse as Japan and Indonesia. Most works make a few general comments before moving to the more comfortable terrain of country-by-country analysis or richly detailed chapters on particular issues.

By contrast, for those engaged in universal theorizing about politics, the problem with the idea of "Asian politics" is that the category is too narrow, rather than too broad. For universalists, politics is best understood from the perspective of all countries taken together. If there are systematic differences, they may have nothing to do with geography. To put it bluntly, adding the fact that a country is situated in Asia will tell us nothing about the nature of its politics that we could not understand by looking at other variables, like social structure or institutions. It may turn out that, as in Fukuyama's discussion of social trust,[45] Japan is more like the United States, while China is more like Italy.

Neither of these perspectives is necessarily incompatible with taking Asian politics seriously. There are indeed complexities and variations within the fourteen states that require careful identification. Moreover, it is often true that these complexities and variations map better onto certain universalistic explanations of politics than any regional explanations do. But by adding the "Asia variable" to our descriptions and explanations of politics in these states, we can often significantly increase the significance and power of our observations. Asian countries are neither totally outside nor totally inside universal political trends but are rather embedded in them in distinctive ways.

A theory of Asian politics might have predicted, for instance, why China, Vietnam, and today perhaps Myanmar would emerge from their self-imposed isolation in the past. It might explain why the region has had no major conflicts since the winding down of the last colonial wars in Vietnam. It might explain why the North Korean regime has endured and why its future might look a lot like China's. A theory of Asian politics is also important for identifying and explaining outliers from the general pattern of political and economic development and public policies, of which the Philippines is the most frequently cited example.

If understanding is not enough, a more strategic reason can also be offered. In recent years, there has been a growing divergence between the foreign policies of Western governments and those of Asian governments on issues like climate change, human rights, economic and financial systems, and international law. Only South Korea and Taiwan have bucked this trend and remain more aligned with "Western" than "Asian" foreign policies. Selig Harrison warned of this trend in his 1978 book *The Widening Gulf*.[46] Today, as Cold War enemies like China and Vietnam converge on Asian norms, and as even Taiwan and South Korea show signs of drifting away from Western alignments, this gulf is growing. What is needed then is a renewed attempt to understand the forces behind the domestic politics of Asia that manifest themselves in these foreign policy directions. As Feigenbaum and Manning point out: "The reality to which the United States must adapt is that Asians are redefining their region, trying to develop a sense of 'Asian' identity and enhance their clout in the global system."[47]

THE ASIAN GOVERNANCE MODEL

A theory of Asian politics should have three key features. One, already mentioned in the previous section, is that it should be comprehensive of politics itself and distinctive from theories of economic development. It should reach deep into the interstices of political life – from political parties to local government – and it should shed light on everything from military strategy to welfare reform. At the same time, it is important for it to note both divergence as well as convergence. A good comparative theory should allow for *both* comparing Asian countries to the rest of the world *and* comparing Asian countries to each other. Of particular importance here is that a good theory of Asian politics should tell us about how the region compares to other developing regions. Too often, Asian politics is compared to politics in the West, which leads to a series of cartoonish statements about the rational, individualistic West and the exotic, communal East. Yet few of these claims would stand up to scrutiny if Asian politics were compared to politics in Africa, Latin America, the Middle East, or the Indian subcontinent. In order to understand what is distinctive about Asia as a developing region that was colonized by the West, we need to compare it mainly to other developing regions that were colonized by the West, not to the West itself.

Secondly, a theory of Asian politics should have a broad geographic scope. Many works on Asia consider only the "tiger" or "dragon" countries. Jones's excellent 1997 work *Political Development in Pacific Asia* is limited to just six of the fourteen countries (South Korea, Taiwan, Singapore, Indonesia, Thailand, and Malaysia).[48] Zhang's 2003 work *Pacific Asia: The Politics of Development* draws its conclusions from the same six plus Japan.[49] What is notable about these works is not only their exclusion of "non-miracle Asia" – Laos, Cambodia, the Philippines, North Korea, and Myanmar – but also the exclusion of the region's giant, China. These "tiger" works can make the region appear hyperactive and single-minded, leaving out key countries whose interpretive value may be greater.

Specifically, no account of Asian politics can fail to include the historical and civilizational behemoths of China, Japan, Vietnam, Thailand, and Indonesia, nor can they fail to wrestle adequately with the tumultuous and slow-developing Philippines. These are the largest two countries in each of the three subclusters identified in the previous section. Below them, attention must be paid to South Korea, Myanmar, and Malaysia, the "second tier" countries in each subregional cluster. Tiny

Singapore – whose population of 5 million (0.2 percent of the Asian total) is less than that of the Chinese city of Shenyang or the Thai capital, Bangkok – probably should not be taken alone as the basis of grand theorizing, however delightful its politics.

Finally, a theory of Asian politics should be Asian. Asia has long been prone to interpretations from the West (just as the West has been prone to interpretations from Asia) that are essentially contrastive and used for self-reflection and strengthening. There is nothing wrong with this, except that it is liable to exaggerate differences, if not mislead altogether. When we call Asia "illiberal" or "communal" or "developmental" or "market-driven," we are often reflecting more on Western experiences and debates than on Asian realities. While these concepts are indispensable, the aim should be to properly describe the reality of Asia rather than to set up neat contrasts with the West, or with any other region for that matter.

With those preliminaries, this book introduces a broad concept called the Asian Governance Model to explain the nature of Asian politics. Briefly, it argues that Asian politics operates according to a model in which *a state with a widely acknowledged political authority allocates political values in a non-patrimonial manner that advances broadly shared development, internal and external security, and social opportunity through a form of governance that is characterized by the traits of rationality, accountability, and propriety.* All of this needs to be unpacked in the course of this book. For now, the model can stand as an ideal type exemplified by the Malaccan example.

The focus of the Asian Governance Model is both <u>how</u> politics operates and <u>what</u> it achieves. Asia is governed by a variety of regimes, institutions, and public policies. What unites the region and makes it coherent as well as important is that politics in Asia is organized in a way that minimizes governance deficiencies, taking into account available resources. The basic idea here is that the state will deliver economic and social advancement, state and territorial sovereignty, and national and cultural renewal, in return for which society will accord it legitimacy and authority.[50]

It would be wrong to call this a form of "social contract," because the model assumes that states constitute society as much as societies constitute states. But in practice, there is an implicit social contract, and Asian citizens protest loudly when the state violates expectations of good governance. In effect, this book argues that the "Asian social contract" is constituted by the balance between the <u>power</u> of a dominant state that enjoys above-average levels of legitimacy, compliance, capacity, effectiveness, and resilience and a correspondingly above-average set of <u>obligations</u> to behave morally, seek social feedback, and remain internally accountable, reformist, meritorious, and rational. This trade-off is evident in the demands on public leaders in the five areas that constitute the five following chapters – state–society relations, development, democracy, governance (regulation and public management), and public policy.

While this is an ideal type for which one can find many egregious counterexamples in modern Asian history – Mao's China or military-led Myanmar – the contention here is that it remains a largely accurate picture of politics and policy in the region. It shapes the expectations and structures of politics and by implication the options for public leadership. A better parallel for the model than the Rousseauvian social contract would be the Aristotelian idea of rule for the common good rather than rule for the good of a particular individual or group. The general contention here is that Asian states more often govern in ways that serve the common good than in ways that serve particular individuals or groups. As the term "common good" suggests, Asian publics are oriented toward governance models and institutions that avoid sectarian interests. This is grounded in norms of public well-being, which in the Chinese case go back as far as the *Analects* of Confucius, in which the sage instructs his followers to "make them prosperous" and then "educate them," because only then will they know enough to obey virtuous rulers.[51]

Both Court Buddhism as it developed in Southeast Asia and Court Confucianism as it developed in Northeast Asia emphasized the notion of the virtuous ruler (having virtue or karma) and its manifestation in national prosperity and stability. It also put a premium on the nonpatrimonial demands of leadership. There was a common good emphasis, because the ruler was seen not as representing a tribe or group but as a cosmic representative on Earth. Daily governance was then parceled out to administrators and family members in accordance with rites and laws. This can be contrasted to publics in Africa in particular, but also to a lesser extent to Latin America and the Middle East and India, where preferential clientelistic or neo-patrimonial governance in return for political support has long been the norm.

Of course, Asian politics, like politics everywhere, is prone to corruption, misrule, legitimacy failures, dysfunction, repression, favoritism, violence, and internal and external governance failures. Asian politics has also seen its fair share of truly disastrous misrule. But today, taking into account developmental levels, Asian politics is characterized by comparatively less of these things than politics elsewhere, or so I will seek to show. These features are so common in the region that it is worth speaking of a distinctive mode of Asian politics, which I summarize in shorthand as the Asian Governance Model.

This model seeks to crystallize our understanding of the region by drawing on the enduring insights of two main schools of thought about Asian politics. One, *Oriental despotism theory*, has been formulated with respect to the Far East in terms of the predominance of strong and institutionalized states that oversee mobilizational bureaucracies.[52] I will say more about this approach in coming chapters, but what is important here is its emphasis on stability, continuity with the past, the "tyranny of history," and unchallenged rule – military, communist, or otherwise. This means that it has blind spots for change, for the obstacle to reform that the state may represent,[53] and for the social bases of state strength and state-led development.

The other, which I will call *Asian dynamism theory*, conceptualizes the region in terms of a rapid change in political, social, and economic structures as a result of an accelerated modernization drive.[54] The emphasis here is on change, disjunctures in history, and populist rule – benevolent authoritarian, democratic, or otherwise. This approach, by contrast, has blind spots for historical continuities, for the obstacles to stability (or sustainability) that rapid change entails,[55] and for the primacy of the state in social and economic change.

One might say that the problem with both schools is that they ignore politics. The political origins of Asian states and the political origins of Asian dynamism need to be exhumed in order to understand the nature of Asian politics. To fully grapple with Asian politics, we need a model that gives politics a central place. The Asian Governance Model does this by stressing the accountability process through which states in the region grow and operate and by stressing the public policy process through which modernization occurs. It provides a conception of Asian politics with an emphasis on both the continuity of state dominance and the continual change in the ways that state dominance is exercised. The story of Asian politics, in other words, is neither an "Oriental" story of fearsome despots nor a "bourgeois" story of the march of progress but a more nuanced story about the ways that societies and states have mutually reshaped one another through constant interactions.

Doré wrote in his 1973 work *The Political Regimes of Asia*: "There are not two Japans – that of military government and bureaucracy and that of parliamentary government – but just one, whose uniqueness lies precisely in the continuity and rupture of these two types of government. There are not two Chinas – one bourgeois ... and one communist ... – but just one, whose ideology is *both* that of Sun Yat-sen *and* that of Mao Zedong."[56] Working through the implications of that tension will absorb the remainder of this book.

Chapter 2 takes up the relationship between states and societies in Asia. It describes the nature and emergence of the modern states of the region and the societies in which they took shape and continue to operate. Theoretically, this chapter is the natural starting point, because it begins with the Oriental despotism literature as it has been developed and applied to Asia. This literature is closely linked, on the social side, to a category of theories that root this despotism in a distinctive set of social preferences or political culture, which are often grouped today under the rubric of Asian Values. The argument here is that strong states are drawn from distinctive social milieus.

Chapter 3 shifts to the study of economic development. The focus here is on the remarkable and yet still little understood causes of rapid growth and development in many Asian countries. Here, I consider developmental state and Asian dynamism theories, which have been central to explanations of politics in the region. The argument here is that we need to recover the political dimensions of the developmental state and Asian dynamism. The developmental state needs to be understood as an outcome of politics, and its behavior needs to be contextualized within politics itself.

Chapter 4 takes up democracy. The study of democracy provides a key insight into the good governance agenda that is at the heart of the Asian Governance Model. By rethinking democracy in terms of good governance rather than liberal values, we can understand how the Asian region has foiled so many antidemocratic predictions and has democratized smoothly and for the most part successfully. The argument here is that democracy is neither inconsistent with nor central to the model but is instrumentally adopted and reformed in order to serve the goals of development, security, and opportunity. However, the politics of democracy for this very reason remains distinctive in Asia as compared to elsewhere. This chapter considers the important ways in which Asia may be shifting the practice of democracy on a global scale through, for instance, its move to embrace majoritarianism.

Chapter 5 considers the various dimensions of governance, regulation, and public management in Asia. The role of bureaucracy in Asia and its relationships to other parts of the state, like executives, courts, and local governments, is critical and yet oddly understudied. Beginning with the idea of the "bureaucratic polity," this chapter traces how public sector reforms have been embraced and used by these state agents to maintain their dominance while maintaining good governance. The rebuilding of state-society networks has been an important and overlooked aspect of this – an aspect that reminds us of the dynamism of Asian governance.

Chapter 6 then looks at the consequences of Asian politics for public policy, first at a general level and then in the fields of welfare, public works, the environment, and foreign policy. If the study of bureaucracy provides the fine-grained account of how politics works inside the state, this chapter provides a similar account of how it operates in society. This is the "on the ground" view of Asian politics, and it shifts from the more process-oriented approach of political science to the outcome-oriented assessment of policy studies.

I refrain from offering a concluding chapter, hoping that the story will help readers draw their own conclusions. There is much to learn from Asian politics. So let's begin.

2

State and Society

While traveling through the Far East in 1892, the British adventurer Henry Norman happened upon a dusty square in the Chinese city of Canton (today Guangzhou), where he witnessed the public execution of fifteen men. As the condemned were led into position, Qing dynasty magistrates carefully removed from each of their pigtails a long piece of paper that had been held in place by a stick of bamboo on which their crimes and death warrants were written. Then, without ceremony, the executioner's sword was raised. "Chop, chop, chop – the heads roll off one after another in as many seconds," Norman wrote. After each stroke, the crowd roared its approval with a hearty "*Hao!*" (roughly "Great!"). "The place is ankle deep in blood, the spectators are yelling with delight and frenzy, the heads are like bowls on a green, the horrible headless bodies are lying about in ghastly grotesque attitudes, the executioner is scarlet to the knees and his hands are dripping." Although reeling from the spectacle, Norman could not resist thrusting several banknotes into the executioner's hands in return for his drenched sword: "It hangs on my wall today," he wrote, "a valuable antidote to much that I read about the advancing civilization of China."[1]

Today, in the early twenty-first century, the death penalty continues to be legal and practiced not only in China but in a large number of Asian states. Only Cambodia and the Philippines have officially abolished it (although the latter wavers constantly), while Laos, South Korea, and Myanmar have not committed executions since the 1980s. As for the other nine states, the death penalty continues to be both legal and practiced to varying degrees, representing a quarter of the countries in the world where this is the case. In the 2000s, China executed more people than any other country in the world, while Singapore executed more people per capita than any other country in the world.

It is no surprise that the region's most authoritarian regimes – China, Vietnam, North Korea, and Myanmar – are retentionist states, because the threat of violence against citizens is an important part of any authoritarian regime's control. The surprise is that many of the region's developed, electoral regimes – Singapore, Malaysia, Indonesia, Japan, Taiwan, and Thailand – continue executions for various crimes, sometimes very ordinary ones. In all six countries, abolitionist civil society groups have mounted vigorous campaigns, but with limited results. The trend, if anything, has been to affirm the importance of the death penalty. With the notable exception of twenty of the fifty subnational state governments in the United States, no developed region of the world practices the death penalty to such an extent.

For some, this is because of a cultural predilection for vengeance and an uncompromising obedience to power and law in Asia. But the cultural basis for capital punishment in Asia is no stronger and no less contested than it is elsewhere.[2] The story of the death penalty in Asia is not some hackneyed recounting of "cruel Orientals" who "do not value life." Rather, the story is one of dominant states that have slowly, through internal processes, regulated and reduced, while not giving up, the use of capital punishment. It is a story of governance in which the public good is largely defined by executives, bureaucracies, and courts rather than legislatures or civil society.

The death penalty is a key indicator of state-society relations because it is literally the systematic taking of citizen lives by the state, making use of its monopoly on the legitimate use of violence. While democratization and left-of-center political parties have reduced capital punishment in Asia as elsewhere, its decline but retention has more to do with the *internal* dynamics of states – calculations by political elites, technocratic deliberations by public administrators, and careful reasoning by judges – toward the appropriate limits of state power. It has been *predemocratic* motivations relating to governance, not *postdemocratic* motivations relating to the sacredness of life or the rights of man, that have determined the uses of the death penalty in Asia. This contrasts with the European experience, where democratic change and rising human rights discourses propelled declines and, ultimately, abolition of the death penalty.

In the Philippines, for example, executions peaked under the elected presidency of Ferdinand Marcos (1965–72) and then declined steeply in the authoritarian Marcos period that followed (1973–86) before being formally abolished by the first democratic government (1987).[3] In South Korea, both the execution and death sentence rates (annual executions and death sentences as a proportion of the population) declined steadily after the rule of strongman Syngman Rhee (1948–61). As in the Philippines, by the time of democratization (1988) and the coming to power of a left-of-center party (1998), the rates were *already* negligible in South Korea. The same is true in Thailand, where executions declined steadily from about six per year in the 1960s and 1970s to about five per year in the 1980s and then to two per year in the three years leading up to the first democratic transition in 1992. In Malaysia, the number of executions fell steadily under the authoritarian National Front rule – from 0.69 per million in 1990 to 0.04 per million by 2006. This same process of a decline in but maintenance of the death penalty *prior to* democratic transition is now observable in China and Vietnam.

It is hard to attribute these predemocratic declines to international pressures, given that the main patron of many Asian regimes in the Cold War was the United States, not Europe, and Washington rarely pressed them on this issue. Johnson and Zimring note "the weakness of challenges to national autonomy on capital punishment" from the international community.[4] To the extent that external influences mattered, there were probably *intra-Asian* (not Western) ones – in particular Taiwan and South Korea wanting to distinguish themselves from the brutality of their communist rivals.

The main motivation, however, was that state actors increasingly came to believe that capital punishment was not an effective tool of social control and governance. "The main arena for death penalty debates and decisions remains the nation state,"[5] note Johnson and Zimring. In the Marcos period, for example, the authoritarian misuse of executions for political purposes created a backlash from the judiciary. When Marcos had three men publicly executed for a gang rape in 1972, a supreme court justice complained that it had been "shamelessly played in television and radio," creating a sense of "lost self-respect" for citizens and bureaucrats alike.[6] In the 1970–87 period in South Korea (i.e., before democratization), the high court reversed 228 death sentences, 53 percent of the total number reviewed, often because of worries that the regime was misusing the National Security Law aimed at communist subversion. The reversal rate after democratization was only slightly higher – in the 60–70 percent range. In Taiwan, after the "White Terror" decade of communist suppression in the 1950s, executions declined sharply, especially under the reformist president Chiang Ching-kuo (1975–88). In Thailand, the king's increased use of pardons from the 1960s onward was a result not of royal changes of heart, nor of democratic pressures, but of the ability of officials in the Ministry of Justice "to influence the flow of pardon petitions that make their way to the throne."[7]

To be sure, Asia has followed broad modernization trajectories – as countries got richer, capital punishment declined. But the means for this was not the empowerment of civil society or the emergence of rights norms. Instead, modernization operated through the rationalization of governance systems by state actors. Capital punishment, as is well known, does not deter crime, is more expensive than lifelong imprisonment, can easily denude the reputation of a state if exculpatory evidence is later uncovered, and is subject to populist political irrationality (whether by autocrats or democrats). On the other hand, it is often seen as a potent symbol of state power. As a result, public administrators in Asia chose to "retain but reduce." The state of violence became a state of pardons.

Today, in most Asian states, executions have become a "low visibility act of administrative government" rather than a high-profile act of democratic politics or public debate.[8] In Japan, the decision to execute is made by the Ministry of Justice following trial after a long review process, in which the dossier passes through "at least 10 and as many as 20 ministry prosecutors."[9] What's more, in several countries, such as the Philippines, Taiwan, and Thailand, democratization has brought renewed populist pressures to *increase* its use. The Philippines, for instance, briefly restored the death penalty in 1993, a highly unusual reversal in the annals of capital punishment globally. Elsewhere, such as in Taiwan and Thailand, democratization led to temporary upsurges in executions as legislatures and populist leaders became more involved in policy making. Then, when populist sentiments urged moratoriums, executives and bureaucracies pushed back.[10]

As with the broader use of state violence in Asia, then, capital punishment reflects the writ over society that allows governors to choose when and how to implement force with very little social resistance.[11] In a 2010 column on Asia's death penalty exceptionalism, *The Economist* noted: "The issue is not between death-row convicts and the rest of the citizenry but of overweening state power over all."[12] Decision making has been retained in the hands of executive and bureaucratic state actors rather than political parties, legislatures, or social movements.

What distinguishes Asia from the irrational and violent myth of Oriental despotism are the rational and measured ways in which this state dominance has been exercised. Confucius, quoting a Chinese proverb, said: "If excellent people managed the state for a hundred years, then certainly they could overcome cruelty and do away with executions."[13] This idea of "excellent" administrators who gradually reduce executions of their own volition over an extended period is largely what happened in Asia. The "advancing civilization" that Norman mentioned did indeed come to Asia (including belatedly to China itself). But it is the heirs of the Qing magistrates, not the heirs of the hooting crowds or the squeamish foreigners, who brought about the change.

REFINED ORIENTAL DESPOTISM

The relationship between societies and the states that hold absolute ("sovereign") power over them is arguably the central question of politics. It is also the place where we need to characterize Asia accurately by emphasizing *both* the strong state of "Oriental despotism" theorizing and the remonstrative society of "dynamic Asia" theorizing. As Han shows for South Korea, this particular state-society relationship found throughout most of Asia, often reflected in geomantic capital cities that emphasize state-society harmony, is at the heart of the region's politics.[14]

The theme of the strong states of Asia holding overweening power over society is an eternal one in Western conceptions of the region. It emerged as part of a broader tradition of characterizing everything to the east of Europe as some form of "Oriental despotism." Aristotle, whose works were the starting point for these attitudes, concluded that those to the east of the classical world were "always in a state of subjection and slavery."[15] While often tainted by imperialistic or racist concerns, this tradition was based on rational inquiry and drew on empirical evidence that cannot simply be brushed aside as irrelevant or false.[16]

In its canonical formulations, Oriental despotism described a form of politics in which political rule was exercised in an unrestrained and often brutal fashion toward all subjects, irrespective of wealth or rank. Turkey's sultans provided the closest examples to Europe of Oriental despotism and thus loomed large in theorizing about the eastern world. Over a long period, other countries and empires were added, including Persia, Russia, India, and the Mongols. In due time, Oriental despotism found its way to the Far East. Montesquieu wrote at length about China and Japan in his 1752 *Spirit of Laws*, in which he argued that "Asia is that region of the world where despotism is, so to speak, naturally domiciled."[17] Much later, the idea that Asia was the place of the most "natural" Oriental despotism would remain a powerful image. Perry Anderson, for instance, argued in his 1974 book, *Lineages of the Absolutist State*, that genuine political absolutism was best seen in feudal Japan (fourteenth to nineteenth centuries), where ties of kinship dominated ties of law, the lord's authority was hierarchical and unquestionable, vassal courts did not exist, legalism was very limited, and there was no estates system.[18] By contrast, in Europe, rulers were constrained by laws, legislatures, property rights, independent cities and provinces, the church, a hereditary aristocracy, and norms of reciprocity and due process.[19] The *politically* absolutist state, Anderson argued, was a myth that never came into being in Europe but found full expression in Japan.

A similar argument could be seen in Benedict Anderson's classic 1972 study of the Javanese state.[20] There was always an "urge towards the center" in Javanese politics, such that aspirant leaders sought to associate themselves with the long-standing state, not to challenge it. The Javanese word *negari* refers to both the capital city and to the kingdom itself, just as the Chinese word for China, *Zhongguo*, translates roughly into "the central state." In both cases, there is the "center" and then there are the "outer regions" that orbit around it, domestically or internationally. There is no notion of equal centers of power, much less of equal citizens organized into a political community.

While Oriental despotism theory migrated to Asia, it was not blind to the subtle but important differences that distinguished the region from the other parts of the Eastern world. Asian despots, it seemed to writers like Montesquieu and Benedict Anderson, ruled according to customs and by using the language of laws (ruling *through* laws but not *under* laws) rather than through arbitrary choices. They also had more institutionalized political systems in which power was exercised by a variety of agents of the state. Most of all, the results of their actions seemed to serve some widely shared understanding of the common good.

Writers often made use of Aristotle's distinction between despotism and tyranny to highlight what was different in Asia. The despot, while absolute in his power, ruled through laws and bureaucracies according to widely held norms, and he held his position by right of tradition. The tyrant, by contrast, had often usurped power and ruled heedless of norms and laws. As Curtis notes, "Unlike tyranny, despotism did not entail illegal rule over involuntary subjects.... [T]yranny was illegal rule or abuse of power or rule in the interests of a particular person, while despotism implied a legal system of arbitrary rule, appropriate for subjects, and often accepted by them as legitimate."[21]

In Asia, Western observers (including Pires in Malacca) found that rulers were despots but not tyrants. The French Jesuit Jean-Baptiste Du Halde, echoing a half dozen other works by French authors in the 1700s,[22] wrote in his 1736 *General History of China* that there is "no monarchy more absolute than that of China ... but no people in the world have better laws of government."[23] China's rulers, these French authors believed, were absolute but chose to act within laws, customs, and their own sense of virtue. It is this "refined Oriental despotism" that forms the basis of the Asian Governance Model: strong states, acting under norms and laws, govern through bureaucracies and according to a conception of the common good. It is "refined" in the sense of being both more specific and more "civilized," to borrow an old term. As the opening sentence of the Thai constitution proclaims, "May There Be Virtue."

The notion of a "unipolar" or "centripetal" state has also derived from modern studies of Asia. Huang describes a "unity of powers" model that "rejects the idea that government branches should be made antagonistic to one another, sees state institutions as being functionally dependent on one another, and argues that they ought to support each other and collaborate for overall state purposes."[24] While the various arms of the state – military, bureaucracy, judiciary, legislature, and local governments – array themselves around the executive, they are not feckless. Rather, they commit themselves to ideals of a refined despotism. The term "executive-led government" was coined by the British to describe their colonial rule in Hong Kong, but it was then adopted there as a permanent model of *self*-rule after 1997.[25]

A second feature of "refined Oriental despotism" is the deployment of state power for the aim of a common good. A paternalistic or personalistic ruler is one who governs through direct, face-to-face interactions and transforms the public exercise of power into a familial (or patrimonial) framework. This has been the common pattern in Africa with its "Big Man Rulers," Latin America with its left populists, and the Middle East with its military sultans. But in Asia, rulers do not derive their status by doling out favors to special groups, from which they win contingent support. Rather, the norm is benign governance that reflects an ordering of Heaven and Earth – a modernizing vision with a national purpose.[26] In Javanese politics, for instance, "fertility, prosperity, stability, and glory" were the signs that power is being used appropriately – indeed, that it *was* power at all. If the state's power and unity were maintained, "popular welfare will necessarily be assured," Benedict Anderson noted.[27] According to this view, Asian leaders do not aspire to be patrons but national heroes.

While Asian strong state theory has been remarkably resilient, there was a brief dissident literature during the heyday of globalization in the 1990s that wondered if times had changed.[28] Case, for instance, argued in his 1998 chapter, "*Sayonara* to the Strong State," that globalization and domestic modernization had created new constraints on the states of Asia. "State apparatuses have withered, their internal discipline evaporating as memories fade of wartime dislocation, poverty, and nationalist commitment."[29] A similar fear had been voiced by Chinese nationalist leader Sun Yat-sen in 1924, when he worried that China had become "a heap of loose sand," even though in retrospect the Republic of China he created was rather impressive.[30] As with the earlier one, this brief existential crisis was overblown and soon passed. Asian states emerged from the liberalizing and challenging conditions of the 1990s with their power wholly intact.

The widely used World Bank Indicator for "government effectiveness" measures roughly 200 countries on how well they can formulate and implement policies, controlling for levels of economic development that are positively associated with stateness everywhere. If stateness were randomly distributed in Asia, we would expect something like seven countries to be above and seven to be below their group averages. In fact, for 2012, only three of the fourteen Asian countries (North Korea, Myanmar, and Laos) had estimates that were below their income group averages. The other eleven exceeded their group averages, sometimes by very large margins. Going back to the earliest measures in 1996, this pattern is repeated throughout the whole period.

Other measures of state capacity reach the same conclusions. For instance, the "relative political reach" of the Performance of Nations dataset measures the ability of governments to mobilize citizens to be economically active in the formal sector. The measure is relative to development levels and economic structure. Of the nine Asian countries covered by the study, only Japan is (slightly) below average.

While the strong states – like Malaysia, Vietnam, and South Korea – may not surprise us, what is notable is how often the supposed "sick men" of Asia – the Philippines, for instance, or Cambodia – prove to be remarkably capable states when properly compared to others. Country specialists of both tend to emphasize their shortcomings.[31] But given their levels of economic development, both are remarkably robust. In 2002, Philippine President Gloria Arroyo pledged to build a "strong Republic" with "the capacity, represented through strong institutions and a strong bureaucracy, to execute good policy and deliver essential services."[32] This reflected a drive in both countries to converge on the strong state models they see elsewhere.

A different argument applies to North Korea (and to a lesser extent Laos). While Pyongyang is certainly a disastrous *government*, it is inaccurate to call it a weak *state*. Indeed, the tragedy of this country has been the brutal ways that the state has been all too sovereign over society. North Korea has managed two successions in the Kim dynasty thanks to its Leninist political institutions, and it firmly imposes its boot on society in both economic and social matters. What really distinguishes North Korea from its Asian counterparts is that it does not advance the common good. To be sure, it is the poor governance record that irritates the leaders of Asia rather than the poor rights record. The line between a civilized despotism and an uncivilized tyranny is nowhere more apparent. Only Myanmar truly embodies a weak (albeit far from failed) state.

The remarkable fact, then, is that there are no weak states in Asia comparatively speaking, with the possible exception of Myanmar, which has begun to take the path to reform. While development levels determine the absolute capacity of any state, Asia enjoys a "stateness premium" that development cannot explain. Moreover, this pattern is true in Southeast Asia as well as Northeast Asia. Living in the shadows of the Confucian Leviathans, Southeast Asian states have often been portrayed as weak.[33] Yet in comparative perspective, they are as likely to fit the ideal type of the Asian strong state as those to the north are. Both Malaysia and Singapore, for instance, have been described as Weberian administrative states,[34] while Thailand and Indonesia have been described as "bureaucratic polities."[35] In addition, Southeast Asian states, like those of the north, use state power to advance a common, rather than particularistic or neo-patrimonial, end. As Kuhonta has noted of Indonesia under Suharto (president from 1967 to 1998), which was long painted as neo-patrimonial by country specialists,[36] the state had technocratic and growth-promoting features that meant "personal whim had to be constrained."[37] Political institutions like the army, party, and courts developed an autonomy and coherence under Suharto that would outlive the dictator himself. "The weight of scholarship leans toward conceiving of the Suharto period as somewhat more institutionalized than patrimonial," Kuhonta writes.[38]

The extension of the enduring ideal of the strong Asian state is the enduring ideal of the unified state. In Asia, only Malaysia is a federation, with some political powers, like land and agriculture, constitutionally vested in thirteen state governments. But even here the constitution gives precedence to any central laws that conflict with state laws, and in practice state autonomy is limited because of the electoral dominance of UMNO and its control of most economic resources.[39] Elsewhere, experiments in federalism in Myanmar (1947 to 1974) and Indonesia (1949 to 1950) were terminated when they were seen to be causing political looseness. Federalism is a rarity everywhere, accounting for only 24 of the world's 161 major states, or 15 percent.[40] But Asian states would be expected to have *more* rather than *fewer* federations, given their huge populations and vast internal diversity. Even in gigantic China, federalism has never been a serious option and was extended to Hong Kong in 1997 only by virtue of a 1984 treaty with Britain. In general, Asia has a strong aversion to the idea of federalism because of the implication of a divided state.[41]

Throughout Asia, local governments enjoy various abilities to administer, share, or assume the authority of the central government (which we return to in Chapter 5). With economic and political modernization in the 1970s and 1980s came pressures for putting more authority into the hands of efficient and responsive local governments. Important acts of devolution occurred in Cambodia, Thailand, Vietnam, China, and the Philippines,[42] and most of all in newly democratic Indonesia.[43] In the analysis by Blume and Voigt of the distinctive ways that central governments can dominate subnational governments, Malaysia, the Philippines, and Japan all have relatively undominated local governments compared to global averages, the former because of formal federalism and the latter two because of an intentional deference to local government traditions.[44] In these countries, the central state shares de facto powers with local governments. Of the others they study, South Korea and Indonesia are relatively typical in their central-local powers, while China and Thailand are relatively centralized. The Asian states they do not measure – North Korea, Cambodia, Laos, Vietnam, Singapore, Myanmar, and Taiwan – are well known for their centralized politics.

While administrative centralization is on the decline in Asia, the "localization of power" has not generally caused a "loss of power" by the central state.[45] The *decentralization of government* (meaning the delegation of executive priorities to local governments) has not led to *decentralized governance* (a loss of initiative and control by the central state to autonomous local governments, civil societies, or parliaments). The *norm* of centralized state power transcends the *institution* of decentralization.[46] Indonesia, for instance, undertook in 2001 the region's most radical decentralization, which placed authority for all but religion, finance, foreign affairs, defense, infrastructure, and justice in the hands of local governments and set out a clear revenue-sharing structure. Nearly 2 million civil servants were transferred from the central government to districts and municipalities, along with authority over more than 40 percent of government expenditures and more than 60 percent of the national development budget.

Despite this, the Suharto-era technocrats in Jakarta continued to exert remarkable control over government. In bypassing the country's thirty-three provinces (which were dismissed as colonial relics), the decentralization was a way to divide regions into relatively powerless units – the powers were held mainly by the roughly 400 districts (*kabupaten*), or cities (*kota*), with half a million people each. A Ministry of Regional Autonomy was abolished after only one year. Taxation powers remain mostly in Jakarta, especially those of income tax and value-added tax.[47] The implementing regulations and revisions to the laws, meanwhile, reclaimed residual and overarching powers for the various central ministries, in forestry and mining for example. These recentralizing tendencies were justified as a response to *ontonomi kebablasan* ("over-acting autonomy") by local governments.[48] Vice President Megawati Sukarnoputri, eldest daughter of the nation's founder, Sukarno, who was obsessed with unity, warned early on: "Can you imagine if we (the nation) disintegrate? We'll have to raise our own flags, sing our own anthems and may well have to have our own militaries."[49] In 2010, President Bambang Yudhoyono reminded the nation that "although we have adopted decentralization, we remain a unitary state and the president is the head of the government." The official news agency added: "President Yudhoyono asked all regional leaders to better comprehend the unitary state concept in order to avoid mistakes in implementing regional autonomy."[50]

In Cambodia, another alleged model of decentralization, the ruling Cambodia People's Party (CPP) and the central Ministry of the Interior used World Bank and UN funding after 2001 to strengthen their control over local governments by putting power into the hands of 1,600 elected local communes, 75–90 percent of which were held by CPP governments. Those communes in turn chose the higher-level local councils that exercised control, in effect locking opposition parties out of local governance in rural areas, where the CPP's support was mainly based.[51] As Huang notes of Asia as a whole, decentralization "has not diminished the dominant role of central government, much less the dominance of state institutions."[52]

Despite the rapid changes of the 1990s and 2000s, then, including globalization, democratization, and two major economic crises, the Asian strong state has survived. It is by now a highly refined version of Oriental despotism – indeed, so refined as to be nearly beyond recognition. The Asian Governance Model is a more appropriate concept for modern Asian states and how they rule. The question remains: What explains this overarching power?

MONEY, COLONIALISM, WAR, AND WATER

For Aristotle, the combination of hereditary rule and law-based precedent explained the endless succession of Oriental despots.[53] But this "constitutional" theory never fit the case of Asia, because hereditary rule was uncommon and formal laws did not emerge in the region until much later. Instead, a variety of nonconstitutional explanations have been offered to explain the strong states of Asia.

For economically minded thinkers, strong states emerge because they extract a lot of money from society.[54] Indeed, effective public finance has been a hallmark of the Asian strong state, as evidenced in the Malacca Sultanate's precise and carefully enforced taxation regime. In China, the history of the state can be read from the sophistication of public finances – the ways in which the central government taxed the population and shared out the revenues among its various levels and branches. From the Tang dynasty onward, fiscal reform was the trademark act of an emperor reasserting his control over the empire. In the late Ming, for instance, a "single whip" tax was introduced to consolidate all exactions on peasants into a single fee, greatly simplifying administration, reducing corruption, and alleviating resentment.[55] The Ming maintained a special library of population and land records on a series of small islands in the middle of a lake in Nanjing from 1381 until 1644 for the purposes of taxation, a library of 700 storage rooms with regular ferry service and a team of four doctors to look after archive staff.[56] In world history, it was the public finance equivalent of the great classical libraries of Alexandria and Cordoba. Then in the Qing, a "fire," or "meltage," fee was established, in which local governments won a fixed portion of national taxes every year to finance their activities, thus solving local fiscal crises and reducing corruption.[57]

The rise of so-called "fiscal states" in early modern Asia from Java to Japan reflected the development of complex, specialized, rules-based political orders.[58] But while public finance can explain *how* Asian states emerged, it cannot explain *why*, because for the most part the bulk of wealth remained in the hands of society, not the state. Truly extractive fiscal states were more common in Europe, which may in part explain its more rapid development. Oriental despotism in Asia was characterized by relatively light taxation, which is consistent with the distinction between despotism and tyranny. Even today, compared to other states with similar economies in terms of structure and level of output, Asian states tend to confiscate *less* economic wealth from their societies than elsewhere (see Chapter 5). Of the nine of our fourteen states included in a study of "relative political extraction" (government revenues compared to other economies of similar structure) for the year 2007,[59] only Thailand had (slightly) above-average extraction. The average score for Asian countries was 0.68 (where 1.0 is average) – nearly a full standard deviation *below* the average. Singapore, despite its state strength, confiscated barely anything from its society in comparative perspective. In other words, the writ of Asian states over their societies is not dependent on economic extraction.

Colonialism, Japanese occupation, and the Cold War have also been cited to explain Asia's strong states. These external pressures, it is argued, motivated political elites around the region to seek new ways to reinvigorate traditional political structures.[60] For example, in Thailand and Japan, which were not colonized, political leaders of the late nineteenth century launched extensive reforms to create modern bureaucracies, legal systems, and development policies. Vu, for instance, has described how local elites stepped into the power vacuum left by retreating Japanese soldiers in 1945 to repress dissent and centralize new state apparatuses.[61] The Cold War, then, seemed to reinforce these colonial and Japanese pressures to "catch-up" to the developed world through state building. Kim writes that "national survival and national development, most urgent tasks for the East Asian states in the course of colonialism and the Cold War, necessitated the concentration of power within one center, be it monolithic party, personal ruler, or some oligarchic power center."[62]

Yet if colonialism, occupation, and the Cold War are responsible for the strong states of Asia, why did those same historical forces not lead to strong states in Africa and the Middle East? While it is important to understand how these factors shaped and propelled Asian states, the critical origins of stateness in Asia must be found elsewhere, if for no other reason than that these factors are not unique to the region. Indeed, the fact that Western observers have been wondering about the causes of the

strong states of Asia since long *before* the colonial period tells us that this
phenomenon has origins that lie much earlier.

As the Malacca Sultanate example reminds us, political order is by no
means a modern phenomenon in Asia. Sandwiched between the ancient
political orders of China and India, much of the region developed administrative specialization, law-based rule, and effective political orders long
before other developing regions, not to mention much of Europe itself.
Javanese, Sumatran, Siamese, Annamese, Chinese, Japanese, Malayan,
and Korean political orders grew and complexified through regional
borrowing. The sprawling Hindu (later Buddhist) Angkor Wat temple of
the Khmer kingdom built in the early 1100s has figured prominently on
the flags of every Cambodian government of the country since a French
protectorate was established there in 1864 – French, monarchic, communist, Vietnamese, and democratic – with the exceptions of the brief
occupations by Japan and the United Nations, who did not see themselves as indigenous rulers. Around 1600, prior to European colonization,
Asia was ruled by the Ming dynasty in China, the Tokugawa shogun-
ate in Japan, the Le dynasty in Vietnam, the Yi dynasty in Korea, the
Ayudhya kingdom in contemporary Thailand, and the various Buddhist
and Islamic kingdoms of the Malay-Indonesian archipelago. All of these
represented political formations with armies, administrations, laws, and
borders. The Ming ascendancy after the fall of the Mongols in China
in 1368 marked the beginnings of the Asian renaissance in world history, a renaissance that was only briefly interrupted from perhaps the
mid-eighteenth century until the conclusion of the wars in Korea (1953)
and Vietnam (1975). By contrast, in Africa tribal and kinship loyalties
were never replaced by political authority, while in Latin America and the
Middle East, Europeanized state structures always had limited reach over
indigenous societies. Asia is the land of Leviathan. Whereas state violence
against society in other parts of the world has always been an "instrumental" act to establish state authority over rival social groups, in Asia
state authority has usually been taken for granted. Instead, state violence
has been "exemplary" and has been used by state leaders to establish new
modes of governance by making an example of victims.[63]

The further question then is: What led these long historical processes
in the direction of state strengthening in Asia? One common explanation
has to do with warfare – namely, that constant warfare forced states
to organize armies and bureaucracies, which in turn strengthened their
domestic sovereignty. Yet this bellic model does not fit the Asian case at
all. While China, for example, fought constant battles to guard its frontier

against Central Asian peoples (and fell to their rule under the Yuan and Qing dynasties), the periods of state building in the Han, Tang, Song, and Ming took place during times of peace, not war. Moreover, in the rest of Asia, major wars between states (although not civil wars) have been rare historically. Asia has always been a zone of relative peace, including over the last forty to sixty years. Malacca, we should not forget, reached its zenith without any wars to speak of.

Myanmar is the only state in the region that fits the bellic model, having been founded and run by the military in a series of wars.[64] Yet this has made Myanmar the only *weak* state in the region. The same was true of South Vietnam and the Republic of China on mainland China (both cases of states that *failed* as a result of war). In Malaysia and the Philippines, by contrast, anticommunist, counterinsurgency operations that could have weakened the state were relatively minor, never allowing military actors to supplant civilian ones or to redirect state priorities from development to war.

One deeper explanation concerns geography and climate. The German scholar Karl Wittfogel, borrowing from Marx, argued in 1957 that the irregular patterns of rainfall in Asia meant that large-scale irrigation projects (rather than farm-based irrigation or dependence on regular rainfall) were the most efficient means of organizing agriculture. The projects included not just agricultural irrigation but also flood control, navigation canals, and drinking-water reservoirs. This prompted the creation of the strong state in China, India, and Thailand – the first of these being "the dominant center of power and cultural advance in Eastern Asia."[65] The careful counting and record keeping of the Chinese state, which was a direct result of its hydraulic works, formed the foundations for the strong state, Wittfogel argued. This strong state was then emulated elsewhere in the region, in particular in Japan and Indonesia. Japan escaped becoming "Western feudalism with wet feet" by absorbing Chinese cultural influences that *transformed* its decentralized farm-irrigation state into a centralized hydraulic state.[66]

The strong Asian state became an "apparatus" in Wittfogel's view, meaning that it could dominate society rather than be dominated by society: "The hydraulic state prevents the non-governmental forces of society from crystallizing into independent bodies strong enough to counterbalance and control the political machine."[67] Yet as he argued, acting on hydraulic conditions and then diffusing them to others depended on particular *cultural* conditions and *political* choices. This is why strong hydraulic states failed to take root in Latin America, Europe, or the Middle

East. In other words, hydraulic states arose from culture and politics. The real puzzle of world history is why some societies *chose* to embrace hydraulic despotism. "[M]an proceeded not as a passive instrument of an irresistible and unilinear developmental force but as a discriminating being, actively participating in shaping his future.... There were recognized alternatives and those who were faced with them were able to make a genuine choice."[68]

More generally, if money, colonialism, war, and water cannot explain the Asian strong state, it may be because these explanations ignore the cultural contexts in which political decisions were made. States cannot be separated from the societies they rule, if for no other reason than state leaders are drawn from society and take with them many of its presumptions. To explain Asian states, we need to understand Asian societies.

THE LEGITIMACY PREMIUM

It may seem ironic to explain Asian strong states that dominate societies as being a result of those societies themselves. Yet in a sense, this is the *only* explanation that can work, for it is the relatively limited "struggle for authority" in Asian countries (something, as mentioned in the previous section, that may be less true in Myanmar and perhaps the Philippines) that signals what is distinctive about Asian strong states: Their claims to rule enjoy an unusual degree of *acceptance* by society. They enjoy what can be called a "legitimacy premium," meaning an unusual degree of being treated as the rightful holders and exercisers of political power.

The notion of Asian states enjoying a high degree of popular acceptance goes back to Aristotle, who wrote that "Asians ... tolerate rule by a master without any complaint."[69] In Boulanger's 1761 *Research Into the Origins of Oriental Despotism*, it was the religious status of the political order that led to an "idolatry" of rulers.[70] Yet like all classical Oriental despotism theory, these works contained only half-truths applied correctly only half the time. To find the emergence of a precise theory of *legitimate* Oriental despotism, one has to fast forward to the modern era, beginning with Weber.

For Weber, the peoples of China and Japan considered their political orders "as eternally given, and so the best of all possible worlds." The reason was that these political orders had taken shape before the emergence of independent peasant or bourgeois classes, such that there was no "pariah intellectualism" (of the lower classes) or "petty bourgeois intellectualism" (of the urban middle classes) to develop "an original attitude toward the meaning of the cosmos." In China "there is no independent, unofficial intellectualism" outside of Confucian scholar-officialdom.[71] As a result, China and other Asian states with similar political cultures enjoyed "an established belief in the sanctity of immemorial traditions" or of "age old rules and powers." The only rebellion possible in such a system was rebellion against an iconoclastic ruler who had violated the traditional basis of the state's right to rule. One could have a "traditionalist revolution" to restore the old order. But the old order itself, as constantly interpreted and modified by acknowledged prophets, remained legitimate. In China, there was a cult of officialdom in which "high mandarins were considered magically qualified."[72]

The Weberian notion of legitimate Oriental despotism has exerted a profound and enduring effect on the study of Asian states. In the study of Southeast Asian states, Heine-Geldern introduced the idea of "the cosmological basis of state and kingship," in which individuals were expected to conform themselves to the natural order embodied by the rulers, who were most attuned to the nature of the cosmos.[73] Likewise, in his classic chapter on the Javanese state, Anderson argued that there was an "urge towards the center," such that aspirant leaders sought to associate themselves with the long-standing state, not to challenge it.[74] In a parallel theory, Schwartz argued that Asian countries were unique because of the "the supreme jurisdiction of the political order in all domains of social and cultural life."[75] This jurisdiction was maintained not by a state religion but by the "religious status of the political order" that was taken to represent the link between Heaven and Earth. Citizens held a "positive evaluation of hierarchy and status" and considered all legitimate social norms and groups to emanate from the political order.

India notably did *not* fit this profile, Schwartz argued, because its modern state had jettisoned Hindu religious order, the traditional basis of authority, which now represented an alternative pole of authority. In Europe, too, the Catholic Church and Roman legalism put limits on the reach of the state. To these examples one might add the role of ethnic groups in Africa, of Islam in the Middle East, and of revolutionary idealism in Latin America. The Ottoman sultans, archetypes of Oriental despotism, were constantly challenged by the autonomy of Islam.

In traditional Asian conceptions of power, the right to rule is assumed. At the same time, the duty to rule well implies that there are good and bad ways of exercising that right (in particular, the need to assure widespread prosperity, stability, and virtue), and potential usurpers of "the way" face expulsion. Confucius averred that "if the people have no

confidence in their rulers, there is no standing for the state," suggesting
that an illegitimate state was not really a state at all.[76] Just as Asian
strong states had an authority lacking elsewhere, they (usually) maintained and used that authority with far more restraint than classical
tyrannies had. McCarthy's *The Political Theory of Tyranny in Singapore
and Burma* contrasts the just despotism of Singapore with the unjust tyranny of Myanmar, noting how Singapore's ruling People's Action Party
has enjoyed widespread legitimacy, while Myanmar's military rulers have
not (and have thus sought reform).[77] Oriental despotism is legitimate in
Asia as long as rulers assert the traditional relationship between state and
society. In other words, legitimacy both created and constrained rulers.
Montesquieu argued that the confiscation of goods was more common
in Europe than in Asia because in the former there was always the protection of the law to limit the abuse of this practice, whereas in the latter
there was not: "The magistrates themselves would be the greatest oppres-
sors" in Asia, and thus "the prince checks his own power."[78]

Because state primacy in Asia is widely acknowledged and civilizational
in nature, it is rarely imposed. The state is dominant but not intrusive or
abusive. Oriental despotism in Asia, in its ideal form, is a *legitimate* despotism, not an imposed one. The modern concept of the state exercising
a "monopoly of coercion" over society is better understood in Asia as a
"monopoly of culture." Indeed, its most notable feature is a benign governance – a tendency to allow markets and society to operate freely within
a framework of assumed control and the assumption of a duty to guide,
but not remake, society. Rulers, Schwartz notes, aspire to be free from
the burdens of day-to-day management, their status as holders of the
Way (*dao*) or Mandate of Heaven (*tianming*) being their most important
"policy issue."

What is notable about Asia, as opposed to, say, the ancient political
orders of the Middle East or Africa, is that these traditional legitimacy
assumptions survived colonialism and modernity. Traditional political
orders were revamped and updated with modern notions of technocratic
rule, state-led development, and modern public administration. Asian
states tapped the benefits of global society without losing their traditional
legitimacy. There was no "Things Fall Apart" in Asia, only a "Things
Revamped along Modern Lines." As Kahin wrote in 1958 regarding
Indonesia:

The idea of individual and state activity harmonizing with the cosmos, so vital to
pre-European and particularly pre-Islamic Indonesia, is not dead today. Although
certainly much less influential now than in the past, it is of greater significance in

the individual and political lives of present-day Javanese than most Westerners are aware. The important contemporary residue of this sort of thinking is still the widely revered idea of harmony – harmony with the forces of nature, harmony within the political community – and conversely the conviction that inharmonious conduct is a disruptive force which society should rightly frown upon.[79]

Pye in 1985 argued similarly that the inheritance of colonial political institutions by deferent political cultures had created a potent combination of enduring legitimacy:

Asians have grown up with the state as though it were a normal part of their world, like their other social institutions. Thus most are routinely socialized to accept without question the sovereignty of their governments ... [In the West] legitimacy is usually thought of as residing in the public as a check on their rulers ... [but] legitimacy has generally been defined in Asia by those with the greatest pretensions of power.... [T]he establishment of the nation-state as the basic framework of politics and government has not weakened, and indeed in many cases has strengthened, the ideals of paternalistic authority.... [T]he demand for unity and conformity has been translated into unquestioning patriotism.... The modernization of Asia is thus going to emphasize state authority.[80]

In the period of political and economic liberalization that swept through Asia in the 1980s and 1990s, Asian legitimacy theories, like Asian strong state theories, were questioned. Indeed, the assumption that legitimacy was on the *decline* in Asia gave rise to the first explicit literature on the subject itself. The 1989 Tiananmen Massacre in China, for instance, set off a wave of theorizing about "legitimacy crisis" in China.[81] A parallel trend could be seen in studies of Southeast Asia.[82] Compton argued that Asian states needed to reconstruct their legitimacy along modern (market-oriented and democratic) lines. "The role of the state will change and probably diminish," as will "the cultural foundations of legitimacy," he predicted.[83] The fall of Suharto in 1998 seemed to confirm the depth of this change.

Since the late 2000s, however, Asian legitimacy premium theories have been resurgent.[84] In China, the heavy keel of state legitimacy unexpectedly righted the ship of the Chinese Communist Party, despite the gale of 1989.[85] The CCP was now an "organizational emperor" of legitimation. In Indonesia, too, scholars found an unexpected relegitimation of the state, despite the storm of 1998.[86] Election-related political crises in Taiwan, the Philippines, and Thailand in the 2000s seemed *not* to upend the state but to reaffirm its centrality. As Dressel and colleagues wrote in 2011: "[H]ierarchical world views (e.g. paternalism, bureaucratic decision making) are deeply entrenched. These hierarchical world views help shape the distinct ways in which politics is conducted in the region."[87]

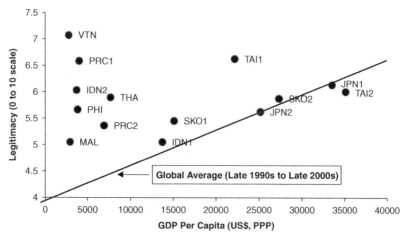

FIGURE 2.1. The Asian legitimacy premium.
Notes: Pooled sample; $n = 124$, $r^2 = 0.33$, p|t|=0.000.
Source: GDP per capita from IMF World Economic Outlook Database, various; legitimacy scores from Gilley (see n. 88).

In Weberian terms, the political storms of the 1980s through the 2000s in Asia were "traditionalist revolutions," in which corrupt and over-reaching rulers were chased from their thrones on the advice of prophets and state intellectuals seeking to introduce new modes of rule. Genuine kings in appropriate raiment returned, and Asian states recovered their accustomed place in society with minimal challenges. According to this interpretation, the 2009 opposition victory in Japan over an increasingly corrupt and incompetent Liberal Democratic Party signaled a "traditionalist revolution" against the postwar American order. The voter turnout for the 2009 general elections was 69 percent, the highest since single-seat districts were introduced in 1996. After the great Tohoku earthquake and tsunami of 2011, there was even evidence of a resurgence of emperor-centered nationalism and *tenno*-ism. When the LDP returned to power in 2012, it had been suitably chastened.

Is the Asian legitimacy premium empirically provable? The answer is yes, according to two separate studies by this author (see Figure 2.1).[88] In both cases, legitimacy was conceptualized and measured for a large number of states – seventy-two in the first study of legitimacy around 2000 and fifty-two in the second study around 2008 – using both survey questions that asked citizens to evaluate their support for the state and behavioral indicators of things like tax-paying, political exclusion, and political violence. In both cases, the legitimacy of states was compared to their development levels and their democracy levels, because these factors are associated with more legitimacy in all countries. In the first study, around 2000, there were no Asian countries that suffered from lower levels of legitimacy than would be predicted from their development or democracy levels and several – notably China and Taiwan, but also the Philippines and Indonesia – that enjoyed much higher legitimacy than would be expected. In the second study, ca. 2008, the pattern repeated: No Asian countries suffered from legitimacy deficits and several – China, Indonesia, Thailand, Vietnam, and Malaysia – over-legitimated.

Neither of these two measurements included five of the fourteen states: Singapore, North Korea, Cambodia, Myanmar, and Laos. However, there is no reason to suspect that legitimacy in authoritarian Singapore and Cambodia or in autocratic and underdeveloped North Korea and Laos is significantly less than what would be predicted from their development or democracy levels. Indeed, a significant amount of literature on these states concerns the surprising ways in which they have been able to legitimate their rule despite dramatic performance failures. In the case of Cambodia, whose flag telegraphs hierarchy and order with the Angkor Wat complex at the center, two scholars concluded that challenges to the state "in Cambodian society have to compete with extremely powerful values which are mobilized to support the organizational principle of hierarchy."[89]

Thus, compared to the rest of the world, Asian states enjoy more legitimacy than expected. What has survived from medieval times is a predisposition to think of the state rather than society as primary, in sharp contrast to the attitudes in the West, Latin America, and Africa. Explaining the "apparatus" of strong states in Asia rests on this high degree of *normative* acceptance, something that cannot be reduced to geography, colonialism, economic calculation, or warfare, much less to some nefarious conspiracy of "false consciousness." The final question, then, concerns the origin of this acceptance.

HEGEL AND ASIAN VALUES

Javanese, Siamese, Khmer, Chinese, Korean, and Japanese political orders go back at least to medieval times. They were sophisticated, "civilizational" orders in the sense that they had detailed rules, high degrees of specialized state functions, and comprehensive, internally coherent written ideologies of interpretation and legitimation. As Asia legitimacy premium theories imply, state strength came from culturally and historically specific assumptions about the primacy of political order, such that states developed in a way that eliminated rival sources of authority, like religion, social tribes, castes, local elites, or law. Asia became temperamentally the zone of Leviathan, although it was one imbued with reciprocal obligations on rulers to deliver collective well-being. Why?

Bentley argues that the political transformation of Asia was possible only because of a prior *cultural* transformation that overtook the region as a result of a distinctive confluence of the traditions of cosmology and realpolitik of Buddhist (and derivative Hindu) India mixed with the centralizing and organizational traditions of Confucian China.[90] Throughout the region, Buddhism and Confucianism formed the cultural presumptions that generated reverence for the state. In Confucianism, the notion of "harmony" (*hexie*) between state and society maintained by the "virtues" (*daode*) of the rulers and the ruled has been central to both ideological claims and ideological education in Asia, and not just within the Sinic sphere. Islamic (Indonesia and Malaysia), Buddhist (Thailand, Cambodia, and Laos) and Christian (Philippines and South Korea) countries have all embraced a version of the Confucian ethic, although usually under the label of national culture. The distinctive "political theology" of Asia is one in which religion, rather than a political agenda, prostrated itself before political order.

The transformation of Confucianism and Buddhism from doctrines of the individual to doctrines of the state is a long and complex story.[91] Over time, both lost their faith in the people and placed their hopes in rulers. This "secularization of the magical concepts of moral and cosmic forces ... [meant] that power became identified with the legitimacy of the existing social order," writes Pye.[92] In their manifest forms, they deterred society from taking an active interest in politics, while at the same time tasking rulers with the onerous responsibility of uplifting the nation (assuring social harmony, peace, virtue, and prosperity). Both Confucianism and Buddhism became unusually accepting of the legitimacy claims of rulers.[93]

In China, there was a noisy debate as late as 1916 about whether Confucianism should be made the state religion.[94] Confucianism's sacrilization of the state, emphasis on harmony rather than pluralism, and assertion of rule by the few put it squarely outside of Western liberal traditions. In Chan's words, Confucianism "has always been concerned with political legitimation and compliance."[95] The revival of Confucianism throughout Asia in the 1990s, especially in China,[96] served mainly, in Chan's words, "to serve the traditional role of providing legitimacy."[97]

Likewise, Buddhism's lack of a social-improvement impulse and disinterest in worldly affairs meant that it was highly vulnerable to co-optation and control. It also tended in Asia to amalgamate with national cultures – Nat Worship in Myanmar, Shinto in Japan, Confucianism in China – that supplemented the state's national integration agenda. In combination with the elitist court traditions of Brahmanism, this created a dynamic of "dependent" subjects owing loyalty to virtuous and blessed rulers.[98] Buddhism, Kitigawa writes, "only asked for protection, support, and freedom, and never embarrassed the state by voicing ethical judgments regarding political issues."[99] It was declared the official religion of the Siamese Ayutthaya kingdom in 1360, a decade after the kingdom was founded, and a community of Buddhist monks was imported from Ceylon to serve as venerators of the throne. After a "traditionalist revolution" against an increasingly decadent King Rama VII in 1932, a new, "modern" constitution was written that affirmed the king's central status and the necessity of his being a Buddhist (and "Protector of Religions" as a whole). The Thai Custom Decree (Rathaniyom) of 1939 reestablished Buddhism as the state religion under the patronage of the monarchy, reaffirming a long tradition of *sasanupathamphok*, or the "royal protection of the sacred religion." Under the constitutional provision (reaffirmed in 2007) that "the State shall provide patronage and protection to Buddhism, which is the religion long practiced by the majority of the Thai people," the Buddhist monkhood, or *Sangha*, became an arm of the state.[100]

So entrenched was this culture that when Islam came to Asia, it did not challenge the state with notions of an autonomous *umma* of believers any more than Christianity had with its distinction between Rome's legions and Peter's church (with the usual exception of the Philippines, whose Catholic Church has long rivaled the state for authority). Indeed, *shariah* law was reduced to the status of customary *adat* law in Indonesia and Malaysia, a mere curiosity within the dominance of state law. Islam never became the potent political force in Malaysia or Indonesia that it became in the Middle East, and it never will. It was indigenized into the political culture of state dominance, co-opted as a new local governance mechanism.[101] The threat of Islam to strip the ruler of his divine pretensions and cast him down as another human groveler before the majesty of God was neutered by the *adat* designation. Just as Confucianism became the "rational religion" of China that supported the state, Islam in Southeast Asia evolved in a similar "rationalist" direction. It is no surprise that Western leaders fearful of radical Islam heap praise on Indonesia and Malaysia.

The Asian tradition, then, has been to exile or incorporate religion, but never to allow it to exist as a rival source of authority. Islam and Catholicism in Singapore, Buddhism in Indo-China, and Islam in Malaysia and Indonesia have all been variously incorporated into the state or repressed when the practitioners refused incorporation: for instance, China's state-sponsored religions and its vicious persecution of the independent Falun Gong Buddhist sect. The Khmer Rouge's failed attempt to destroy Buddhism led its successors to incorporate it fully. Japanese Shinto is often an adjunct of state power, vividly demonstrated at the Yasukuni shrine of war dead.

The claim of Keyes, Kendall, and Hardacre that "Asian states have … failed to subordinate religious authority to state authority" may be true in some absolute sense,[102] but it is patently false in any comparative sense. It was the transformation from premodern cultural states to modern bureaucratic states that led to the extensive management of religion in a way that had not hitherto been necessary. Certain "fine traditions" of indigenous religious practice were preserved (in the name of national identity), while other "superstitious" practices were abolished (in the name of modernization).[103] Hermits and sages could continue to exist outside of state power in Javanese and Chinese traditional political culture, so long as they did not challenge it. The Chinese reaction against the idea of "public intellectuals" who are both engaged and critical of the state reflects a view that the "proper" place for moral challengers is to be sealed away in caves, or their modern-day equivalent, universities. The "engaged Buddhism" that some see emerging in the region is at most a remonstrative nudge to rulers.[104]

State patronage of Buddhism and Confucianism thus created the social foundations of state legitimacy in Asia by putting rulers at the center of veneration under an expectation to rule well but without regularized mechanisms of dissent. While Northeast and Southeast Asia do not share the same political culture, what they do share is a view of the state as both natural and sacred, which emanates from the long interplay of Indian and Chinese political cultures. The cultural and institutional diffusion from hydraulic states – like China, Thailand, and India, and then again from Indonesia and Japan – created the social basis for subsequent political orders. In many ways, the political cultures that developed under these conditions differed across the region. But in this respect, they were similar. Countries like China, Japan, South Korea, Indonesia, Singapore, and Thailand might borrow Western techniques, but politics always favors the state over society. As Jones put it: "This East Asian social logic consequently failed to value either the articulation of an alternative viewpoint, or the need to consult interests, to separate public and private, or to maintain inalienable rights."[105]

Civic life in Asia is thus ineluctably conditioned by the presumption of an authoritative state. Societies work hand in glove with their governments to achieve socioeconomic goals in ways that governments elsewhere in the world – especially in Africa and Latin America, with their traditions of social distancing from the state – would envy (we return to this in Chapter 5). The state is seen as ontologically (that is to say, theoretically) prior to society. There is no imagined prepolitical social life into which the state intrudes. Rather, there is an imagined presocial political order into whose hands society is delivered. As Pye put it: "The dominant theme has been that, at the beginning, idealized forms of power existed."[106]

This means that the experience of "civil society" is different in Asia from elsewhere. To be a civil society activist in Asia is to critique state goals and propose alternatives. But unlike elsewhere, civil society operates within the normative confines of the state, is shaped by state policies and discourses, and often finds itself directly incorporated into state policy processes. The unipolar state gives rise to a form of state-society relations that is best described as "embeddedness." Social groups and actors gain their legitimacy and efficacy, indeed their identity, from their statuses and relationships with the state. It was widely noted during the 1989 Tiananmen protests in China, for example, that the three students who broke through the police cordon and rushed up the steps of the Great Hall of the People on April 22 proceeded to kneel in obeisance with their petition before it was finally taken by a lowly state functionary. Societies do not dominate the state because social forces are seen as chaotic and partial, whereas the state is rational and organic. A civil society embedded in affective social relations and a political culture of state primacy is bound to operate differently from a society in which social relations are more market-based, civic-based, or religious-based and where the legitimacy of the state is always in question.[107] What distinguishes Asia is an underlying assumption that society belongs to the state, not vice versa. "We the rulers ..."

Within Western political thought, there is a small amount of dissident literature that justifies the primacy of the state, although it has never sat well with the central liberal tradition, much less with radical ideology, both of which share a suspicion of the state as an apparatus of repression. In the theories of the early nineteenth-century German philosopher

Georg Hegel, the modern state embodies the highest ideals and the most just consensus of a fractious society. For Hegel, writing after the chaos of the French Revolution, the state should be altruistic, non-partisan, public good-oriented, rational, and the bulwark and creator of a *civil* society. Freedom, indeed happiness itself, was impossible without this ordering and dominance of the state.[108] A citizen's "highest duty is to be a member of the state,"[109] and citizens must be rational enough to realize that their own ends are achieved only within the overarching power of the state. The state's legitimacy derives from its essential rightness in this respect. "Men trust in the stability of the state, and suppose that in it only the particular interest can come into being."[110] The disharmony of individuals and prepolitical society is brought together into a "serene totality" by the state, which delivers "objective liberty" that individuals learn to appreciate.[111] Unrestrained mob rule is not "the general will." If it "overturns the ministry ... and becomes the new government," it will immediately find itself the target of new challenges. The solution is an organic state, created over time and embodying the objective general will.[112] What citizens needed, Hegel believed, was not revolution based on abstractions but organization based on reason.

The fusion of state and society in Hegel's vision is a remarkably good fit for the conception of the modern state in Asia. In Singapore, for instance, "civil society literature is filled with leitmotifs of descriptions of a strong state, political legitimacy and a weak civil society."[113] The demands placed on the Hegelian state prevent patrimonial, undevelopmental, or tyrannical rule. The relentless focus on "self-renewal" by Asian states reflects these Hegelian imperatives to rule well if the traditional legitimacy premium is to be enjoyed. Cumings described South Korean developmental dictator Park Chung-hee, who oversaw that country's economic transformation under his incorporative "Revitalization" (*Yusin*) democracy, as "the Korean agent of the Hegelian conception of the fused state."[114]

Besides Hegel, another Western writer who played a key role in providing modern justification for the Asian strong state was Herbert Spencer, who wrote in the late 1800s.[115] Spencer believed that societies that embraced utilitarian norms (to maximize the greatest good of the greatest number) would tend to "survive and spread." Individual conduct in such societies, he said, "call[s] out no antagonistic passions, favors harmonious cooperation, profits the group, and, by implication, profits the average of its individuals." While Spencer's ideas were employed in Europe to justify a market-driven social policy with a minimal state, they were employed in Asia to justify a state-driven social policy with a dominant state. Indeed, the Asian interpretation is probably closer to the overall spirit of Spencer, who in his later years became increasingly convinced of the importance of a strong state that delivered social goods and enforced tax collection.[116] For Spencer, a dominant state was crucial to the strengthening of society.

In Meiji Japan, whose influence over state builders elsewhere in the region was profound, Spencer's ideas were employed to create domestic theories of state-led modernization – economic reform, representative institutions, rational public administration, centralized rule, and scientific progress.[117] The 1882 book *Jinken Shinsetsu* (*A New Theory of Human Rights*) by Kato Hiroyuki, a member of the "Meiji Six" group of regime intellectuals, "was intended to justify the supremacy of the state, which he felt was rightfully in a position to determine the best course of action for the people, now essentialized as *shakai* (society)."[118] Hiroyuki, who served as president of the University of Tokyo from 1881 to 1886 and again from 1890 to 1893 when it was Tokyo Imperial University, turned the egalitarian ethos of social Darwinism on its head by arguing that it instead justified the special status of the emperor, who had emerged on top after a long historical struggle: "He argued that the emperor's authority derived from his earliest ancestors being the fittest and, as such, able to offer protection to people in exchange for acquiescence to their authority. No other Japanese had subsequently been fitter to rule than those in the Imperial line."[119]

Hegel and Spencer were thus the Western theorists who meshed with the underlying presumptions of state-supporting Confucianism and Buddhism. Neo-Confucian and neo-Buddhist theorists, some explicitly borrowing from Hegel, have been widely influential in Asia.[120] The Asian communitarian, or "Asian Values" theories, associated most clearly with Singapore leader Lee Kuan Yew,[121] for instance, had strong Hegelian overtones, especially in their emphases on the state as the organic expression of a fractious society and on the duty of citizens to obey, even in the face of performance failures. The new discourse emphasized trust in the state and a state-ordering of civil society to maintain community.[122] Asian Values emphasized national integration, collectivism, the priority of the community over the individual, and the organic nature of the state as the representative of all of society.

Jayasuriya linked Asian Values to the German tradition of "reactionary modernism" spawned by Hegel that aimed, in Herf's words, to "restore the primacy of politics and the state," amidst the challenges of the market (and today's globalization).[123] Asian Values was a reassertion of conservative values as an illiberal pathway to modernity that emphasized social discipline, technocracy, and a strong state. It was an attempt to rearticulate ancient political cultures in modern terms. Herf's concept fits Asian Values in its harnessing of the challenge of modernity and the political culture of illiberal states for the purposes of stateness. What is important is that this new interpretation of political culture by Asian elites was unthinkable in the absence of the state-dominant political cultures of the past. We need *both* historical cultural conditions and modern political choices to explain how Asian stateness came into being.

INTEGRATIVE NATIONALISM

With this explanation of the cultural foundations of state legitimacy, we can better understand nationalism in Asia. Nationalism throughout Asia emerged as a state project with an unflinching focus on social integration and national development, consistent with "modernization" theories of nationalism. Nationalism was a project directed at *internal*, not *external* challenges. The purpose of nationalism was to solve what used to be called "the communal problem," namely, loyalties to groups that did not overlap with the boundaries of the nation.

Asia is a bracing tonic for claims that colonialism exacerbated ethnic tensions, for Asia shows that such tensions arose instead because of the absence of a precolonial political order. In Asia, colonial powers ruled mainly through such orders, which were themselves legitimate. As a result, modern nationalism in Asia was never a struggle against the state or, really, against the West. Rather, it was a struggle against attempts to delegitimize the state in favor of communal loyalties. National movements focused on sovereignty, national integration, and national uplift. Nationalism in Asia was focused on creating internal, Weberian sovereignty and on speeding up national development – it was *integrative* and *developmental*. The movements, noted Ball in 1952, "seek to revive and foster national art and culture, to subordinate the narrower loyalties to family or clan to a wider loyalty to the nation."[124] In Indonesia, Benedict Anderson noted, "nationalism expresses a fundamental drive to solidarity and unity in the face of the disintegration of traditional society." The nationalist state sought to be "syncretic and absorptive" in order to re-create the primordial bond between people and ruler.[125]

The trinity seen throughout Asia was to unite the nation, the value system, and the political order into a seamless whole. In the view of two modern scholars of Asian nationalism, Claudia Derichs and Thomas Heberer,

[S]ociety is perceived as an organic unity and the state as an embodiment of the interests of this imagined entity. The task of the state is to enforce or preserve this unity and thus the concept of nation-building. That is why authoritarian states in East and Southeast Asia in the name of preserving national unity and stability attempt to eradicate particularising interests of single social or ethnic groups, and to prevent political contest and the formation of parallel power structures.[126]

This reinvention of traditional political ideas in nationalistic terms was evident throughout the region. Siam's government under Marshal Phibun renamed the country Thailand in 1939, allied itself with the pan-Asian nationalism of fascist Japan, and espoused Buddhist ideals of loyalty to the newly modernist spirit of saluting the flag, wearing hats, and playing rugby. In China, Yuan Shikai issued a proclamation in 1913 demanding that all colleges, schools, and public bodies revive the Confucian sacrificial cere- monies in order to engender loyalty to the new republic. The nationalistic Confucians were later defeated by an even more ferociously state-centered ideology, Leninism, which has lately overseen a Confucian revival.

By making integration the focus of nationalism, states in Asia became less susceptible to political breakdown in the face of internal conflicts, economic crises, governance failures, external threats, or environmental catastrophes. Strong states were upheld by a national project of integra- tion that was built on the foundations of Hegelian legitimacy. Asian states have weathered crises of internal conflict (the secession of East Timor), economic crisis (the 1997–98 Asian Financial Crisis), external threat (the post-Tiananmen sanctions of 1989–91), governance failure (the convic- tion on corruption charges of two former presidents of South Korea in 1995 and 1996), famine (China, North Korea, Cambodia), and environ- mental catastrophe (everywhere) without any resulting state failure.

Another consequence of the distinctive civic or integrative form of Asian nationalism is that ethnicized or divisive exhibits of nationalism, whether by majorities or minorities, are sternly repressed. This is where Asia parts ways with the ethnicized Hegelianism of Nazi Germany. Chinese regimes in Singapore and China regularly punish behavior regarded as "Han chauvinism." In Malaysia, where the ruling UMNO party cynically manipulated a race riot in 1969 in order to expand its electoral control,[127] the ethnicized nationalism of *bumiputra* (Malay) uplift became civilized through the establishment of a National Front coalition with the major Chinese and Indian parties. The ruling coalition successfully responded to an electoral setback in 2008 with a "1Malaysia" campaign – equating opposition with national disintegration.[128] Meanwhile, minorities that seek a separate identity throughout Asia are usually crushed, often with the direct assistance of neighboring states who share the same ethnicity as the dissenting group (Malaysia in the case of Malays in southern Thailand, for example, or North Korea in the case of Koreans in China).[129] Mindanao in the Philippines and Aceh in Indonesia are the only places in Asia with an autonomy of sorts. Elsewhere ethnic demands have been met with repression. Leninist China, for example, does not mind that Taiwan is governed independently by nationalist Confucians under a "one China" principle, so long as Taiwanese nationalism is suppressed.[130] In Thailand's southern Malay Muslim areas, autonomy is variously described as "not an option" or "unthinkable,"[131] while neighboring Malaysia is equally suspicious of attempts by the insurgents to reestablish the ancient Malay sultanate of Pattani. The Thai Queen in 2004 urged Buddhists in the region to take shooting lessons in order to preserve national rule and promised to do the same herself.[132] The Thai word for autonomy, *ekkarat*, means independence, and thus, writes McCargo, "calling for any form of substantive decentralization in Thailand's southern border provinces is fraught with dangers, since anyone supporting such ideas risks being accused of disloyalty to the nation and the monarchy."[133] The issue is managed under what Askew calls "a policy orthodoxy that aims to resolve the southern unrest primarily through economic development and pronouncements of a shared Thai character that exists under the king's benevolence."[134] Because Buddhism has long been an adjunct of state power, it is of little surprise that Buddhist monasteries are used for concealing soldiers and as sentry posts in the area.[135]

In Malaysia, meanwhile, non-Malays are expected to accept the Malay-based national identity as the only stable basis of national unity. For the Chinese, who do well economically, it has been a price worth paying. But for poor Indians, the deal has been less attractive. While Chinese graveyards are regularly plowed under by the developmental state with minimal protest, the destruction of Hindu temples by local Islamic governments in Malaysia in 2007 sparked protests by Indians in Kuala Lumpur. The leaders of the Hindu Rights Action Force were quickly arrested. While Yugoslavia collapsed with the overthrow of its authoritarian regime in 1991, the even more pluralized and developed Indonesia, the "Balkans of the Orient,"[136] did not, despite many scholarly predictions that it would.[137] In all of these cases, ethnic demands for autonomy have no market within political cultures built on foundations of state dominance and assumed legitimacy.

This does not mean that Asian states are tyrannical in their treatment of ethnic demands. Indeed, the Asian Governance Model and refined Oriental despotism inform a rational and careful approach characterized by innovation, incentives, and a long-term outlook. Various mechanisms of good governance, including some forms of decentralization, have been introduced. Development is usually the overarching strategy of integration. But those seeking a separate identity and a separate authority are frustrated. There is no "liberal conscience" that spurs rulers to "accommodate" such demands and to recognize separate nations.[138] The accommodative recommendations of a National Reconciliation Commission for southern Thailand in 2006 were "largely ignored" by the state,[139] as were the proposals for autonomy for Tibet floated briefly by China's top leader, Hu Yaobang, in 1980.

Another aspect of Asian nationalism is its general rejection of anti-Western bombast. Unlike in the Indian cultural sphere (or among those of Indian descent, like Singapore grandee Kishore Mahbubani), where an obsessive anticolonialism still dominates, Asians were never particularly concerned about the imagined depredations of the West. Cordial, even close, relations were maintained with Western powers that had been colonizers or even invaders – the Dutch in Indonesia, the French in Cambodia, the British in Malaysia, and the United States in the Philippines and today in Vietnam. Ho Chi Minh was much enamored of France and attempted initially to achieve a peaceful French condominium over Vietnam. Filipino nationalist José Rizal wanted to promote Western classical music, while Sukarno wanted "crisply tailored" uniforms for officials and trousers for men. Even the Taiwanese look fondly on their period under Japanese colonialism. The simple fact is that colonialism was largely benign or beneficial to Asia, and Asian leaders were far too embedded in precolonial political cultures to care much after independence. Colonialism came and went like a summer monsoon.

Because Asian nationalism is developmental, it makes little sense to cut off ties with advanced countries. "Nationalism in East and Southeast Asia is less an aggressive, externally oriented ideology but rather entertains domestic functions," write Derichs and Heberer.[140] To the extent that it exists, anti-Westernism in Asia is about surpassing, not blaming, the West.[141] This is in stark contrast to the nationalisms of India, the Middle East, Latin America, and Africa, where anticolonial and antimodern obsessions often replaced development as the basis for state legitimacy.

In this respect, as in so many ways, nationalism in Asia was pragmatic and developmental, not utopian or aggressive. Where it did fall prey to anti-Western bombast – Pol Pot in Cambodia, the Kim dynasty in North Korea – it offended fellow Asian countries more than it offended the West. Even in Vietnam and Indonesia, where armed struggles were waged for independence, there was (and remains to this day) a remarkable absence of the sort of "colonial victimization" narratives that animate, say, the political cultures of India or Africa. The *indignées* of Asia are mainly indignant about not catching up fast enough.

The presumption of authority even in the face of colonial incursion was vividly memorialized by Burmese court scribes after the kingdom's defeat by British forces in 1824. The king, they wrote in the official annals, had "from the motives of piety and regard for life, made no preparations whatever to oppose them." To explain a large indemnity, it was written that the king "in his clemency and generosity [had] sent them large sums of money to pay their expenses back." After that, he had "ordered them out of the country."[142] Asian states have roots that run far deeper than colonialism. In this sense, the Asian experience of state building is difficult to transfer to other countries or regions. But clearly, legitimacy is central to building state capacity, and questions of social cohesion (not just government performance) lie at the heart of building legitimacy.[143] Tracing the implications of this state-society relationship for Asian politics will occupy much of the rest of this book.

3

Development

The Second World War was a time of opportunity for Wu Ho-su.[1] Born in 1919 into a poor household in northern Taiwan, Wu took a job with a Japanese-owned cloth distributor in the capital, Taipei, in 1935, where he first worked as a dockhand and then as a salesman. By 1939, at age twenty, he was appointed by the Japanese owner to comanage sales of a new cloth company. When war came, Wu took advantage of the shortages caused by Allied bombing raids (Taiwan had been under Japanese occupation since 1895) to make profitable purchasing trips to Japan and to buy up properties in Taipei from fleeing residents.

Japan was defeated in 1945, and Wu found himself in control of the Taiwan side of the business, which he renamed the Shinkong (*xinguang*), or New Bright, Company. Although he invested money to produce goods that were in short supply, like tea, sugar, and coal, his heart remained in the rag trade. But business conditions for a native Taiwanese entrepreneur deteriorated sharply with the retreat to the island in 1948 and 1949 of the Kuomintang (Nationalist Party) government that had lost China's civil war. Besides establishing three state-owned textile factories, the KMT's new Taiwan Production Board gave preference for cotton imports to seven textile companies from Shanghai that had fled China with the regime.

To avoid direct competition with the state-backed companies, Wu established a small dyeing and spinning factory in his hometown of Hsinchu in 1951 and decided to focus on the new fabric of rayon ("artificial silk"), which was cooler and more fashionable than cotton. But obstacles remained. Because he was not approved to use the national power grid, Wu had to strip a fifty-horsepower diesel generator from his tea factory at Laotienliao to provide electricity. To get around a prohibition on importing textile-making equipment, he had 50 machines disassembled into about 1,000 parts each in Japan and shipped to Taiwan as "spare parts." Finally, to get a permit to import the raw materials to make rayon, he organized a trade fair of Japanese rayon and invited KMT officials to attend. Frightened at the prospect of a surge in imported Japanese rayon, the officials slapped a 160 percent tariff on the fabric and gave Wu a permit to make it in Taiwan. The first swatches were shipped in 1952, and Shinkong was soon exporting them around the world.

Wu next attempted to make the raw materials (mainly artificial fibers) that went into rayon. For this, he sought the support of K. Y. Yin (Yin Zhongrong), Taiwan's economic czar from 1951 until 1963. But Yin was resistant. He believed that Wu could not succeed, and in any case, he was captive to the spoils system controlled by the émigré and state-sector textile owners, for whom "spinning yarn was like spinning gold thread, while printing cloth was like printing banknotes."[2] As Wu recalled:

From the very beginning, Mr. Yin had contempt for me because I appeared to be merely a young fellow. He flatly told me: "Young fellow, what qualifications do you have for making artificial fibers? Even though mainland China is so large, they can't find anyone with the right talents to do such a thing. It's certainly impossible for you to have any success in this enterprise. You're only a kid, and a Taiwanese local yokel. You have absolutely no special background or experience." Although he addressed me in a condescending attitude, I still vigorously contended with him. Almost every day, I scurried over to his office to argue the matter.[3]

Eventually Yin relented, telling Wu that if he could raise NT$20 million for the venture (the equivalent of about US$5 million in 2012 dollars), Yin would seek U.S. aid for a matching amount. Using his connections in the textile industry, Wu persuaded a close ally of President Chiang Kai-shek and one of the big Shanghai émigré textile manufacturers to put up half the sum, while he raised the rest. The China Artificial Fibers Company was established in 1954 in Toufen, and Wu was managing director. A few years later, when the émigré investor wanted to sell his shares in the profitable company to Wu, the deal was scuppered because "some bureaucrats at the government's finance ministry opposed handing over such a large-scale industry to a young Taiwanese entrepreneur." But Wu cared more about business success than official status: "What difference would the title and status of 'chairman' make to me anyway!"[4]

The bureaucratic challenges that Wo Ho-su faced in expanding his businesses in other sectors were similar. Throughout the 1950s, he wined and dined officials, while seeking a permit to build a glass factory to compete with the state-sponsored Hsinchu Glass. They rejected his requests. But the émigré managers at Hsinchu were constantly embezzling funds and fighting among themselves, so bureaucrats invited Wu to take over there as managing director. Wu accepted but soon left the "rotten mess" that the company had become under state sponsorship.[5] Hsinchu Glass collapsed, and its former émigré president went on to become the godfather of one of Taiwan's most notorious criminal gangs, the Supreme Alliance. Wu, meanwhile, helped a fellow native Taiwan entrepreneur set up a new company, Taiwan Glass, passing on his connections with the famed Japanese glassmaker Asahi. Taiwan Glass became the island's preeminent glass maker.

In setting up the life insurance business that would become Shinkong's second core business, Wu faced equally daunting bureaucratic obstacles. One official "was very hard to find," while another "frequently pestered and put the squeeze on some of us for things like 'rights and privileges money.'"[6] Wu's solution was to cofound the business with an influential KMT party member, whom he made chairman of the board when the business was established in 1963.[7] By 1964, Shinkong was the largest unlisted private company in Taiwan by capital, and the twenty-first largest overall.

In classical works on the Asian "developmental state," K. Y. Yin and other Taiwan planners are portrayed as enlightened technocrats who brilliantly steered industrial development.[8] Indeed, compared to the "presidential office" faction in Taiwan's post-1949 politics, which favored a mostly state-owned economy, Yin himself was a pragmatist. For him, the choice between public or private ownership, trade or protection, and foreign or domestic capital depended on the situation. But above all, he believed in the state's right to make those decisions.[9] Taiwan's development, he wrote, relies "on the government's involvement in economic activities, sound plans, and supervision of the implementation of the plans.... Here 'plan' means that after considering the whole situation and keeping its eye on the common good, the government decides the direction and goals of industrial development for a certain period.... Meanwhile, each industry and each enterprise within the sector have ample freedom to perform."[10]

What's wrong with this account? From the perspective of the entrepreneurs like Wu who created the economic miracle in Taiwan, the problem with the "wise technocrat" theory is that it ignores the politicized, ad hoc, episodic, and frequently counterproductive nature of such interventions. Wu's story, writes Tillman, "provides further evidence ... that the short-sightedness of government officials, like K. Y. Yin, unnecessarily *delayed* some aspects of Taiwan's industrialization.... Mr. Wu's account shows that it was sometimes the government meritocracy itself that needed to be prodded."[11] As Wu meekly concluded: "My viewpoint came from many years of accumulated experience, and even though my view didn't draw on any economist's grand theory, I believe most people would agree with me."[12]

Rethinking the Wu Ho-su story in terms of the Asian Governance Model makes more sense. State officials like Yin had a genuine commitment to shared development, no doubt. But their prescriptions were frequently wrong or constrained by intrastate politics. State interventions in the textile sector did not create Taiwan's economic textile boom;[13] they constrained it. What made development succeed was the state's embeddedness in accountability pressures from society, in particular those from the private sector, which forced it to revise and restrain its policies.

Historians and analysts have long been mesmerized by the elegant plans and authoritative-sounding institutions that accompanied Asian growth. But the economic history of the developing world is littered with similar plans and institutions that caused growth disasters. As Ngo says of the Taiwan case: "A closer look at the way these planning bodies functioned reveals that their jurisdiction was arbitrary, their status was ambivalent, and their life span was short. Very often, planning and coordination were undertaken by agents not entrusted with the responsibility to plan."[14]

Recent work suggests that neither a neoclassical market-based account, nor a *dirigiste* state-based account captures the essential causes of Asian economic success.[15] Instead, economic success was caused by "growth alliances" between state and society (discussed further later in this chapter), in which entrepreneurs like Wu were supported by growth-supporting state policies in areas like education, industrial clustering, cheap credit, and innovation incentives. Rather than debating the arid "state versus market" question about Asian success, we need to understand the particular roles and contributions of bureaucrats, businessmen, technicians, white-collar staff, and blue-collar workers. In particular, we need to understand the *shared* drive for innovation and productivity by all actors alike. Above all, this collaborative endeavor was a creation of politics. To understand Asian economic development, a political perspective that explains *how* the state behaved and what constrained it will shed more light on the issue than a purely "institutional" account of miraculous state agencies. As Wade puts it: "How has the use of public power been disciplined?"[16]

In his classic study, Gold concluded that American pressures "played a decisive role" in forcing the KMT to be accountable to society.[17] But the Shinkong story shows that a different accountability dynamic, one grounded in a historical Asian tradition, was far more important. Getting this story right is critical to development theory, because all too often Asia has been looked upon wistfully by advocates of state intervention or market liberalization as the solution to development woes.[18] But companies like Shinkong prospered because of the particular *politics*, not the particular *institutions*, of development.

At the microeconomic level, the Taiwanese state could neither pick winners, nor manage companies. Its political survival strategy protected the domestic market for lumbering state enterprises and a few large, private firms set up by loyal mainland refugees. Conflicts among the army, the state companies, and the government were legion – most famously in the case of Taiwan Sugar, whose general manager was sentenced to death for treason in 1951 for building railways, irrigation canals, and shipping facilities that the paranoid army believed were intended to facilitate a communist invasion.[19] State-backed ventures in automobiles, heavy trucks, and Japanese-style trading companies all ended in failure. In 1962, the government's attempts to squeeze out private savings schemes in favor of state banks unintentionally caused the bankruptcy (and nationalization) of Tangrong Iron Corporation, which made 60 percent of the island's steel and employed 4,500 people.

The clumsy state interventions paradoxically created conditions for nimble, smaller enterprises to dominate the export market and to step into fast-changing market conditions. Globally competitive industries, like textiles and petrochemicals, developed in spite of, not because of, government policies. As a 1968 study of Taiwan by the Asian Productivity Organization concluded: "The small-scale factory type of enterprise, while profiting from the favorable industrial climate created through public policies and industrial planning, has largely grown and developed on its own resources – a tribute to the remarkable resilience and ingenuity of the family enterprise." What had spurred development in Taiwan was "a large proportion of persons ready to assume risks, explore market opportunities and experiment with new products, materials, technology, and processes – in short, persons possessing a high degree of innovative talent."[20]

At the macroeconomic level, the Taiwan state mobilized savings, undertook land reform, improved education, expanded infrastructure, created an effective commercial legal system, maintained a stable and low-inflation currency, and encouraged foreign trade and investment. But these cannot constitute an explanation of Asian economic growth, because many developing countries have technocrats and institutions that intend to do these things but do not. The reason why the Taiwan state succeeded was that it was constrained by the overarching normative pressures of the Asian Governance Model, namely, a political sociology of delivering broad prosperity and national stability, which in the case of economic issues manifested itself in a distinctive pro-growth politics. To understand Asian growth, studying institutions is not enough. Instead, we need to consider sociology, culture, and above all politics. By building political survival strategies around the concept of rapid development – strategies that were rooted in political cultures of "refined" Oriental despotism – Asian governments like that in Taiwan were impelled by political pressures to adjust, abandon, and repurpose public policies that were not working. As Ngo concludes: "The basis of state agency is political not technocratic."[21]

In Taiwan, as elsewhere in Asia, the particularities of developmental politics varied over time. Initially, the KMT talked of the need to "retake China." By the 1970s, it had shifted its focus to gaining legitimacy in the eyes of the Taiwanese population. Both were conceptualized in terms of rapid development (as opposed to, say, military buildups or the personalization of power). This urge toward development meant that political goals were seen in developmental terms and that public policies were subject to comparatively rigorous cost-effectiveness and efficiency criterion. By the 1970s, the KMT was abandoning state controls and ownership as the small and medium enterprise sector flourished. A private entrepreneur joined the government's economic planning advisory council for the first time in 1981, the same year that a small business administration was established. "The main role of government is to find ways to help everyone to earn money," the finance minister declared in 1975.[22]

Back at Shinkong, the KMT's shift toward cultivating Taiwanese entrepreneurs was a blessing. Wu was able to open his own synthetic fibers company, Shinkong Synthetic Fibers, which competed against the state-backed company he still managed, China Artificial Fibers. President Chiang Ching-kuo visited the new company in 1978, praising Wu's role in Taiwan's export boom. By the mid-1970s, Shinkong was the ninth largest private enterprise group in Taiwan.[23] New businesses opened in natural gas, tires, retail, and food processing.

Wu Ho-su died in 1986. By then, Shinkong was no longer struggling against the politics of the state. When Wu's third son was kidnapped and ransomed for $3.8 million in 1990, police found and executed the alleged kidnappers and recovered most of the money within a year. In 1992, during the first national legislative elections, Wu's eldest son won a seat as a KMT candidate, one of thirty-five "golden oxen" to successfully contest for parliamentary seats that year. Wu's three sons took over management of Shinkong, and four of his six children married into other prominent Taiwanese industrial families.[24] While many family businesses collapsed after the death of the founder, Shinkong had many professional managers and had offered enough shares in most of its firms to ensure external accountability. The family's net worth was estimated to be $5 billion in the early 1990s, making it one of Asia's richest.

In the 1990s, the group diversified into the aerospace technology, semiconductors, railways, and banking, all the while retaining the core businesses in textiles and insurance. Shinkong breezed through the Asian financial crisis of 1997–98, using the brief slump in Taiwan to consolidate its top position in the insurance and department store businesses. Shinkong was Taiwan's third largest business group by revenues in 2000.

In the 2000s, Taiwan's politics was again reshaped, this time by a growing reconciliation with China that was driven by both political and economic considerations. Shinkong's investments expanded in China, where it opened four new department stores by 2011. The liberalization of direct travel to and from China meant the company was also attracting mainland clients for medical tourism to its reputable Shinkong Wu Ho-su Memorial Hospital in Taipei. A business dispute between Shinkong and one of its Chinese department store partners in 2007 led to high-level political interventions by governments on both sides. Shinkong footed the $10 million bill for a new panda house in the Taipei Zoo for two pandas sent by China in 2009. Shinkong had by now fully transformed from an upstart Taiwanese business into a member of the corporate and political establishment. With power came responsibility, however: The group was publicly upbraided by Taiwan's premier for making too large a profit (about $100 million) on the flipping of a piece of land in Taipei in 2010.

Today, Shinkong is one of thousands of corporate success stories in Asia that reflect the broader developmental success of the region. The politics of development is the obvious place to start in understanding Asian politics, because development has been so fundamental to the self-identity of the region.[25] The study of economic development, wrote two scholars in 2005, "has grabbed and held the political science of Asia by the throat for more than 25 years."[26]

While there is more to politics than development alone, development cannot be explained without politics. In the words of one scholar: "What coalitions of political and economic actors have combined, and in what way, to shape these [economic] changes? How have the costs and benefits been distributed, by whom, and on what grounds?"[27] There is at present an underappreciation of the political nature of Asian development.

The Shinkong story provides an entrée to this feast. It tells us to look at the dynamic, contentious politics that went into Asia's developmental miracle and that continues to shape its trajectory. It suggests the need to politicize the question of Asian development in order to understand it better.

AN INPUTS MIRACLE

The rapid development of Asia after World War II came as a surprise to the world. Asian versions of Oriental despotism theory had emphasized the anticommercial ethos of Confucianism and the indolent fatalism of Buddhism. Schwartz noted that "no strong orientation to economic development seems to have arisen" in ancient Asia, because rulers were satisfied with averting famines.[28] Under these conditions, an "Asiatic mode of production" had emerged, as Marx termed it in the 1850s, working mainly from the writings of the East India Company College economist Richard Jones, in which land was managed by family-based communities without any specialization of labor and was owned by despotic rulers who exacted rents and corvée labor at random. All of this was seen as inhospitable to capitalist development, which even Marx admitted was a precondition for rapid growth. John Stuart Mill introduced the term "Chinese stagnation" as a general economic concept. Moreover, Asia was burdened with high population densities, limited natural resources, and multiple political conflicts. The glory days of Asian prosperity, it was believed, had passed. In its 1949 survey of the region, the United Nations Economic Commission for Asia and the Far East warned of the "serious decline in the region's position in the world" and concluded: "It would be totally unrealistic to talk in terms of a rapid increase in the standard of living and welfare of the peoples of Asia and the Far East."[29]

In the 1950s, pessimism about Asian growth became more pervasive, because under the prevailing theories of the time, developing countries needed either vast infusions of foreign aid or strict isolation to break their "dependency" on the rapacious West. Postcolonial Asia, from this perspective, was getting it all wrong by limiting its use of foreign aid, relying on the private sector, and encouraging exports and foreign investment. Only Mao's China, Sukarno's Indonesia, and Kim's North Korea stood a chance of developing because of their "self-reliance" policies.

In 1958, the Burmese economist Hla Myint published a now-classic paper, in which he advocated the export-led model. Myint was not keen on import protection, which he believed preserved inefficiencies. Instead, he argued that governments should promote export industries. Indonesia, for instance, should prevent its profitable sugar and rubber lands from being taken over by subsistence rice farmers, a policy that had once been pursued by its Dutch rulers. "To pursue their development plans successfully it is vitally important for [developing countries] to carry out the export-drive policies, which in their technical properties, may not be very different from those of the colonial governments in the past."[30]

It was not until the late 1960s that some economists began to notice that the countries of Asia that were following Myint's advice were booming. In his 1969 work, *Japan Surges Ahead: The Story of an Economic Miracle*, Stone observed that "Japan has emerged so brilliantly and so swiftly" from its wartime slump that other Asian nations were taking notice.[31] In the following two decades, the term "economic miracle" was used to describe other countries in the region.[32] The recognition of a fundamental change was given its fullest expression in the World Bank report of 1993, entitled *The East Asian Miracle*.[33] Even after a brief but severe economic slump in 1997 and 1998, the region returned to rapid growth. Since the 2000s, there has been a resurgence of inquiry into the causes of rapid growth in Asia.

In comparative perspective, Asia's development record is astounding. Using the average growth in four major developing countries (India, Egypt, Nigeria, and Brazil) as a standard of comparison, and using the longest postwar growth data available for each of the fourteen Asian countries, growth has been above-average in ten of fourteen countries (see Figure 3.1).

In most of these cases, it has been *substantially* faster. While the developing world has generally grown in real terms at about 2 percent per capita per year since 1950, Asia has grown at about 4 percent. *The East Asian Miracle* identified seven of the ten – Japan, South Korea, Taiwan,

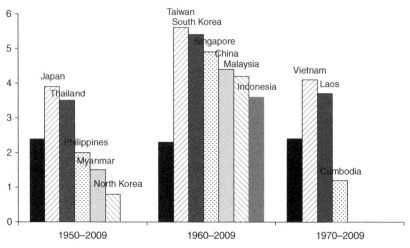

FIGURE 3.1. Comparative economic growth of Asia.
Notes: Average annual real growth in GDP per capita using purchasing power
equivalent exchange rates. Comparison (black bar) to average of growth rates
1950 to 2009 of Brazil, Egypt, India, and Nigeria.
Source: All data from Penn World Tables.

Singapore, Malaysia, Thailand, and Indonesia – as high-performing
Asian economies. Within a few years it was trumpeting the successes of
economically liberalizing China, Vietnam, and Laos, as well. In 1950,
the fourteen major countries of Asia accounted for 11 percent of global
GDP.[34] By 2012, that portion had risen to 28 percent, more than any
other region.[35] Taiwan's GDP per capita was half of Cuba's in 1960 but
three times Cuba's by 2009. More than half of the global output by value
of steel, textiles, cars, and semiconductors is now made in Asia.

Even among the four growth laggards of the region, three of them –
the Philippines, Cambodia, and Myanmar – have not substantially under-
performed developing country averages. Indeed, in the 2010s, Cambodia
and Myanmar were seen as emerging into their own "miracle" phases,
while growth in the Philippines accelerated. North Korea stands as the
lone developmental disaster of Asia for the entire postwar period. Few
doubt that when its deadly regime is overthrown, North Korea will
boom, as well.

The second important dimension of Asian growth is that it has been
widely shared, meaning that the income of the poorest people has risen
rapidly in absolute terms and often more rapidly than those in better-off
categories. The proportion of the population living on less than $2.00

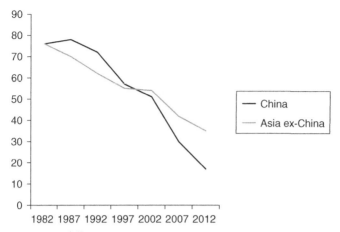

FIGURE 3.2. Asia's falling poverty.
Note: Proportion of population with incomes below $2 per day.
Source: World Bank.

per day in local purchasing power terms has declined more dramatically in China and the rest of Asia than in any other part of the world (see Figure 3.2). In the 2000s, a virtually unnoticed miracle of poverty reduction occurred in the region, driving the proportion of the population living on less than $2.00 per day down from 52 percent in 2002 to 25 percent by 2013.

Finding so many high and pro-poor growth states in a geographic cluster is statistically improbable, unless they are either acting on the same model or influencing one another directly. This suggests that there are some common and important factors driving growth in the region. Explanations of Asian economic success have run the gamut: the development state, market-led growth, labor repression, crony capitalism, Asian Values, and the "bamboo network" of Chinese entrepreneurs, to name just a few. As we will see, each of these concepts captures a partial view of Asian economic success. The key to uniting them is the pro-growth alliances that gave rise to a form of contentious politics in which effective policies were maintained and bad ones were curtailed. As a result, government delivered needed public goods while also maintaining strong incentives for entrepreneurship and social effort.

In order to explain why economies grow, economists work backward from the most proximate to the most distant causes. In a strict accounting sense, economic output (everything from dry-cleaning services to freight logistics) is a result of labor mixing with machines and equipment.

The more labor and the more capital applied, and the more knowledge embodied in each, the more an economy will grow. Looking only at savings rates since 1975, for instance, Asian countries have outperformed every other region and major developing economy. Gross domestic savings as a percentage of the GDP in Asia has generally hovered around the 30–35 percent range, compared to about 20 percent in the rest of the world. Other indicators of "input mobilization" tell the same story: For instance, the proportion of workers putting in more than sixty hours per week is consistently higher in Asia than elsewhere – 11 percent in Japan and Indonesia in 2008 compared to 4–5 percent in the United States and Britain.[36]

If the actual growth of an economy exceeds the growth of these inputs, economists add a residual fudge factor called "total factor productivity" that is supposed to capture things like work practices, effort, managerial and organizational efficiency, scale, financial innovations, and unexpected positive shocks to supply and demand. An economic "miracle" implies a large TFP residual. In a well-known 1994 article, the economist Paul Krugman argued that there was no TFP-driven miracle in Asia; there were only massive increases in labor and capital.[37] Asian countries grew so rapidly not because of "subtleties of East Asian government intervention" or "fewer civil liberties and more planning" but simply because of an "extraordinary mobilization of resources," which took the form of more education, more employment, and more machines and equipment that were bought with savings. "If Asian success reflects the benefits of strategic trade and industrial policies, those benefits should surely be manifested in an unusual and impressive rate of growth in the efficiency of the economy. And there is no sign of such exceptional efficiency growth," he wrote.

Krugman's claim created a cottage industry in total factor productivity studies of Asia. One rejoinder is that while the overall picture is correct, certain key sectors in Asian economies did experience miraculous efficiency gains, and it was these sectors, especially the export-oriented ones,[38] that spurred wider growth in their economies.[39] Another is that the overestimation of embodied efficiency gains in the labor and capital measures (better machines, more educated workers), a common accounting problem in high-growth economies, tends to underplay what would otherwise have been measured as total factor productivity gains.[40] Either way, since Krugman's 1994 article, the region seems to have experienced an uptick in the contribution of total factor productivity to growth.[41]

The fact that Asian countries have managed to pave their roads, electrify their villages, educate and house their populations, and commercialize their land at rapid rates and without the usual drop-off in returns is itself important.[42] In some countries (Taiwan, China, Vietnam, South Korea), these activities involved significant land reform to create more agricultural owner-operators. In other countries (Singapore, Malaysia, Thailand), the gains came more through education and urbanization. Thus, even if Krugman was right, it does not necessarily imply that growth has not been miraculous. An inputs miracle alone is worthy of note, for the remarkable thing about development in Asia is that it is largely led by the private sector, not by Soviet-style state planning, and it has generated demand through export markets.[43] Through the actions of states that are fiscally prudent and invest in education, as well as societies that save their income and push members to improve their skills, Asian countries excel. In other words, the "extraordinary mobilization of resources" in Asia requires an explanation, regardless of how we measure it.

The next proximate step is to examine the factors that cause this syndrome of rapid input and efficiency growth. Once Asia began to boom in the 1960s and 1970s, analysts began to look more closely at cultural and other fixed factors. Among cultural factors, a wide propensity to save, a trading and risk-taking ethos, and social business networks constituted by families, ethnicities, or hometown linkages have been widely studied. Of the top thirty business groups in Thailand in 2000, twenty-five were owned by families of Chinese descent. This family-based Chinese entrepreneurial ethos pervades the region.[44] Or to take another cultural example, the concept of "death by overwork" (*karoshi*) is only half-jokingly referred to as Japan's first major export to Asia. Beyond this, Asia's port-based maritime geography, its early access to U.S. markets during the Cold War, and the post–World War II U.S. defense umbrella seem to help its growth prospects. At its peak in 1972, for instance, the combined U.S. trade deficit and defense spending in Japan was the equivalent of $24 billion in 2012 dollars.[45]

But if Krugman's thesis was too proximate to growth to explain it, cultural and geographic theories are too distant.[46] In the case of culture, for instance, while it may operate directly on growth, its most important effect is probably in steering policy makers to adopt pro-growth policies. The fact that Asian cultures sometimes produced growth disasters – Mao's China, for instance, or Pol Pot's Kampuchea – reminds us that culture (like geography) may be useful, but it is not sufficient to

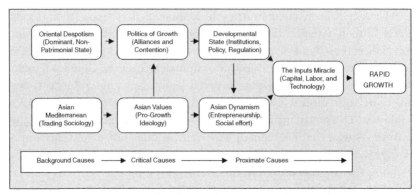

FIGURE 3.3. Explaining Asian economic growth.

explain growth. Rather, it is how culture is transformed into an operative ideology and how that ideology in turn shapes political alliances and institutions that is decisive. To understand Asian development means understanding how state-society relations so often generate a pro-growth politics and how economic institutions and policies emerge within this politics to deliver an inputs miracle.

Politics and policy are the "intervening variables" through which culture (or geography or the international system) operates. It is somewhere in this intervening space between the background factors of trading and prosperity-oriented cultures and the immediate factors of an "inputs miracle" that our explanation must be found. As Gray notes:

The national culture and the economic values that it generates interact with the political system to affect the set of policies in force by virtue of either positive support for growth-oriented policies or a docility, the willingness to accept the advice or orders of authority, on the part of the electorate in the face of the implementation of policies more likely to benefit future than current generations.[47]

Politics, in other words, is the best explanation of Asian growth, because it is both separate from growth (unlike the inputs miracle) and yet variable enough to observe different causal effects over time (see Figure 3.3 for a conceptual framework).

The story of Wu Ho-su and Shinkong remind us that the puzzle is not how Asian development *escapes* politics or insulates bureaucrats from it, but how politics delivers pro-growth, rather than growth-restraining, institutions and policies most of the time. The challenge is to describe the political logic of Asia's economic miracle.

GROWTH ALLIANCES AND REGIMES

When workers of Japan's massive Matsushita Electric Company reported for work each morning in the 1960s, they stood in serried rows, limbering up for the day's labors and singing the company song[48]:

> *For the building of the new Japan*
> *Let's put our strength and minds together.*
> *Doing our best to promote production*
> *Sending our goods to the people of the world.*
> *Endlessly and continuously*
> *Like water gushing from a fountain*
> *Grow industry, grow, grow, grow!*
> *Harmony and sincerity*
> *Matsushita Electric!*

Around the same time, South Korea's government popularized the song "Let's Live Affluently," which included the lyrics: "Let's work! Let's work! Rich countries over the sun were not created overnight!"[49]

Fifty years later, a similar refrain could be heard every morning on the streets of Shanghai, where employees of Ping An Insurance gathered in their office courtyard to sing[50]:

> *We are hand in hand in this world*
> *Choosing Ping An is what we want*
> *Sincerity, trust, positive thinking, accomplishment*
> *Our beliefs will not change ever*
> *Prestige is tops*
> *Efficiency is tops*
> *Customers rank highest*
> *Service is No. 1*
> *Ping An Insurance!*

Underlying the politics of growth in Asia is a widespread social consensus in favor of economic growth as an overarching priority. This pro-growth ideology has emerged from a trading and prosperity ethos that has been around at least as long as the Malacca Sultanate. In 1975, Butwell noted the "strong belief in the inevitability of progress, or primarily economic development" in Southeast Asia, which "contrasts sharply with the sense of despair" elsewhere in the developing world.[51] In 2010, *The Economist* wrote in a similar vein of Asia as "a joint venture, namely the pursuit of materialism based on rapid economic development."[52] Survey data from the widely used World Values Survey shows a preference for pro-growth values in Asia compared to other countries in the world. Using four measures of pro-growth values from the survey, the eight Asian countries for which data is available are more pro-growth than the global averages in twenty-three out of thirty-two (or 72 percent) of the cases.[53] At its most basic, the politics of development in Asia reflects how a consensus for rapid growth in society emerges and is then institutionalized through politics.[54]

While the seeds of pro-growth social values have been sown over many centuries through the trading and small business ethos of the region, their modern manifestations are contained in pro-growth nationalisms and pro-growth ideologies. To become sovereign and self-governing in Asia has always meant to become developed.[55] The rice and cotton sheaves on the national emblem of Indonesia were intended by Sukarno to represent the *Pancasila* (Five Principles) notion of widely shared prosperity. South Korean strongman Park Chung-Hee, who ruled from 1961 to 1979, advocated the stirring slogan of "nation building through export promotion" (*suchul ipguk*).[56] "Asian Values," meanwhile, is primarily an ideology of state-society relations, but it is distinguished from other communitarian philosophies of the developing world by its decisively pro-market stance.

The immediate manifestation of pro-growth social preferences is that partisan politics in growth phases has always begun with what Huang called "growth alliances."[57] Social forces have organized themselves into competing groups that claim to deliver more rapid and broadly shared prosperity. This contrasts with the "distributive alliances" of labor versus capital, indigenous versus globalized, peasant versus urban, or disadvantaged versus middle class that are often found in other developing countries. Of particular note is that growth alliances in Asia have usually included rural constituencies, whose interests in marketization and growth have been strengthened by land redistribution and privatization (creating a countryside full of owner-operators), by rural industrialization and infrastructure, and by opportunities of migration to urban areas. In South Korea, the proportion of farm households that were owner-operators rose from less than 10 percent to 70 percent by 1965 under a land transfer program involving half of all farmland.[58] In both Vietnam and China, it was the peasants who caused the post-Stalinist growth miracles through their early pressures and efforts to break down growth-killing communes.[59]

These growth alliances were forged in different ways in Asian countries – the grand ethnic coalition in Malaysia, the corporatist "iron triangle" in Japan, the "red capitalist" party in China, the military coalition in Indonesia, and the "mutual hostage" arrangement in South Korea between the industrial groups (*chaebol*) and the regime.[60] As democratization spread, these alliances took on new forms, generally as majoritarian ruling parties, as we shall see in Chapter 4. These political alignments and their maintenance through shifting coalitions have provided the bedrock on which growth has emerged. As Leftwich noted, long before we start looking at what states actually do to foster development in Asia, we need to explain "the enormity of the political change that is required for it to happen."[61]

Growth alliances and regimes are part of what Underhill and Zhang call a "state-market condominium" in Asian politics, which brings together social and state actors into competing networks that debate, deliberate, and sometimes collide over competing plans for national development. "State agencies are reflective of the social conflicts of the markets," they write.[62] To understand Asian development, one needs to begin by understanding these political coalitions and policy networks.

One indicator of the depth of pro-growth politics in Asia is the absence of strong, unified labor movements and social welfare parties.[63] This was easy to ascribe to repression during periods of authoritarian rule. But worker or welfare movements never gained much traction in Asian politics, even after controls on independent unions were lifted with democratization. Social preferences tend to reject zero-sum approaches to development. In his 1969 book on Japan, Stone noted the pervasive "idea that certain persons or organizations should be allowed to accumulate such wealth so that it may be productively invested to produce more wealth."[64] Whereas contemporary Europeans had "too much Robin Hood," Asians were more like Protestants who had achieved a fusion of good business with good morality. Japan, Taiwan, and Thailand never had Robin Hood politics, while attempts elsewhere either self-destructed (China and Vietnam), were defeated by growth nationalism (Indonesia, South Korea, Cambodia, the Philippines), or reformed themselves (Singapore and Malaysia).

Often the question has been asked why Asian citizens obey the pro-growth state. But the question is misplaced. As the creation of societies themselves, it should come as no surprise that pro-growth states command wide obedience. They are congruent with social preferences and therefore enjoy the legitimacy that generates policy compliance. The overarching reason for the effectiveness of the pro-growth state in Asia is not repression, exclusion, or co-optation but the legitimation of regimes through good performance.[65]

Pro-growth states emerged in Asia as a result of political ruptures, in which class-based movements were defeated by pro-growth movements.

We can see this vividly in Indonesia in 1965–66, where the independent Indonesian Peasants Front was replaced by the Indonesian Peasant's Harmony Association affiliated with GOLKAR, the new regime's ruling party. In launching the Cultural Revolution in China in 1966, Mao was fighting against the "traditionalist revolution" that sought to restore rationality and development after seven years of gross mismanagement. Mao torched the palace rather than allowing it to be retaken by the technocrats. By 1970, when an agricultural work conference for northern China rejected growth-impeding Maoism in favor of pro-growth technical expertise (seeds, fertilizers, mechanization, electrification), the palace was smoldering, and 74 percent of China's population lived in poverty, using the $1 a day standard. The restorationists included not just Deng Xiaoping but also many "revolutionary" elders, like Ye Jianying and Chen Yun, who had fought to make China develop, not decay. Once Mao died in 1976, the miracle began – the Gang of Four was arrested, Mao's successor Hua Guofeng was sidelined, and the pragmatists took command.

The resolution of growing tensions over development was a new social contract, a restoration of what I have called the Asian Governance Model, in which the state delivers rapid growth in return for a quiescent civil society and an absence of Robin Hood politics. Over time, this social contract has changed, as those middle class beneficiaries and supporters of the pro-growth state have developed broader preferences (including for democracy and freedoms). But what has not changed in Asian politics is the model of a state-society alliance for capitalist expansion.

Once we understand the state-society alliances grounded in the political culture of the Asian Governance Model, the forms and leadership of Asian regimes become more explicable. Because political regimes are seen as instrumental, authoritarianism is more or less stable, to the extent that it is delivering rapid growth. In their rapid-growth stages, countries as diverse as South Korea, China, Indonesia, Vietnam, and Malaysia kept labor unions weak and wages low, repressed consumption through low exchange rates and import tariffs, directed savings into state banks, and kept economic decisions away from the grasp of rent-seeking groups. This worked only when a pro-growth alliance was in place and to the extent that state institutions were effective. Authoritarianism in the absence of a growth alliance (Mao's China, Ho's Vietnam, junta-run Myanmar, or today's North Korea) was a failure. Moreover, as economic policy needs have changed, authoritarianism has withered. The authoritarian developmental state will increasingly be a liability in China, Vietnam, Malaysia, and Cambodia.

Leaders, meanwhile, are chosen for their perceived economic competence, and they in turn focus on broadly shared development in order to legitimate their rule. Suharto paraded himself as the "father of development" (*bapak pembangunan*), and Deng considered himself the "architect of reforms" (*gaige zongshejishi*). Leaders in Asia derive their goals and efficacy from social forces, not the other way around. For this reason, and despite the adulation lavished on leaders like Deng, both China and Indonesia would likely have boomed without them. Japan's "misunderstood miracle," as Friedman calls it,[66] was the work of prewar corporate formations that combined with a highly trusting growth-oriented society to generate the political orientations and capabilities of the bureaucracy and the leadership. Japan's near-mythical Ministry of International Trade and Industry (which was a revival of its prewar Ministry of Commerce and Industry) could neither exist nor function without the society in which it was embedded.

It is this embeddedness in the psychology and sociology of the Asian Governance Model that explains why Asian leaders offer credible commitments to pursue pro-growth policies and why they actually pursue them. "Growth ideology," as Suehiro calls it,[67] is the underlying constant, even as leaders, regimes, institutions, and policies change. Li uses the term "economism" to describe the politics of Asia because of this overarching emphasis on growth.[68] For Park, the one indisputable feature of Asian development is that "governments set economic growth and industrialization as their first priority" and pursue it consistently and rationally, even to the exclusion of other domestic and international goals.[69] In short, the political logic of Asian regimes is centered on rapid growth, which maintains the traditional legitimacy that states enjoy.[70] Populations elsewhere might be swayed by anti-Western, class warfare, or ethnic appeals. But in Asia such appeals usually fail.

Cambodia is a "hard case" for this theory, because on the surface it never had the shift in political forces that was necessary to set it on the path of rapid economic growth. The Communist Party of Kampuchea installed by Vietnam in 1979 was rebranded as the Cambodian People's Party after peace accords were signed in 1991. After elections in 1993, the CPP used its dominance to limit opposition, sideline the king, and control local governments. Since 1985, Hun Sen has continuously held the position of prime minister. Acemoglu and Robinson predicted that Cambodia would be a growth disaster because of this unreformed soft authoritarianism.[71] Yet pro-growth ideology and rational legitimation processes pushed the CPP into governance reforms both within the party and in its management of society that delivered broadly shared growth. For instance, agricultural productivity rose steeply as a result of the 2003 Land Management and Administration Program that, among other things, issued secure land titles to peasants for a nominal fee.[72] The economy grew by 7.4 percent a year during the 1990s and by 9.7 percent a year during the 2000s, the fastest pace in Asia after China. Poverty fell from 47 percent of the population in 1993 to 21 percent by 2008.[73] Pure-form institutionalism that ignores the political culture of Asia predicts a growth failure. Instead, Cambodia is an Asian miracle.

THE RATIONAL STATE

How then do pro-growth *bureaucracies* and *policies* emerge against this backdrop of growth alliances and leaderships? While the answer to this question might seem to belong in a footnote, Asia's experience shows that there is much political contention at this stage. Politics is necessary not just for the emergence of the developmental state but also for its success.

Again, it is useful to work backward (refer again to Figure 3.3). If growth miracles in Asia are a result of inputs/efficiency miracles, then these in turn are most directly shaped by economic institutions and policies. Virtually all of the attention given to Asian development has been focused on this link, and to be sure, it is key. Growth alliances are not sufficient to generate the incentives to learn, work, save, and invest without the right policies and institutions. Agencies like the World Bank focus on this "good governance" agenda, if only because the question of "how to get good governance" would draw it too deeply into political and social analysis.

To begin with a concrete example, Asia's shipping business has become a world leader and an important reason for the region's export success, accounting for fifteen of the largest twenty-five container ports by throughput in the world in 2010 (compared to two in 1970). Most immediately, this is because of an inputs and efficiency miracle that has involved the rapid expansion of shipping fleets, port facilities, and dock-side roads and storage facilities alongside steady worker upgrading. This in turn has depended critically on key state policies in the shipping sector that have stimulated private-sector initiative. While Anglo-American countries tend to develop ports on a purely private-sector basis (expecting users to pay all of the costs, even those of navigational beacons), European ones develop them on a purely government-run basis (never expecting the port to break even and setting low tariffs for users). Neither approach, however, has led to much success, judging by cost-effectiveness criteria and export competitiveness.[74]

In Asia, by contrast, governments act in part like those in Europe by making the state, not the private sector, the main investor in ports and their associated infrastructure. "Asian port developments have been driven by multi-dimensional roles of central governments as port designer, developer, operator, port pricing maker, mediator and investor," write Lee and Flynn.[75] Governments in Asia also invest in adjacent economic zones, rail links, and customs clearance facilities to keep port tariffs low as part of a public good rationale.

But Asia departs from the European model in using competition among multiple privately contracted port operators and adjacent facility owners to ensure efficient operations. This also means that tariffs are not set so low that the operators (even without overhead costs to bear) cannot make a profit. Asia's ports are also more flexible than Europe's are – for instance, they devolve functions to local governments or government port authorities to ensure more efficient resource allocation and prevent extortionate unions. While often beginning with a bigger government and nonmarket profile than those of ports in Europe, Asian ports transform more quickly to private-sector and market-oriented management, often under flexible new government agencies. "The dilemma is to pick when, by whom and how to transform the port and push it forward to a participation of private capital to maximize its economic efficiency," write Lee and Flynn.[76] In effect, Asian governments mimic what an ideal private sector would look like if it had sufficient capital, risk tolerance, time horizons, and influence over the planning process. Of particular interest culturally is how ports in Hong Kong and Malaysia (Tanjung Pelepas) that were begun under Anglo-American premises in the 1960s have gradually transformed into more Asian-looking facilities today.

The ports example highlights several functions that economic bureaucracies and policies play in order to stimulate the inputs miracle. These include the normal prescriptions of prudent macroeconomic management, secure property rights, and well-functioning and minimally distorted goods and credit markets. Relative to their developmental levels, virtually all Asian countries outperform their peers in measures of global economic competitiveness. While there is a great debate about whether commercial law or industrial finance is the Asian developmental state's greatest contribution, there is no doubt that the region's states have been able to deliver both.[77] Asia's growth is not so much driven by

globalization. Rather, its success in globalization is a result of its domestically driven growth.[78] Beyond this, several unique features are worth
noting.

Most important is the concentration of power in a series of state
agencies that have both the technical and administrative means, as well
as the political and social authority, to enact and implement growth-
enhancing policies.[79] Such agencies have the ability to break the tragedy of the economic commons by limiting the particularistic demands of
politically salient sectors – unions that resist innovation and efficiency,
money-losing state enterprises, regime cronies, unproductive landowners, or monopoly concession holders. When Stone visited the Japanese
government's Camera Inspection Institute in central Tokyo in 1965, for
instance, he found more than one hundred highly trained inspectors randomly sampling batches of cameras bound for export and rejecting entire
shipments when only a small percent were defective. Having a shipment
rejected caused "loss of face and bureaucratic displeasure" for the manu-
facturer.[80] The following year, Japan overtook Germany as the world's
largest camera exporter.

In China, the empowerment of a growth alliance under Deng Xiaoping
still left many entrenched interests that could resist competent economic
regulation and policies. It took the post-Tiananmen empowerment of the
hard-nosed Zhu Rongji (vice premier and then premier from 1991 until
2003) to resolve the country's "triangular crisis" of money-losing state
firms, insolvent state banks, and a tax-starved central government. As
with Cambodia, outsiders surmised that the obstacles to reform were too
great. What they underestimated was the strength of politically powerful
growth alliances in society, which could prod institutions to be reformed
and overcome opposition from protected social interests. The newly
unemployed state enterprise and government workers did not revolt but
instead "leapt into the sea of business" (*xiahai*). Like China, Vietnam has
prodded its state enterprises into consolidation, managerial reforms, and
hard budgets, pushing the country onto the well-worn path of market-
oriented, state-led Asian development.[81]

The economic bureaucracies and policies of Southeast Asia (except for
Singapore) have often been seen as a pale imitation of those of Northeast
Asia. But compared to the rest of the developing world, they more closely
fit the Asian pattern.[82] Suharto's first acts in office, advised by the so-
called "Berkeley Mafia" of returned economists, were to curtail trade
and price protection, cut spending and monetary expansion (including
a balanced budget law), join the IMF and World Bank, and enact laws

protecting multinational investors. Per capita growth rose dramatically –
from -0.5 percent between 1960 and 1967 to 5.4 percent between 1967
and 1981.[83] In the 1980s, the Suharto government introduced the developing world's first value-added tax in order to eliminate tax unfairness
and loopholes, as well as a new property tax; this time it was aided by
Harvard economists.[84] When Pertamina, the state oil company, defaulted
on its foreign loans in 1975, Suharto sacked his close ally General Ibnu
Sutowo from his position as head of the company and put the company
under the control of the state's Bank of Indonesia. In 1985, Suharto
hired the Swiss firm SGS to inspect all shipments at the Jakarta port of
Tanjung Priok, firing 6,000 government inspectors. Control was partially restored to the government inspectors under SGS guidance in 1991
and then fully restored under a newly professionalized customs service
in 1997. Indonesia's exports boomed. Growth in the 1990s remained at
more than 5 percent on a real per capita basis, and the number of people
in poverty plummeted from 60 million to less than 20 million.

What is important is that the pro-growth bureaucracy and policies in
Indonesia did not disappear once the increasingly corrupt Suharto was
chased from office in 1998. After a string of weak and scandal-prone
presidents, Indonesia regained its pro-growth state under retired general
Susilo Bambang Yudhoyono, who was elected as president in 2004 and
reelected in 2009. Under Yudhoyono, the macroeconomic stability created after the Asian Financial Crisis was reinforced by microeconomic
reforms, which included liberalizing changes to investment, tax, customs
and excise, and labor laws. A so-called Rainbow Cabinet was appointed
to ensure the growth alliance.

Indeed, the continuities of state-led development in Indonesia are
remarkable. In rural areas, for instance, peasant smallholders and ten-
ants seized 170,000 hectares of state-owned and private rubber, cocoa,
and teak plantation lands after 1997, replanting them with cassava, rice,
banana, durian, and oil palm. But decentralization and land-to-the-tiller
were exactly what the Indonesian state now *wanted*, so "what started
out as a community-based ideology intended to wrest control of tightly
controlled forest resources from the central government was soon being
represented ... as both a neoliberal strategy for reducing big government
and a mobilizing/organizing strategy for agrarian reform."[85] As with the
ports example, the pro-growth state managed the transition from state
ownership to privatization without missing a beat. In 2006, the government
announced that after a forty year hiatus, land reform would be resumed,
and 8.15 million hectares of state land, an area larger than Panama, were

marked for redistribution. The central state was now the agrarian radical, pushing marketizing reforms that spurred development.

Economic bureaucracies in Asian states, in other words, are guided by a strong sense of policy rationality. Policies are chosen based on sufficient information and adequate forecasting, and they are then implemented in a cautious manner with an emphasis on cost-effectiveness, monitoring, and revision. It was Silberman, an expert on Japan, who coined the term "the rational state" and then brought the concept back to Europe.[86] As Lee writes, the difference between Asia and other developing countries "lies clearly in strategic orientation and in institutional capacity in formulating and implementing a program" of national development.[87]

Again, while Southeast Asia has often been seen as less rational or results-oriented than Northeast Asia, what is astounding is how often it escaped growth-retarding policies despite political turmoil. The Malaysian electronics sector, for example, was initially conceived in 1969 as a way to attract foreign capital that could be co-opted into the country's pro-Malay discrimination policies to squeeze out Chinese electronics entrepreneurs following ethnic riots between 1965 and 1969.[88] Yet this hampered the industry, because it was those Chinese-run small electronics firms that were needed to service the foreign-invested firms.[89] In 1971, the state shifted strategies by opening an industrial zone in the Chinese-dominated state of Penang, whose local government (especially the Penang Development Corporation and the Penang Industrial Coordination Council) was allowed to encourage race-blind and investor-friendly economic policies.[90] The Penang cluster then led a national boom in electronics, which became the country's chief export earner and largest source of industrial value-added by 1980.

While much less has been written about the financial and monetary aspects of the developmental state in Asia, these are no less critical than its fiscal, investment, and regulatory roles. Financial repression (meaning directing savings into a limited number of banks, which in turn are limited in their lending activities) and monetary stringency (low inflation and pegged or managed exchange rates) were the norm in Asia throughout the boom years of the 1960s until the 1990s. One problem with the state-led financial model was that is discouraged prudent risk analysis and management by the private sector, because actors assumed that the bureaucracy either was playing that role or would bail them out. The result was the Asian Financial Crisis of 1997–98, in which prominent banks and investment companies in the region went bust. The resulting financial reforms were intended to bring more shared governance to financial markets by putting more responsibility on private sector actors. In many ways, it was the exact opposite problem that led to the Global Financial Crisis of 2008–9: The private-led financial model in the West discouraged prudent risk analysis and management by the state, because bureaucrats assumed that the private sector was playing that role. The resulting reforms also sought to reintroduce shared governance, in this case working from the opposite direction. For Asia, the early start on shared risk regulation allowed the region to escape relatively unscathed from the global crisis of 2008–9.[91]

Of course, there are significant differences in the ways that economic bureaucracies operate and the sorts of policies they adopt throughout Asia. The varieties of pro-growth states in Asia mean that any "Asian model" is at best a stylized picture that does not fit any country particularly well. Foreign investment, for example, has always played a bigger role in China than in Indonesia. The banking sector is more strictly controlled in Japan than in Thailand. Small businesses are more critical to Taiwan than to Vietnam. State ownership matters more in Singapore than in South Korea. Agricultural reform was more important in Taiwan and China than almost anywhere else.[92] Moreover, rational pro-growth states have changed significantly in Asia in the 2000s as a result of globalization, changes in innovation, and the rise of China.

The one thing that appears notably absent is the successful industrial intervention by states in creating new industrial companies. To be sure, Asian states set policies to encourage certain sectors through subsidies, infrastructure, research, and state-led coordination.[93] Khan referred to this as "growth-enhancing corruption," because in effect what the state does is tilt the playing field in favor of socially productive capitalists rather than landed elites or consumers.[94] Others have noted that industrial policy, when it works, does not involve providing open-ended protection and input subsidies to state-owned companies, but instead it takes the form of encouraging private firms to become competitive in world markets through export incentives and research grants.[95] The World Bank, in both its original 1993 *The East Asian Miracle* and its 2001 *Rethinking the East Asia Miracle*,[96] noted the lack of evidence showing that industrial interventions were a major part of the growth story in the region and the surplus of evidence showing that they were more often implicated in white elephants.

The history of interventions in the auto sector, for instance, is dismal. In Japan, bureaucrats tried to prevent motorcycle-maker Honda from entering the car market in order to protect Toyota and Nissan. Thankfully, that attempt failed. In Malaysia, the state-backed Proton car company, which began making cars in 1985, caused huge welfare losses while delivering a second-rate auto industry that cannot compete in export markets to this day. Proton, in the words of *The Economist*, is "a firm born of national-ist ideals not commercial rationale, protected by old-style cronyism, and never exposed to real competition."[97] In Taiwan, talks with Toyota in 1984 about building a massive auto base in the country fell apart over the KMT's insistence on protecting mainlander-owned Yue-Loong and Lio-Ho.[98] Taiwan's auto sector never recovered.

In South Korea, the country's two largest "developmental state" proj-ects of the 1970s, Pohang Steel and the Changwon Industrial Complex, experienced very different fates. Pohang became a leading integrated steel producer, mainly because it was given a protected domestic market and was then left to its own devices. The various state-run machinery, equip-ment, appliance, auto parts, and defense equipment factories at Changwon (created in 1974), by contrast, wallowed in management divisions, labor unrest, and cost overruns. Because the government was reimbursing all infrastructure costs and was lending to companies at 4 percent below market rates, the public return on investment was low to non-existent.[99]

Today, industrial interventions in rapidly developing Asian states are increasingly rare, in part because Asian nations have bound themselves through both international and regional trade agreements. But the deeper story is that state interventions in propping up companies rarely worked and were abandoned, and that this logic has become truer in the postin-dustrial era of innovation and services. While fans of industrial policy look to Asia for instances of successful intervention, "few sustained such policies for a significant length of time and several intervened in ways that cannot be reconciled" with the theory, notes Petri.[100] Indeed, one might argue, as do Campos and Root, that "economic growth has been durable in Asia precisely because leadership established institutions, rules, and procedures that limited government discretion over economic policy."[101]

CONTENTIOUS DEVELOPMENT POLITICS

What makes economic bureaucracies and policies work so well in Asia (and what makes them sometimes fail)? We can complete the circle (again, see Figure 3.3) by linking back to the pro-growth alliances and regimes that underpin them. These alliances and regimes are not simply midwives of the rational state. Rather, they are active and contentious stewards of it. The most forgotten aspect of the politics of development in Asia is that it *is* political. Without the explanation provided by the study of contentious politics, economic bureaucracies and policies can appear "as a *deus ex machina* in the drama of economic development," wrote Chan and Clark.[102] It is the <u>operation</u>, as well as the <u>design</u>, of the pro-growth state that is at issue. As Pei puts it, the real question is not how developmental states govern the economy but how they govern themselves.[103] If social accountability pressures are what created growth alliances and regimes, then it must be the continuous behavior of these alliances and regimes that explains the effectiveness of economic institutions. As Haggard suggests: "The preoccupation with institutions ... has obscured more fundamental political and social processes that are themselves determinants of institutional form and quality."[104]

Again, we can return to the ports example. One of the most rapidly and successfully developed hub ports of the region is South Korea's Busan (Pusan), which managed to put itself at the center of Asian traffic, despite being slightly off the main Singapore to Japan routes and far away from Seoul, the financial center.[105] Its first container terminal opened in 1978, and by 2010 it was the third largest port in Asia. The central government's Ministry of Maritime Affairs and Fisheries took the lead, devolving authority first to the Korea Container Terminal Authority (1990), and then later to the Busan Port Authority (2003), a partially privatized public corporation that operated under private-sector accounting principles.[106]

While one can tell a story about the wise, efficient, and unencumbered developmental state that created the Busan port, it does not take much to unpack the black box and find a highly politicized process. When construction began in 1974, the building of the first container terminal faced opposition from the neighboring port of Gwangyang, which forced the government to adopt a "two-port" strategy.[107] In the early 1990s, when the second wave of expansion began at Busan, contentious politics again arose over the unlevel playing field for rival ports, congestion on the road to Seoul, and planning decisions made by the Busan municipal government. For instance, when the port attempted to shift some transshipment activities to the vicinity of the railway station, the city government successfully objected on the grounds that the area should be set aside for residential development. In 1994, the expansion of Busan's municipal boundary through the annexation of 44 1/2 square miles (115 square kilometers) of land from neighboring Kyungnam province met with strenuous opposition from Kyungnam officials.[108] Seoul's attempts to mediate the dispute from the top failed, leading to the introduction of a decentralized, collaborative planning council.

Then in 2002, in an attempt to slow the port's expansion, the city decided to extend a special tariff on container traffic that had been in place since 1992. The Korea International Trade Association called the plan "outrageous" and lobbied the central government, which forced the city to relent.[109] On the waterfront, meanwhile, strikes and strike threats by the Federation of Korean Seafarers' Unions revolved as much around questions of professionalism and governance as they did around wages and working conditions.[110] In the 2000s, when the central government decided to build a new port to the west of the existing facility in order to alleviate growth pressures, the governor of the adjacent province, where most of the new port was located, pledged to block construction until the local government and industry signed off on the project.[111] At the national level, meanwhile, critics of the spending on the new port forced the central government to roll back its contribution to construction costs from nearly 50 percent to an estimated 25 percent of the total.[112] More generally, after the creation of the BPA in 2003, there was constant tension between the demands of the private sector and what Song calls "vestigial cobwebs of inefficiency and inertia left by many years of external bureaucratic control."[113]

Seen from this perspective, Busan's success is inseparable from a contentious politics that remains constrained by rational debate. Busan thrives not because it is insulated from politics, but because the politics in which it is embedded is one in which labor groups, exporters, terminal operators, and elected city and provincial officials fight over the difficult issues of efficiency and equity in a rational manner. The only appeals possible in this politics are appeals to sensible growth policies.

Contentious politics have always been at the center of economic policy making in Asia.[114] If we focus only on rational *policy* and ignore contentious *politics*, note Andersson and Gunnarsson, we will "underestimate the processes and structures under which these policy choices are made." [115] While this contention has occasionally been on display in the media or in protests, for the most part it is an organized contention that takes place through discussions between the government and the private sector. In Haggard's phrase, state-market relations in Asia are "an ongoing negotiation," which ranges from "close alignments, to arms-lengths relationships, to open antagonism."[116] The purpose of these discussions is not simply to better inform government policy: It is also to ensure that no one gets special favors. For, as Campos and Root note, "when rules, procedures, and regulations are discussed openly among the relevant parties and input from all parties is encouraged, a more transparent and impartial policy environment emerges."[117]

While there were indeed state favors available, what distinguishes Asia is that there is an open competition for these favors (what economists call "rents") that is based on rational performance targets, such as exports or competitiveness. In Kang's account,[118] regime corruption was just as widespread in South Korea as it was in the Philippines. The difference was that in the former, regime and business interests were balanced and thus mutually constraining, while in the latter, first business (1946 to 1972) and then the regime (1972 to 1986) were dominant and thus able to plunder the economy. Japan's Council on Economic and Fiscal Policy, which was established in 2001 with wide powers to set economic policy, was mandated to have at least four of its ten members come from the private sector and to publish its full minutes three days after every meeting. It succeeded in tackling difficult fiscal and regulatory issues that had been seen as insolvable during Japan's "lost decade" of slow growth in the 1990s.[119]

The claim by Jones that Asian developmental states are built on a "feudal cultural legacy, emphasizing hierarchy, conformity, and loyalty to the group" is thus only a partial truth.[120] Since their earliest years, state-society relations have been characterized by contention and pressures to perform. As Yap has shown using statistical models,[121] when Asian states fail to perform, citizens withdraw their support by striking, underpaying taxes, and delaying investments. Governments then respond to these social pressures by sacking officials, restructuring institutions and policies, and offering apologies and compensation to those who are unfairly harmed by policy mistakes. Only then do they demonstrate the credible commitment to restore social support for the developmental state. Chang has used the term "developmental citizenship" to describe the dominant political culture in many Asian countries, under which citizenship is mainly conceived in terms of rights and obligations relating to economic development, and grassroots activism revolves around economic issues.

In 1973 and 1974, for instance, pro-growth authoritarian regimes in Taiwan and Malaysia, responding to the growth slowdown caused by the first oil shock, took harsh steps to arrest corrupt officials, streamline administration, and abolish ineffective institutions. In Malaysia, the ruling party's chief minister in the powerhouse state of Selangor was expelled for corruption, while in Taiwan a presidential aide and the head of party personnel was convicted of graft relating to two state agricultural cooperatives. In the same period, both regimes expanded their popular base, with the KMT's installation of a native Taiwanese to the post of provincial governor in Taiwan and the formation of the National Front cross-ethnic coalition in Malaysia.

From this perspective, what is notable about the Asian Financial Crisis of 1997–98 is not how quickly social support was withdrawn and economies crashed, but how quickly social support (and growth) resumed following appropriate government responses. In the hardest-hit economy, Indonesia, a regime change occurred, while in hard-hit Malaysia, South Korea, and Thailand, governments created ad hoc bodies, like Malaysia's National Economic Action Council or Thailand's Nukul Commission to resolve bank insolvencies and investigate financial corruption. The Nukul Commission criticized the Bank of Thailand for its lax oversight and corrupt protection of the crony-ridden Bangkok Bank of Commerce, which it bailed out at a cost of $7 billion in 1996, only to see it fail nonetheless with $3 billion in debt, taking fifty other financial institutions with it. The Bank of Thailand's former governor was sued for gross negligence in 2001, resulting in a $4.6 billion fine, the largest in Thai history (it remains under appeal at this writing), while the former Bangkok Bank of Commerce president was jailed for twenty years. By 1999 and 2000, real per capita growth in all three countries had rebounded to near its high-growth levels. Books pouring off the presses about the "end of the Asian Miracle" were wrong,[122] because they misunderstood the social pressures that keep Asian developmental states effective.

Of course, major reforms of the policies and institutions of growth resulted from the Asian Financial Crisis and broader globalization pressures. Pro-growth states that once intervened to support key industries and subsidize investment, innovation, and education cut back, restructuring themselves from developmental states into regulatory states. But contrary to the dire warnings of critics of "neoliberalism,"[123] growth continued. State authority is no less necessary for a liberalized economy than it is for a state-directed one, and Asian states remained embedded in the shared growth imperatives of the AGM. Just as they could insert themselves neutrally and effectively into economic life in the early stages of development, so too could they withdraw themselves to become omnipresent, neutral, and effective regulators and market watchdogs in the postindustrial phase.

Strong states were pro-growth in both their interventionist and "neoliberal" stages. The Asian model is about growth, not intervention, and it can be selectively pruned when it no longer serves the growth imperative. As Robinson and colleagues note: "The apparatus of the state and that ensemble of power relations embedded within it remains intact."[124] Growth alliances (especially middle-class segments) in countries like Thailand, South Korea, Taiwan, and Indonesia generally *demanded* neo-liberal reforms – "economic democracy," as it is called in South Korea – to ensure fairness against a growing backdrop of conglomerate-based corruption. Domestic growth alliances in South Korea and Thailand benefitted from IMF intervention in the Asian Financial Crisis, because the breakup of state-controlled financial markets and industrial conglomerates unleashed faster growth.[125] Globalization and liberalization have not undermined developmental states in Asia but instead have played to their strengths.

Read this way, the contentious politics of China's 1989 Tiananmen Square movement can be seen as a response to the economic failures of the early pro-growth regime. The movement was fuelled by complaints about rising inflation, official corruption, and the inequities associated with the partial reform that allowed some lucky enterprises and sellers to make a killing. What changed after the movement was a sharp official retrenchment against inflation, a crackdown on elite corruption, and a rapid liberalization intended to level the playing field. By the late 1990s, China's accountable pro-growth regime had begun sacking senior ministers for policy failures – the Minister of Water Resources in 1998, the Minister of Land and Resources in 2003, the head of food safety in 2008, the Minister of Railways in 2011. Because there is no perfectly representative Asian development model, China's particularities do not make it less of a good fit. In key aspects – its rational state that encouraged investment, exports, and industrialization; its focus on market-based competition; its strong social growth alliance and resulting politics that minimized Robin Hood and cronyistic politics; and its prudent macro-economic policies – it fits the regional pattern well, especially when compared to developing nations as a whole.[126]

In short, the developmental state cannot be abstracted from the social and political contexts in which it operates. By making credible commitments to reform, Asian growth states regain the social support necessary to spur investment and employment. That is why trying to replicate Asian success by announcing export promotion boards or national avionics corporations almost always fails elsewhere. Krugman was right that Asia is an inputs miracle. But achieving that requires a deeply political process of growth alliances and regimes that create and then sustain growth-enhancing economic bureaucracies and policies. It is politics, not institutions, that explains Asian development.

Does this model explain growth elsewhere? Phases of rapid growth can result from a number of contingent conditions: the settlement of new lands; the return of political stability; one-off gains in productivity associated with putting capital and labor to better use; or a resource boom. But the Asian model depends in part on historical legacies and cultural orientations that are not as prevalent elsewhere, especially in the developing world. That is why the fate of Asia's slow developers is of such interest.

Although economic failure is not normally associated with Asia, the region has seen its fair share of growth disasters since World War II. Indeed, in terms of total lives lost, Mao's China easily tops historical records, while in terms of lives lost as a proportion of the population, Pol Pot's Kampuchea (about one-fifth of the population[127]) and Kim Jong-Il's North Korea (about one-twentieth of the population[128]) know no equal. While state-led development is an Asian specialty, so is state-led genocide. Besides the ongoing grand tragedy in North Korea, the region has experienced two low-intensity developmental failures, in the Philippines and in Myanmar. To complete the analysis, it is important to understand the politics behind these three developmental failures.

In the Philippines, which had the second highest income per capita after Japan among Asian countries in 1955, institutions alone were never sufficient. Under Ferdinand Marcos between 1965 and 1986, a developmental state was constructed that looked much like those in South Korea and Indonesia. The Eleven Priority Industries Project identified sectors like aluminum refining, phosphor-based fertilizers, cement, and transport equipment as strategic key industries for state support, leading to an armada of 327 state enterprises by 1985. A Labor Coordinating Center was created to control unions and keep wage demands in check, while an Employers Confederation interacted with the private sector on industrial policies. Investment in education surged, and a National Development Bank steered record-high capital accumulation into key companies. Institutions were created to boost agricultural productivity.[129]

But as we have seen, effective institutions are a *consequence*, not cause, of development drivers. Marcos could build institutions, but he could not restructure the divisive Robin Hood politics of the country, diagnosed by Landé in 1965,[130] even after imposing martial law in 1972. His new political party, the New Society Movement, failed to develop as a broad growth alliance. Landed elites remained aloof. Without the political creation of a growth alliance and the ongoing politics of growth accountability, institutions fail, as they did under Marcos and afterward. Rather than pro-growth ideologies, the Philippines has every manner of anti-growth ideology. It is the only Asian country where radical dependency theory and its attendant resentments against the World Bank, multinational corporations, and free trade ever took hold.[131] It is also the only Asian country where the national civic culture and state are seriously challenged by an amoral familistic culture built around a religious organization, the Catholic Bishops' Conference of the Philippines, which has opposed everything from hydroelectric dams to foreign investment in the mining industry through "social action centers" that were established in every diocese.[132]

The political center cannot hold in such a context. Under Marcos, "economic profitability" was only one of thirty-one criteria used to evaluate an investment project, with a 4.4 percent weighting.[133] Economic institutions and policies are pulled in every direction except the one that delivers growth. Under these conditions, tourists and foreign investors steer clear, while patronage politics thrives. The IMF found that the Philippines actually fell further behind average developing country growth after its 1986 democratization (from about 81 percent of the average growth in GDP per capita in twenty-three key developing countries from 1969 to 1983 to just 29 percent from 1985 to 2008).[134] "People Power," as the name suggests, was too infused by Robin Hood politics and not enough by growth politics, despite the best efforts of the country's bureaucrats. Having been undermined first by business oligarchs from 1946 to 1972 and then by a predatory regime from 1972 to 1986, the Philippines economy reverted to a kind of oligarchic putrefaction under democracy. Political parties, rather than being competing growth coalitions, range from the personalistic to the perverse. The 1987 constitution made provision for an independent National Economic and Development Authority, but successive governments never passed enabling legislation to give it the promised autonomy from the cabinet. A 1998 executive order prohibiting government departments from lending money to target beneficiaries – a rational move that was taken long ago by other Asian countries – was rescinded in 2006 under pressure from "anti-poverty" activists.[135] This volatility of public policies and this weakness of public institutions are hallmarks of Latin American economies, which is one reason why the Philippines is often considered to be the Argentina of Asia. Filipino leaders since Marcos have had the right ideas but have lacked the pro-growth politics (in particular, the alliance with pro-growth social interests) that are needed to make them work. The question about the Philippines is not why elite bosses and *trapos* (traditional politicians) plunder, but why people follow them, or why they challenge the system by associating with Maoist communists or anti-growth bishops.

Political culture is not fate, however; it can change. The "Asianization" of the Philippines can occur through deliberate learning and action. Since the early 2000s, several groups have pioneered a "new politics" that rejects the growth-inhibiting plagues of both the *trapos* and the bishops. The indigenous concept of *bayanihan*, or coming together to solve problems, has been used in recent experiments in Palawan province to improve public services while bypassing patronage politics *and* rejecting anti-market solutions.[136] It is a long and uncertain road, but recovery begins with recognizing the problem.

In the cases of Myanmar and North Korea, the problem is more straightforward: the absence of growth institutions and policies. Under a socialist military dictatorship from 1962 to 1988 and then a predatory military junta from 1988 to 2011, Myanmar leaders showed no interest in fostering a capitalist economy.[137] Economic activity was first nationalized and then embezzled by successive military rulers. In 2008, the junta spent more on the military than on health and education combined; among Asian countries, only North Korea did the same. The official exchange rate was overvalued by 21,000 percent in that year.[138] Withdrawals from the Myanmar Agricultural Development Bank were illegal, which predictably kept most savings in the informal sector. Once the rice bowl of Asia, Myanmar was reduced to exporting only low-quality, "broken rice" to Africa. North Korea, for all its differences, is similar in that it is also a predatory regime that is able to cut itself off from the accountability pressures normally expected within the Asian Governance Model framework.

Ironically, this means that both Myanmar and North Korea probably have better growth prospects than the Philippines. Unlike the Philippines, both countries have strong national cultures and an absence of Robin Hood politics. Their links to China and embeddedness in a political sociology that is more typical of Asian countries mean that once "bad rulers" are chased from office and proper institutions are put in place, the political conditions needed to make them succeed are more likely to emerge.

Myanmar's sudden shift to an inclusive growth alliance in 2010 is laying the foundations for a typical Asian developmental state.[139]

The politics of development in Asia, then, have two key lessons for countries struggling to ignite rapid growth. First of all, while state direction remains a critical part of the development story in Asia, it is notable for its pro-market and pro-private sector biases. One might say that Asian states are the key capitalists of Asian countries. In the countries of Asia that embraced any form of antimarket bias in their economic policies – China and Vietnam before reforms, the Philippines under the influence of *dependencistas* and antiglobalization advocates, the predatory state in Myanmar and North Korea, or the affirmative action welfare state in Malaysia – growth has slowed and poverty has risen. Rationality in economic policies means allowing markets and the private sector to take the lead in economic development, while retaining an episodic and limited role for state intervention alongside ongoing state efforts to maintain the macroeconomic conditions needed for growth and the microeconomic public policies needed to maximize social opportunity and minimize inequality.

Secondly, institutions alone will produce nothing unless they are backed by a growth alliance in society that is replicated by a pro-growth regime and political leadership. To escape from slow growth requires first and foremost a social recognition of failure, secondly a "traditionalist revolution" to oust the pretenders, and thirdly the translation of this new pro-growth politics into effective economic institutions and policies. The "fence-breaking" (*pha rao*) in Vietnam was the same as the "fake collectives" (*jia jiti*) in China – bottom-up attempts to reestablish private ownership and market signals as state planning failed. The rapidity with which China ditched Maoism for *gaige kaifang* (reform and opening) and with which Vietnam ditched socialization for *doi moi* (restructuring) is astounding. Top-down recognition of these failures lagged bottom-up pressures in both countries. The pro-growth developmental state, in other words, needed to be constructed from below before it could take shape at the top.

Put in these terms, development in Asia is interesting precisely because it is so dependent on political conditions. Rapid growth can easily give way to slow growth because of the overthrow of pro-growth institutions or because of the breakdown of the social consensus for growth. In many ways, the former seems unlikely in an era when most countries have embraced some version of prudent and growth-oriented economic policies. Rather, the challenges to development in Asia are today more likely to arise from the breakdown of a social consensus for growth, given the emergence of a democratic politics that makes it easier to construct particularistic social movements. Yet democracy has also brought new tools of accountability that may counterbalance those tendencies. Democracy is the topic we turn to next.

4

Democracy

Since the 1980s, Asian politics has been transformed by the spread of democracy. Understanding democracy in the region requires understanding the long historical trajectories in which it is embedded. For that purpose, there is no better case than Indonesia, the region's second biggest country after China.

The borders of Indonesia were roughly outlined by the great Majapahit kingdom of Java, which extended its influence over much of the contemporary country from about 1300 to about 1500 before breaking up into several kingdoms and sultanates. A hundred years later, those same boundaries became the target of the Dutch, who began their conquest with a trading post at the eastern Java town of Bantam in 1602 and continued to reclaim control over the Majapahit region until Bali was finally conquered on the eve of World War I.

While the power of the various sultans and indigenous rulers was subordinated under colonial law, the Dutch left most of those sultans and rulers in place and outfitted them with the apparatus of a modern state. The traditional conceptions of power and propriety that had arisen in the Javanese and Sumatran kingdoms of the Malay archipelago from the 600s to the 1500s remained remarkably resilient in the face of European colonization. If anything, Dutch rule tended to reinforce these conceptions, which were reinvented as what Kingsbury called "an authoritarian parody of traditional style."[1] What later became "Indonesian tradition" was largely an invention of colonialism.

World War II strengthened this emerging Indonesian identity. It was not just that the Dutch were defeated, which suggested the fragility of their rule and the plausibility of an independent Indonesia. More importantly, the Japanese occupation from 1942 to 1945 stimulated new thinking about national identity and political organization. The militaristic organization, developmental ideology, and social integration of the Japanese period seminally shaped the ideas of Indonesian nationalists about a "Great Indonesia" (*Indonesia Raya*). A Japanese film made during the period shows, according to accompanying notes, "scenes of martial parades, banners declaring Japanese-Indonesian solidarity, and soldiers in training, against a background of Indonesian music."[2] The 35,000-strong militia organized by the Japanese formed the basis of the new Indonesian army, and it was the Japanese-created Preparatory Committee for Indonesian Independence led by Sukarno and Hatta that declared independence days after Japanese withdrawal. As elsewhere in Asia, Japanese imperialism and occupation had a profound impact on national identity in the region.[3] The independent Republic of Indonesia was proclaimed in 1945, and after a four year war against the spiritless Dutch, Sukarno was sworn in as the first president in 1949.

From 1949 until 1957, Indonesia experimented with democracy. The nearby democracies in India and Burma and the redemocratization of Japan had inspired a belief that democracy was essential for creating a modern state. But freed from Dutch and Japanese control, Indonesian society found it difficult to regroup. Seventeen coalition governments rose and fell in this period, while dozens of regional insurgencies simmered following the abandonment of federalism. Indonesians felt that multiparty democracy had thrown them into a "rut," writes Feith.[4] Sukarno decried the "liberal politics, in which the votes of the majority of the people are exploited, black-marketed, and corrupted by various groups."[5] In 1956, Sukarno said in a speech that his dream was that political leaders would "join together to bury all parties."[6]

The Indonesian experiment with democracy ended in 1957 when Sukarno imposed martial law and introduced a "guided democracy," in which political parties would cooperate with a newly strengthened presidential office backed by the military, which now played an explicit political role. In 1959, he dissolved parliament, ended the deliberations of a constitutional assembly, and began to rule by decree. Regional revolts and a bizarre new ideology that Sukarno called *nas-a-kom* (combining the terms for *nationalism*, *agama*, or syncretic Islamic religion, and *communism*) led to a precipitous decline in government performance and economic growth. Inflation, debt, and shortages grew. With both democracy and left-wing authoritarianism discredited, an army general named Suharto seized power in 1965 under a "New Order" government.

From 1966 onward, Suharto's New Order was a typical incorporative and developmental dictatorship on the Asian model – one that borrowed explicitly from the New Order of Japan in World War II.[7] The ruling party was called the Joint Secretariat for Functional Groups (*Sekretariat Bersama Golongan Karya*, or *Golkar* for short), suggesting that state-society relations were being formed along integrationist, Hegelian lines. Each segment of state and society – army, bureaucracy, villagers, business – would be seamlessly integrated into a whole. The functional group concept had emerged in Europe from the guild system and had been used by the fascists in Italy and Germany, as well as by the Japanese in their occupations throughout Asia. All traditional political parties were "buried" and reorganized into two new token parties in 1973. In the six legislative elections held during the New Order period, Golkar won an average of 71 percent of the contested seats (the military was given its own seats).

In the 1980s, the New Order was at its most secure. The legislature ceased to function. Dissent and protest left over from the 1965–66 turmoil was extinguished. A conviction grew among experts that the authoritarian personality was deeply embedded in the Indonesian psychology and that authoritarian interests were deeply embedded in the Indonesian political economy.[8] "There is no Indonesian tradition of public debate or loyal opposition," avers Jones.[9] Thompson in 1993 wrote that the New Order "has been stabilized by a growing economy and hopes for orderly succession," and that this "Asian model of development dictatorship may become a kind of alterative political model to Western democracy."[10]

Indeed, Suharto's New Order drew support from well beyond the army and bureaucracy, including from Islamic groups and urban middle classes who feared a renewed communist insurgency. Aspinall wrote that "the New Order possessed a strong institutional base in the army and bureaucracy and considerable civilian support" while its leaders considered it to be "the natural and final form of government for Indonesia."[11] Prominent intellectuals and middle-class groups worried more about national disintegration and social unrest than about political repression.

Despite the apparent success of the New Order, social and economic change was transforming Indonesian politics. The impetus for this was a series of rapid, market-based economic reforms that Suharto undertook between 1983 and 1988. These undid a large part of the import-substitution and investment-regulation system that been created in the 1970s, when Indonesia cashed in on an oil export boom. In a 1980 report, the World Bank referred to the system as a "bureaucratic mess" and began pressing for changes.[12] When oil prices collapsed, Suharto's advisors agreed. Under the changes, new banks were approved, foreign investors were welcomed, and virtually all regulatory constraints were removed from domestic investments in key areas, like maritime transportation (whose importance in a country of more than 1,000 permanently settled islands is akin to that of the U.S. or European highway systems). Almost half of the 1,700 items that required a special license to import were removed from the list, ending the biggest distortion and source of corruption in Indonesia's trade policy.[13] The number of permits needed to start a business fell from thirty-five to fifteen, and export bans on items like coffee and rattan and export quotas on items like fertilizer and rice were lifted.

All of this had a deep and transformative effect on Indonesian society, especially outside of the major cities. The number of nongovernmental organizations spiraled from just 200 in 1981 to 3,200 by 1989 and to 8,000 by 1996.[14] This social mobilization was primarily developmental in nature – marketing cooperatives, water management committees, etc. But the result was a rising demand for accountability. Judges started to make rulings against the regime on issues like press freedoms and labor rights. Indonesia's GDP per capita surpassed $3,000 (using 2005 prices and PPP estimates) in 1996, during the early stages of the developmental phase, when many authoritarian regimes succumb to liberalizing pressures. "State dominance over society is still strong, but not as complete as the authoritarian leaders wish," wrote Uhlin in 1997.[15]

Within society, popular resentment was growing as an increasingly free media reported on the economic misadventures of Suharto's family and friends. In the 1995 hit song "The Pain Remains the Same," the popular Surabaya-based, heavy metal band *Slowdeath* sung:

> *Arise against this unjust system that always fooled us*
> *Chronic corruption never put to an end*
> *Political distortion manipulates the system*
> *Social sterilization sacrificing the people.*
> *Crusade against these feudalistic norms that enslave us*
> *Collusion between entrepreneurs and officials*
> *Colonialist patterns brought again to life*
> *Exploiting the people for their own profit*
> *Only a few million poor left? That's a big lie*
> *Never trust their propaganda.*

Bored with their lies
Stop this wrong system, something must be done
Why must we go on, to satisfy their gains?
There's no difference between
D. C. [Dutch Colonialism]
and the N. O. [New Order]
So, all that we can say is:
The pain remains the same![16]

At the same time, Indonesia's external environment was changing. The end of the Cold War ushered in a new era in which advocating human rights and tackling official corruption loomed larger than fighting communism. Within Asia, a thirty-year authoritarian slumber was ending. Successful democratic movements in the Philippines, South Korea, and Thailand and failed democratic movements in Burma and China had been closely watched in Jakarta.[17] Political "openness" (*keterbukaan*) was widely debated beginning in 1989. The legislature and army started to issue reports on things like multicandidate presidential elections and legislative powers.[18]

Suharto, aged seventy-five in 1996, responded cautiously, affirming the basic principles of the New Order but also making changes, like reducing the military's seats in the 500-seat legislature from 100 to 75. There were even occasional discussions, including by Suharto himself, of the need for a new president following his reelection in 1993. The talk of openness and succession gave the New Order a fin de siècle sense by the early 1990s. Still, most observers believed Suharto's regime was resilient and strong. Liddle in 1996 wrote that "democracy seems further away in this country ... The regime looks solid and highly efficient, and despite recent unrest, faces no serious inside or outside threat, at least as long as Suharto remains in power."[19]

In 1996, Suharto clumsily removed Megawati Sukarnoputri from her position as chair of one of the token opposition parties, the Indonesian Democratic Party (IDP). Megawati, Sukarno's daughter, had suggested that she might run against Suharto for president in 1998. As punishment, she was unceremoniously sacked by an "extraordinary" congress of her own party, and the media was told to refer to her using her husband's last name, rather than Sukarno's. When she resisted (with a lawsuit), the party headquarters became the center of anti-Suharto protests, which led to a military crackdown in July of that year. Despite being an uninspired and reluctant leader, Megawati was idealized for reclaiming the Sukarnoist ideals of traditional nationalism and social justice (she was a great admirer and close friend of the late North Korean dictator Kim

Jong Il).²⁰ Military figures warned of an "Aquino phenomenon," referring
to the leader of the People Power Revolution in the Philippines.

The Asian financial crisis came close on the heels of the crackdown.
Indonesia abandoned its managed exchange rate in August 1997, and the
rupiah promptly lost more than half of its value. Student groups began
protesting "corruption, collusion and nepotism." Suharto was forced to
sign bailouts with the IMF in October 1997 and again in January 1998.
The IMF was seen as having imposed itself on Indonesia's hard-won
sovereignty, not least in a famous photo that shows Suharto signing the
January package at a desk, with the IMF managing director towering
over him imperiously, arms crossed like a strict headmaster.

The first crack appeared in February 1998, when a former Suharto
cabinet minister offered himself as a rival candidate to Suharto's preferred vice-presidential candidate, B. J. Habibie, for the upcoming
presidential "election" (conducted by an upper house, known as the
People's Consultative Assembly, or PCA, which was composed of half
appointees and half legislators). But hopes that this would create a broad
democratic opposition proved premature, given that no one would
openly challenge Suharto. "If only Father Suharto could prepare someone to learn more closely how to lead the nation, it would be much more
reassuring," the country's leading newspaper, *Media Indonesia*, wrote
meekly in a front-page editorial.²¹

After Suharto was "reelected" president in March 1998, he formed
a new cabinet made up of cronies, golfing partners, and family members. Political reforms would begin in 2003, he declared. Street protests
quickly swelled, demanding "total reform." General Wiranto, commander
of the military, appointed an American-educated reformer in the military, Susilo Bambang Yudhoyono, to head a special military committee
to study political reform options for the country, because the military
had always asserted its "dual function" of protecting both external and
internal stability.

The shooting of four students at the Trisakti University on May 12,
1998 broke the regime's spell on Indonesia. Ever since students of the
School for the Training of Native Doctors of Batavia had set up the country's first nationalist organization, which was named Beautiful Endeavor,
in 1908, students in Indonesia (as elsewhere in Asia) had always pro-
fessed their loyalty to the symbols and ideals of the nation, while claiming
to be a moral force that could correct the deviations of the current rulers.
As one prominent student leader of the 1970s put it in 1994, students
"did not wish to form a force but rather wished to communicate with

someone we trusted," and "if the government caught the issue it would mean that our job would be finished."[22] Responding to student protests over the shootings, Suharto suggested he would step down to become the *pandhita* ("sage") or *begawan* ("wise man who guides from behind") of the nation.[23] This was not enough. On May 16, Sukarno was told by the Golkar and PCA chairmen that "there had been a paradigm shift in people's mood."[24] Two days later, May 18, with Suharto still unmoved, the chairman of Golkar, the speaker of the legislature, and General Wiranto all publicly called for his resignation. The Golkar legislative caucus voted 160 to 125 in favor of his resignation. "The public and student pressure was growing and we had to face the reality that we could no longer hold onto Suharto," one Golkar legislator recalled.[25]

In meetings with leading Muslim leaders on May 19, Suharto declared that he was "fed up" (*saya kapok*) with being president but worried that Habibie was incompetent and widely disliked. "If I resign is there any guarantee all this trouble will end?"[26] Instead, he announced that he would reshuffle the cabinet and introduce political reforms. But fourteen members of the proposed new cabinet, as well as most of the forty-five members of a proposed political reform council, refused to serve. The political elites of Indonesia had abandoned their king. Students forced their way into the legislature to demand his resignation.

In a dramatic meeting at Suharto's home on the evening of May 20, General Wiranto promised Suharto that the military would support a handover to Habibie as sufficient fulfillment of the protestors' demands.[27] Everyone seemed to agree that continuity with the New Order was paramount to ensure national stability. On May 21, President Suharto announced his resignation, and Habibie was sworn in as Indonesia's third president to serve out the remainder of the 1998 to 2003 presidential term. Of the thirty-six ministers in Habibie's first cabinet, twenty were from Suharto's abortive "reform cabinet." Students now celebrated.

The handover to Habibie was symbolically important, because as Minister for Research and Technology, he had been at the forefront of several "developmental state" projects in fields like aviation, shipbuilding, and engineering. More broadly, the entire democratic transition in Indonesia is interesting because it *was* a transition, despite its strong continuist elements. In some ways, it is the story of what did *not* happen that needs to be told – namely, that there was no repeat of People Power in the Philippines.

There were two key leaders of the "Muslim street" who might potentially have led a People Power democratic revolution in Indonesia – Amien

Rais, head of the 28-million member *Muhammadiyah*, or Followers of Muhammad, and Adi Sasono, former secretary-general of the government-linked Indonesian Council of Muslim Intellectuals (ICMI). Both had been widely quoted in the 1990s for their work in trying to reconcile Islam and democracy and for their moral critiques of the regime. Both men had been forced out of the ICMI by Suharto in 1997, and Sasono had also been stripped of his PCA seat.

In January 1998, as street protests swelled, Rais proposed the formation of an opposition alliance between himself, Megawati, and Abdurrahman Wahid, a leading Muslim intellectual whose organization had withdrawn from the token Islamic political party, the United Development Party (UDP), in 1984. This "grand clean coalition" would exercise presidential functions until a new election could be held for the legislature and thus the PCA. But Rais was distrusted by Wahid and Megawati, both of whom were concerned with ensuring the peaceful nature of any transition.[28] Sasono, meanwhile, proposed a "national dialog" between regime and opposition, an explicit attempt to create a pact that would have represented a halfway point between a People Power revolution and New Order continuity.[29] Again, he was judged as not sufficiently credible by political elites searching for solutions to the political crisis.

The failure of these attempts to break with the New Order led both Rais and Sasono in more radical directions. As student protests rose in March and April, Rais became more critical, openly calling for a "mass movement" to overthrow the New Order. He expressed the hope that the students "will become the vanguard of the people's aspirations [because they] do not have vested political interests."[30] On May 14, Rais announced the formation of a fifty-five-member "Council of the People's Mandate" that would assume power after Suharto fell.[31] It excluded Megawati and Wahid and was made up largely of nonestablishment intellectuals. This attempt to seize the "mandate" to rule from the state and place it in the hands of society was the most explicit attempt at a People Power overthrow in Indonesia's transition.

At the same time, Sasano proposed a new cabinet that would exclude all of Suharto's cronies and holdovers.[32] The Golkar chairman, General Wiranto, the chairman of the PCA, and even Habibie himself all gave their conditional support, unsure of which direction the political winds were blowing. Expecting to take power, Rais and Sasono even held a meeting with the head of the agency handling the financial crisis. But when it came to enacting People Power, the key political elites – especially Wiranto and Habibie, but also Megawati and Wahid – ultimately balked.

Fearing a disaster, they realized they could probably defuse the crisis with a continuist transition. Indonesian political elites repeatedly referred to the Philippines as a danger to be avoided.[33] Even the people themselves seemed unsure. One Muslim leader accused Rais's Council of the People's Mandate of "rushing ahead like a locomotive and leaving all the coaches behind in confusion."[34]

Once it became clear to Rais and Sasano that the window for People Power was closing, Rais threatened to send 1 million protestors into the streets on May 20, National Awakening Day, which "raised the political temperature in the capital to an all-point high."[35] But by then, the political elite had regrouped around the idea of a Habibie transition. General Wiranto warned Rais that the military would not hesitate to reenact China's 1989 Tiananmen bloodbath. Rais then admitted defeat, accepted the succession plan,[36] and "told his supporters to stay home and pray."[37]

The failure of an Indonesian People Power movement is the great unexplored question of Indonesia's democratization. The explanation lies in the strong state tradition of Asia. As Sukma notes, aside from the students and the "street" leaders, "the opposition forces did not consist of radically different political groups from outside the regime. They were partly derived from within the regime itself. They did not challenge the whole regime, but only its top leadership, namely, President Suharto."[38] In a society-led transition, Rais and Sasano would have led a new government, while in a "pacted" transition, they would have shared power in some grand coalition that included people like Megawati and Habibie. But in this case, despite the massive social mobilization, the transition was regime-led and Rais and Sasono were left out in the cold.

To say that the transition was regime-led *because* the opposition was divided, as is often claimed, is to confuse cause and effect. Rather, the opposition was divided because in the strong state context of Indonesian politics, a united opposition was nearly impossible. The state did not actively repress or divide the opposition. Instead, it crowded it out of the political imagination. The strong state tradition "allowed the bulk of the old governing elite to abandon Suharto, as a concession to the societal upsurge, yet retain power," concludes Aspinall.[39]

At the same time, one should note the central role that was played by social forces in forcing Suharto to resign. The "paradigm shift" took place first in society, not among political elites. Megawati merely filed a lawsuit against her ouster, but her supporters stormed the legislature. That is why, despite the apparently cosmetic nature of the change, new president Habibie acted quickly to initiate real political liberalization.

In the months after the handover, more than 200 political prisoners were released; opposition parties were legalized and eighty new ones were approved; military seats in the 500-seat legislature were cut to 38; government control of the press and protests was vastly curtailed; legislative approval was introduced for all presidential appointments; the PCA was empowered to meet annually to review the president's performance; plans for regional devolution were introduced; and the requirement that civil servants and their families vote for Golkar dropped. Even more telling was Habibie's rapid acquiescence to demands for a snap presidential election alongside the promised legislative elections of 1999.

This balance of social demands and state leadership was evident in the results of the 1999 elections, in which forty-eight parties competed. The three New Order parties (Megawati's IDP, Golkar, and the Islamic UDP) won 67 percent of the votes, while Rais's newly formed National Mandate Party won a mere 7 percent. There was to be no "electoral revolution" to complete the continuist transition here. Given the rivalries among the traditional New Order parties, the PCA decided to elect Wahid, whose party had garnered only 13 percent of the vote, as president. The sorts of elite conflicts that every strategic theory would have predicted for Indonesia did not arise. Indeed, Wahid appointed Megawati as his vice president and promoted the reformist general Yudhoyono to the cabinet – both of whom were his rivals for power. (Wahid was then censured by the parliament for incompetence in 2000 and replaced by Megawati in 2001.) Habibie, meanwhile, shuffled off stage having played his historic role as an interim leader in a state-led democratic transition. In all of these ways, the unity of Indonesia's political elite during a wrenching economic crisis and political transition remains remarkable and largely unremarked on, precisely because it was not newsworthy.

The fact that Indonesia had democratized at the early stages of the typical transition zone in terms of development levels meant that its prospects for consolidation seemed dim. Moreover, with a presidential system and a past military involvement in politics, Indonesia looked a lot like Latin American democracies that had repeatedly failed. Add in an Islamist movement and roiling regional insurgencies in East Timor, Aceh, and Papua, and democratic prospects looked bleak indeed. In a country of 171 million eligible voters in 2004, the obstacles seemed insurmountable.

But despite the political challenges, Indonesia quickly became a consolidated democracy. In particular, the decision by the PCA in 2002 to clip its own wings by giving up its power to appoint the president defied predictions that had been made based on strategic self-interest. "Under conditions of considerable instability, this kind of cooperation among state elites confounds rational choice explanations," Davidson notes.[40] The reason is that Indonesian elites were motivated by genuine nationalist and democratic sentiments that overrode those incentives, sentiments that were strongly influenced by broad social pressures operating on the state.

Both the 2004 and 2009 presidential elections were won by Yudhoyono as head of his newly formed Democratic Party. Yet despite the continuation of the New Order elite, Indonesia made further rapid democratic advances. New institutions were created – a national audit agency, an anticorruption commission, a constitutional court, an elections commission – that acted with neutrality and effectiveness. The military gave up its remaining seats in parliament and formally renounced its "dual function" political and military role. As Davidson notes: "Early pessimism about the capture of new institutions by New Order elites and other predatory politico-economic forces has given way to renewed confidence in democratization as something genuinely supported by state elites and the populace at large."[41] Suharto's death in 2008, at age eighty-six, triggered neither authoritarian nostalgia nor new demands for "restorative justice," reflecting a remarkably stable consensus on the terms of the democratic transition. Among the leading candidates for president in 2014, one was a prominent general from the New Order period who had married one of Suharto's daughters, while another had been hand-picked by Megawati to lead her party's ticket. The Hegelian notions of the organic unity between state and society and the integrational role of the state continued to dominate Indonesian politics.[42]

To explain the paradox – a strongly continuist democratic transition, in which People Power was foiled yet which rapidly and unexpectedly delivered a consolidated democracy – we need recourse to some theory of democratization that fits the Indonesian case. The overarching framework of the Asian Governance Model – a strong state tradition embedded in social accountability pressures – provides such a theory. As with Cambodia's unexpectedly successful economic development despite the continuities of CPP rule, Indonesia's unexpectedly successful political development despite the continuities of New Order elites cannot be explained by pure-form rational institutionalism, which ignores social accountability mechanisms and norms.

Indonesia is now the world's third largest democracy after India and the United States. In its 2014 elections, it had 187 million eligible voters.

If someday China were to democratize (something we consider in the final section of this chapter), then democracy as a form of government would become a predominantly Asian phenomenon. Democratic citizens everywhere have much to learn from Asia.

Democracy is a system of government in which control over political power is held by the people as a whole; all are considered political equals. It is a political system of *inclusion* as political equals and of *shared responsibility* for self-rule. These two core principles of democracy – what Beetham calls *political equality* and *popular control* – can be extraordinarily hard to measure.[43] As a result, the tendency has been to pay attention to elections, which provide an easily observed litmus test of how well a country is doing in upholding democratic principles. From this practical standpoint, the best measure of democracy is whether executive and legislative power at the national level is awarded through regularly held, free, and fair elections. The extent to which a country meets this standard does not equate to democracy, but it is a strongly suggestive indicator that can be easily observed.

Japan was the first country to create a democracy in Asia. During the period from the first election of a legislature with a constitutional role in 1890 until the overthrow of the constitutional government by militarists in 1931, Japan became what we would call today a minimal democracy with a competitive and fairly elected legislature but with "tutelary" powers held by the emperor and limited civil rights, a system sometimes known as the "Taisho democracy." In 1925, the Taisho reformers introduced wider suffrage for the legislature, expanding the number of voters to 12 million males, or one-third of the adult population. The spirit of the Taisho reformers was consciously liberal, albeit with strong Confucian overtones and with an emphasis on government *for* rather than *by* the people.[44] This led to tensions with the military and with supporters of the emperor-centered, rather than citizen-centered, polity. The result was the demise of the Taisho experiment in Asian liberalism.

In the postwar period, newly created constitutional governments throughout Asia shared a commitment to democracy that would be a model for the world. Mao spoke of a "new democracy" that would take shape in revolutionary China. Malaysia's first prime minister, Tunku Abdul Rahman, wrote in *Foreign Affairs* that the world needed "thousands and thousands of people willing to preach and practice democracy with fervor and faith and when necessary to fight for it."[45] But by the late 1950s, democracy was under strain. In short order, multiparty electoral democracies were overthrown by military or dominant-party rulers in China (1953), Thailand (1957), Indonesia (1957), South Korea (1961), Myanmar (1962), Malaysia (1969), Cambodia (1970), and the Philippines (1972). From 1972 to 1986, Japan was the only democracy in Asia (aside from a brief democratic episode in Thailand from 1974 to 1976). Not a single developing Asian country followed India after its independence in preserving democracy, a reminder of the ways that India differs fundamentally from the Asian core. Rather, they shelved democracy in pursuit of national integration, security, and development.

The period of democratic regress proved to be short-lived. Domestic modernization and an easing of Cold War tensions reignited democratic movements in Asia in the early 1980s. Just as quickly as they had fallen, democracies rose again in the Philippines, South Korea, and Thailand, while momentous attempts at democratic transition were crushed by the military in China (1989) and Myanmar (1990). In the 1990s, Indonesia and Taiwan transitioned to democracy, and Malaysia and Myanmar are probably not far behind.

By the early 2010s, six of the core fourteen Asian countries (Japan, South Korea, Taiwan, the Philippines, Indonesia, and Thailand) were "electoral democracies," according to Freedom House, meaning that they held regular, competitive, and relatively free multiparty elections with universal suffrage for national executive and legislative positions, and the results were fairly tabulated and reflected the public will. Four other countries – Singapore, Malaysia, Cambodia, and Myanmar – have semicompetitive elections for national government. This type of liberalized authoritarianism has been common throughout the world and is not particularly Asian.[46] In a democratic age, most authoritarian regimes have some form of elections, even very competitive ones, while retaining behind-the-scenes power structures and limits on civil liberties that preclude those regimes from being called full democracies.[47] Only the four communist states of Asia – China, North Korea, Vietnam, and Laos – have steadfastly resisted the global electoral and broader democratic waves. Indeed, communism itself has become an Asian regime type. All of this means that Asia is more diverse in its regime profile than any other region (see Figure 4.1).

The emergence of democracy in Asia may be something of a surprise in light of the previous chapters. Indeed, the conventional wisdom has long been that Asia's dominant and developmental states would resist

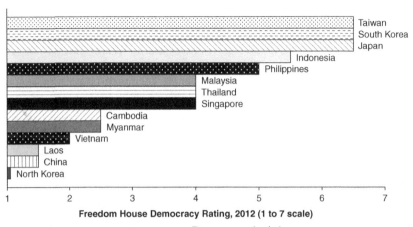

Freedom House Democracy Rating, 2012 (1 to 7 scale)

FIGURE 4.1. Democracy in Asia.

democracy.[48] In Oriental despotism theorizing, institutions of vertical accountability (from society to state) were weak. When he suspended democracy in 1957, Sukarno argued that "the principles of Western democracy, the parliamentary democracy of Western countries, incorporate the concept of an active opposition, and it is precisely the adoption of this concept that has given rise to the difficulties we have experienced over the last eleven years."[49] Harvard political scientist Samuel Huntington, looking at Asia in 1984, saw few prospects for democratic advance. Despite rapid growth, "cultural traditions, social structure, and a general weakness of democratic norms among key elites all impede movement in a democratic direction."[50] Huntington believed that Asia was proof that culture trumped economics in political development. A year later, in 1985, fellow Harvard professor Lucian Pye argued that "prospects for democracy, as understood in the West, are not good [in Asia].... Distaste for open criticism of authority, fear of upsetting the unity of the community, and knowledge that any violation of the community's rules of propriety will lead to ostracism, all combine to limit the appeal of Western democracy."[51] In the 1990s, this antidemocratic discourse found expression in the concept of "Asian Values" that was espoused mainly by the leaders of Singapore and Malaysia.[52]

So how is democracy possible in this political and cultural setting? If we return to the fundamental tenets of the Asian Governance Model, we can see that democracy could, under certain conditions, be both desirable and possible in Asian politics. Democracy in Asia can be explained as an indigenous response to new governance challenges. As we have seen, state dominance in Asia is part of a legitimate and contingent relationship with society that depends on political contention. Seen in this way, democracy in Asia does not need to be dismissed or rationalized as a means of maintaining elite rule or as authoritarianism in a new guise (the latter was used to characterize Japan until the opposition party finally won power in 2009[53]). Rather, it can be seen as a natural and, in many ways, predictable result of the fundamental notions of accountability embedded in Asian politics.

The founder of modern China, Sun Yat-sen, was clear in his writings, especially in the *Three Principles of the People* of 1923, that, in the words of one interpreter, "democratic government provides the best expression of a nationally integrated society and an administrative structure to co-ordinate collective efforts and priorities."[54] Even the "liberal" father of democracy in Japan, Yoshino Sakuzo, who wrote his 1905 doctoral dissertation on Hegel, believed that "the spirit of democracy ... consists in the just and equitable conduct of government in consultation with the majority of the people."[55] McCormick is worth quoting at length here, given the importance of the Japanese example to the rest of Asia:

Yoshino believed that the democratization of the political process and the expansion of the suffrage would alter the way the government treated the people. It would be in the government's own best interest to ensure that the population was thoroughly educated and capable of making rational and informed electoral decisions. He also believed that democratization would change the way the people viewed the government. By learning, living and internalizing the democratic ideology, citizens would come to respect their own political interests and needs as well as those of the nation, which would create national harmony and consensus. Furthermore, unlike the political domination of the privileged classes, consensus through democracy would encourage voluntary commitment to national goals. Yoshino's theories were in this way a form of democratic nationalism.[56]

This particular ideological embrace of democracy as a means to achieve the national purpose indicates that the causes, practices, and consequences of democracy need to be carefully specified in terms of the Asian experience. The global spread of democracy is, after all, due to its adaptability to local conditions. Democracy in Asia has always been understood as state-preserving, developmental, majoritarian, and consensus-based in its essentials. The emphasis has been *not* on the "rights of man" and the claims of difference but on the revitalization of government and the mandate of the people as a whole. The view of democracy as a form of paternalistic meritocracy is one that pervades the Asian region, as Shin shows using survey data; indeed, it is a view that is slightly stronger in Southeast Asia (59 percent of respondents were classified as strong supporters of the principle in the 2005–8 period) than in Northeast Asia (55 percent).[57]

Still, we should not assume that because the Asian experience seems contrastive to the conventional image of democratization in the West that it is not typical of the non-Western world or representative of a better understanding of the West itself. The question of national integration, for instance, was central to the democratization process in nineteenth-century Italy and Germany. Meanwhile, democracy was seen also by American founder Alexander Hamilton as a means to improved government.[58] "The vigor of government is essential to the security of liberty," he argued, because "a dangerous ambition more often lurks behind the specious mask of zeal for the rights of the people than under the forbidding appearance of zeal for the firmness and efficiency of government."[59] Hamilton wanted "energy in the executive" to protect the state against domestic threats that took the form of corrupt officials, law-breaking citizens, monopolistic companies, and fractious parties and interest groups.[60] For Hamilton, as well as many others, democracy was a means to strengthen government and guard against unfettered individualism.

What *may* be true of Asia is that the rival democratic emphasis on individual rights, limited government, and political equality – values often paraded under the banner of Jeffersonianism in the United States, Whiggishness in the United Kingdom, or *égalite* during the French Revolution – is comparatively weak in the region. In Africa, the state was challenged by democrats as a remnant of colonialism, while Latin American populists have challenged the state in the name of "Bolivarian revolution." In India, whose separateness from the Asian core is most vivid in the case of democracy, democracy was a powerful means of redressing caste inequalities and was thus highly prized by the lower castes as a means of individual empowerment.[61] In all of these regions, particularistic ethnic and class demands have loomed large as part of democratic struggles.

In Asia, by contrast, democratic movements position themselves as redeemers of the state and as vessels of a *shared* national purpose. Democracy is not seen as a "liberation," and much less as an overthrow of the state, but rather as a new way to advance common interests through the reinvigoration of state institutions (effective legislatures, professionalized militaries, decentralized bureaucracies, remonstrative courts, and revitalized constitutions). For Compton,[62] democracy in Asia was a natural progression within elite-led and dominant states away from the earlier challenges of national integration and rapid development. Political party competition and fair elections were means by which societies responded proactively to the challenges of modernization and globalization. In a similar vein, Jones described democracy in Asia as driven by neither "demand for the polymorphous delights of an independent media and political pluralism." nor by "an authoritarian response to pressure from civil society," but rather by "the anxious and often proactive attempt by a virtuous rulership to maintain harmony, balance, and economic growth," an attempt that is underpinned by "an Asian understanding of power as the capacity to syncretize difference and project an ethical understanding."[63]

For these and other scholars,[64] democracy in Asia is "instrumentalist," in the sense that the underlying motivations are not the Whiggish (or Jeffersonian) concerns with individual freedom but rather the Tory (or Hamiltonian) concerns of national integration and strong government. Jones describes the preferred form of democracy as "a technocratic administrative one that embraces flexible and pragmatic leadership by a dominant party, subject to a mechanism of regular elections and a degree of economic transparency."[65] From this perspective, democracy is a mechanism of accountability, of state building, and of legitimation in the face of new pluralist demands. One might say that democracy is a means to maintain the "political order" that Hamiltonians prize so highly.[66] As Kim summarizes, democracy in Asia has been a "reflection of the state's need for more efficient management of the society and economy."[67] As the Indonesian case shows, it is not about "taking back power" but about "placing power in the hands of better rulers" who will maintain national integration, rapid development, and uncorrupt rule.

Still, we need not see democracy in Asia as some degraded or diminished version of true democracy. The problem with calling Asian understandings of democracy "illiberal" or "instrumentalist" is that doing so begs the question of why such motivations would render less service to democracy's core principles – political equality and popular control. While rights and citizenship contribute positively to these principles, so too do national integration and effective government. Indeed, the challenges of democracy in countries with weak governments and social fragmentation show how human rights and civil society often suffer. Put another way, democracy is a means to advance the common good agenda of the Asian Governance Model, which, according to a certain interpretation, can be no less true to democratic principles than alternative models can be. At the level of theory, at least, it is clear why refined Oriental despotism can produce Oriental democracy.

MARKETS AND MODERNIZATION

While the philosophical justifications for democracy in Asia may be unique, the process by which democracy has emerged in the region is less so. The starting point for much theorizing about the process of democratization is the American sociologist Seymour Martin Lipset's classic 1959 article, entitled "Some Social Requisites of Democracy,"[68] which outlined what has become known as the modernization theory of democracy. Civil society, urbanization, education, and industrialization, he wrote, would fundamentally transform society, creating new demands for participation and accountability because of shifts in both social ideas and social interests. Democracy would be more likely and more successful if these requisites were in place.

The best statement of modernization theory in the case of Asia came from Morley and Crouch's "driven by growth" framework, which posited a fairly typical relationship between economic growth, resulting structural shifts (such as urbanization, education, and communication), social mobilization, and finally, political change.[69] The fact that wealthy Japan had democratized first was a key finding, they noted, for it was Japan, more than any other single country, that represented the region's future.

Using the World Bank's democracy indicator and a country's income per capita (in purchasing power terms) as a proxy for modernization, Lipset's thesis is a remarkably good fit for the modern world. Development levels alone can explain about a third of the overall variations in democratic attainments. There is a strong probability that as a country gets richer, its politics will become more democratic. Moreover, Asia fits the model rather well, too. Japan, Taiwan, and South Korea are the richest states in Asia and also its most democratic, while North Korea, Myanmar, Vietnam, and Laos are the poorest and least democratic. Thailand and Malaysia are somewhere in between on both counts. The main outliers from this pattern occur in both directions – Singapore and China are less democratic than their income levels would predict (and become greater outliers as they develop), while both Indonesia and the Philippines are more democratic than their income levels would predict (but become lesser outliers as they develop). Thus, modernization theory works as well for Asia as it does for the world as a whole and, to the extent that it does not work, the surprises are not just a few "delayed democratizations" but also a few "precocious democratizations." There is no better place to study democracy than Asia. As Friedman writes, it is "not merely that

East Asia's experience fits general rules but that East Asia's experience can usefully be taken as paradigmatic for *all* democratization."[70]

The fact that democracy has emerged more or less consistently with modernization predictions in Asia means that the notion of "delayed democratization," which has been so central to discussions of democracy in the region since the writings of Sun Yat-sen, is more of a hortatory phenomenon than an empirical one. Asian rulers have always claimed that democracy needed to be delayed until the citizenry were better-educated, the economic base was more developed, and threats to sovereignty (internal or external) were vanquished. But democracy delayed has almost never become democracy denied in Asia. Cambodia, for example, remains a low-quality democracy not because of the devious ploys of Hun Sen, but because the country has a GDP per capita of just a few thousand dollars (half that of Indonesia or the Philippines). Continued economic growth, notes Un, will "expand and transform the country's currently narrow middle class, who could then aspire to greater personal freedoms and call for democratic deepening."[71] Hun Sen may preach delayed democracy, but democracy will not likely be delayed. Tiny Singapore is the only genuine example of delayed democracy in the region, and it will be several decades before China can claim a similar analytic weight.

Interestingly, in most developmental state ideologies in Asia, democracy was never *intended* to be denied. China's reform architect Deng Xiaoping, like Sukarno, believed that democracy could be reconciled with a strong and centralized state led by a dominant party. Deng predicted that China would create "the broadest democracy ever in history."[72] The successors to Deng and Sukarno at first sought to repudiate the earlier formulations. Yet social pressures rejected this attempt to derail democratization. In the final stages, the debates became about *how* and *when* to democratize. Political elites in Indonesia eventually got the message, noting the "paradigm shift" in society, while those in China probably will as well (more of which is discussed later in this chapter).

One important feature of the modernization process in Asia has been the role of markets. The expanding role of markets in allocating labor, capital, and goods has been an important driver of demands for political representation in Asia, both because it creates new demands on government to protect and promote economic interests and because it increases the individual autonomy and sense of efficacy that spill over into the political realm.[73] This has been especially the case in Asia because of the relatively equitable (pro-poor) growth in the region, which created an educated middle class seeking voice and property protection, as well as a working class unmoored by a serf-like dependence on the state. Elsewhere, as in Eastern Europe and Russia,[74] Latin America,[75] as well as much of Africa, marketization *followed* democratization, thus creating the well-known challenges of the "dual transition" that left many people blaming markets for the problems of democracies and blaming democracies for the problems of markets. In other words, while markets and democracy are often in conflict elsewhere, in Asia the regional tendency for market-led development led to a peculiar trajectory, in which markets created pressures for democracy but were never implicated in its problems. Attempts to rally against neoliberalism in Asia fall on deaf ears, because it is a region that grew up on a trading and market-oriented political economy. There is no psychological shock of the market in Asia, and as a result, capitalism tends to drive democracy in the predicted ways – whether they are viewed critically, as by Karl Marx and Thorstein Veblen, or approvingly, as by Francis Fukuyama and others.[76]

What is most remarkable about the Asian Financial Crisis of 1997–98 is how resilient the affected democratic regimes (South Korea, Thailand, and the Philippines) proved to be, despite comparative evidence that economic crises make democracies vulnerable to collapse.[77] In the authoritarian regimes that suffered, by contrast, democratization pressures arose in direct proportion to the degree of perceived governance failure. In Indonesia, as we have seen, the crisis was final evidence of a governance failure that required democratization. But in Singapore and Malaysia, the regimes were able to demonstrate that they could respond proactively with a renewed "good governance" agenda. "Good governance," a term introduced by the World Bank in 1989 as a euphemism for democracy, became in Singapore and Malaysia (and later in China) a euphemism for delayed democracy.[78]

In Singapore, the PAP used the Asian financial crisis of 1997–98 and the global economic crisis of 2008–9 as opportunities to reinforce *both* the imperatives of global capitalism *and* the centrality of the Singaporean state. The regime embraced the crises with unsettling gusto, using its historical record of managing past crises to tackle the challenges successfully through both fiscal retrenchment and further liberalization. For the most part, this occurred through the technocratic state in consultation with foreign and local business. As Chong wrote: "Apart from regular and fair elections, structured dialogue, and feedback through ... corporatist channels, democratization was not encouraged."[79]

Malaysia is a mixed case because, unlike Singapore, both the 1997–98 and 2008–09 economic crises *did* create and strengthen a significant antiregime movement. But that movement did not immediately succeed. The reason is that the crises revealed the mixed governance record of the Malaysian regime. The government's poor decisions during the Asian financial crisis revealed the patronage network of the ruling party.[80] It allowed the linked company Renong, which was linked to the ruling party, to be bailed out by cash-rich United Engineers Malaysia without triggering a general offer to shareholders, and it had the state oil company, Petronas, bail out Konsortium Perkapalan Berhad (KPB), a shipping company owned by prime minister Mahathir Mohamad's son. As a result of such interventions, including the imposition of controls on capital outflows for twelve months, the stock market value of Mahathir-linked companies rose about 17–20 percent more than others did.[81] Dissent within the regime led Mahathir to sack his deputy prime minister, Anwar Ibrahim, who would go on to found the Justice Party, which, in alliance with the Islamic party PAS, would form the electoral face of the opposition *Reformasi* movement.

But while the creation of *Reformasi* indicated that authoritarianism in Malaysia was entering its fin de siècle stage, it could not dislodge the regime immediately, because the regime continued to act with sufficient prudence and efficiency on other issues. The capital controls, for instance, may have given a fillip to regime cronies, but they also gave a larger fillip to economic recovery – lowering interest rates, cushioning stocks, and delivering banking liquidity – because they were market-driven in both planning and execution. As Ali Abbas and Espinoza concluded in their exhaustive study of the capital controls: "Malaysia's preference for a market-based control-regime and its adherence to good financial policies, make the 'success' of the exchange control regime a success of the orthodoxy!"[82] Like the earlier imposition of controls on capital inflows in 1994, the 1999 controls served as a symbol of an activist, but still market-based, state. Given that Taiwan, an economic star, had avoided the 1997–98 crisis because of its capital controls, the 1999 controls could hardly be smeared as antimarket radicalism. Good governance and "national economic autonomy,"[83] when linked to a successful pro-poor growth policy, were powerful political arguments that allowed the ruling party to survive, albeit with an increasingly strong democratization movement in tow.

Of course, given the state-led nature of development in Asia, the embrace of democracy was neither simple nor inevitable. Markets nurtured by strong states created forms of capitalism that were dependent on state support. This meant that the process of marketization was incremental and was managed in such a way that its political repercussions were state-preserving and governance-preserving. In China, for instance, state control of key sectors, as well as the dominance of state capital in financial markets, meant that the democratizing effects of marketization were muted by what Zhang calls the "Southern Jiangsu model" of state-led development.[84] There is much debate today about how China has managed to create "capitalism without democracy" by maintaining the privileged status of the state and by co-opting much of the private sector into dependence.[85] A better way to put this is that China, like other Asian states before it, is managing to create "democracy without capitalist crisis." Rulers in Asia have managed the marketization process through an iterative process of change and social accountability, so that by the time marketization has created sufficient demands for democracy, both the market economy and the good governance of the state have been preserved. Suharto's economic reforms of the 1980s leading to democratization in 1998 are a vivid example.

Singapore is the exception that proves the rule. Uniquely, the developmental state in Singapore has achieved marketization without fundamentally altering the political economy, in which middle-class and labor groups remain highly state dependent. Between 1961 and 1967, the PAP banned all opposition to capitalism (the Socialist Front was outlawed in 1961) and at the same time introduced a form of capitalism in which the state was the key actor. "This entailed not just a powerful new class of politico-bureaucrats but also a form of state capitalism that rendered many Singaporeans directly or indirectly dependent on the state for economic and social resources, including housing, employment, business contracts and access to personal savings," wrote Rodan and Jayasuriya. "This structural relationship has fostered vulnerability to political co-optation and intimidation and further undermined the possibility of alternative social and economic bases from which challenges to the PAP can be effectively mounted."[86]

Why was this possible in Singapore but not elsewhere? Although he is remembered as the father of modernization theory, Lipset believed that authoritarianism could survive if the political system operated "autonomously" of socioeconomic conditions or if "unique historical factors" came into play.[87] Several unique historical factors have allowed authoritarian rule to persist in Singapore, chief among them its small size and relentlessly striving Chinese political leadership driven by high anxiety about the "sea of Malay peoples" that surrounds it. For these reasons, Singapore is a model of what is *not* possible elsewhere, where effective developmental states required democracy to survive because of the monitoring and accountability problems created by a larger size and weaker political traditions. In Taiwan, South Korea, and Indonesia, capitalists broke free from the state, and the middle class was willing to support the voices who argued that the kings had lost their legitimacy. Courtiers then did their duty to introduce democracy.

Another particular feature of modernization in Asia is related to this. While marketization is critical for providing the social space for dissent, the developmental state nonetheless demobilizes the three groups that are typically at the forefront of (rather than merely supportive of) democratic movements – labor groups, the urban middle class, and ethnic minorities. Jones argued that the behavior of the middle class in Asia, in both wanting democracy and yet ceding control over the pace, direction, and final forms of that democracy to street actors and regime players, cannot be explained with recourse to "some neo-Marxist sophistry concerning the structure of class coalitions." Rather, Asia's middle classes were both the beneficiaries of state-led economic growth, as well as the primary targets of the "selective reinvention of Asian traditions of deference, bureaucracy, and consensus,"[88] which were inculcated through education and media. In other words, middle class passivity is as much cultural as it is economic. Democracy allowed Asian rulers to reinvent governance traditions in Hegelian form. In the 1990s, Beijing rediscovered Confucianism, while Kuala Lumpur rediscovered the Malacca Sultanate. Asian educational curriculums emphasize the consanguinity between the national spirit and the state, so that the middle class that emerges from the educational system is thoroughly convinced that the values of technocracy, moralism, hierarchy, and harmony can be realized *only* within the existing political order. As a result, middle-class political opposition to authoritarian regimes in Asia is largely remonstrative and moderate. When the middle class emerges from the shadows to side with the street actors in the clash between "kings [and] people,"[89] they prostrate themselves and ask forgiveness for being so bold as to ask for moral improvements to the kingdom. This imposes a moral obligation on the kings to respond.

Just as Singapore is an outlier to the markets-democracy nexus, the Philippines is an outlier to the "moderate middle class" hypothesis.[90] People Power was a broad-based movement of the urban middle class and labor groups, who not only voted early and often for the core principles of democracy but did so in a belief that the existing political order needed to be abolished, not reformed. The Corazon Aquino presidency that took over in 1986 undertook a thorough dismantling of the Marcos state. Having first considered declaring a "revolutionary government,"[91] Aquino dismissed both the supreme court and sitting legislature and, symbolically, expelled U.S. forces from their permanent bases. Health ministry bureaucrats launched one of the biggest protests of her presidency in 1991 over her plans to transfer health policy to elected local governments. The results were perhaps predictable: economic crisis, a breakdown of social order, and political instability in the form of nine coup attempts during the Aquino years. This paved the way for the restorationist figure Fidel Ramos, a former Marcos general, who was elected president in 1992, by which time not only the middle class but much of the working class had blanched at the results (Marcos's wife also ran and won 10 percent of the vote).

Except for the Philippines, political opposition in democratizing Asia generally is not led by the middle class and is not revolutionary. The baton of active, visible opposition is held jointly by two very different sorts of groups: marginal social actors, like students, artists, intellectuals, priests, and monks; and loyal state actors, like technocrats, vice presidents, former cabinet members, generals, and party hacks. Students in particular are unusually prominent in political reform movements in Asia. While student activism is universal, Asia is "the most consistent host to evocative, potentially transformative student movements," write Weiss, Aspinall, and Thompson. The reason is that they see themselves as a "moral vanguard" or as the "conscience of the nation" rather than as simply another interest group. "Students claimed political voice in respect of their moral purity, legacy as past kingmakers, and lack of obvious material interest in the outcomes they sought."[92] That gives them both a strong voice and a weak hand. They are the court jesters whose job it is to refurbish the state when it goes amiss.

The causes of democracy in Asia, then, are both a ringing affirmation of the universalism of modernization theory, as well as a reminder that below every universal theory lies a particular reality. If there is one lesson to be learned, it is that the beneficiaries of markets may be moderate, but they are not meek. Asian states have managed market reforms so as to preserve governance and the state. But they cannot preserve dictatorship without betraying the national purpose.

RESPONSIVE TRANSITIONS

Market-based modernization with a good governance agenda may be a good way to explain *why* countries in Asia transition to democracy. But the question of *how* is no less important. Not surprisingly, contingency and drama are often at the center of the analysis of transitions – as we saw with Indonesia's 1997 to 1999 transition.

Democratic transitions are characterized by two important features: the strength of protest movements; and the question of who exercises political leadership during the transition. It is no surprise that in the seventy-six democratic transitions that took place around the world between 1972 and 2012, strong protest movements were both common occurrences (present in about half of all cases), as well as a good predictors of more rapid democratic gains; it is also no surprise that an absence of opposition actors in the transition leadership (which occurred in 21 percent of all cases) was the worst possible condition for subsequent democratic gains.[93]

How do Asian democratic transitions compare? There are six cases to consider aside from Japan – Taiwan, the Philippines, South Korea, Thailand, Cambodia, and Indonesia. In general, Asia is typical in having had significant social mobilization in most cases (Cambodia is the exception because it had weak social mobilization) and the presence of social actors in the transition leaderships (again, Cambodia's externally imposed democracy is the lone exception). At the same time, states have, with only one exception (the Philippines), never wholly ceded control over the transition to social movements. Transitions led by state actors alone or social actors alone accounted for half of transitions globally but only one in eight in Asia. Put another way, despite the presence of strong social forces in five of the six transitions, only one democratic transition in Asia resulted in a society-led transition (compared to a global average of 40 percent). Indonesia, Thailand, Taiwan, and South Korea (and probably Malaysia and Myanmar in the future) tell us that even when society is well-organized, the state almost always remains at the center of political change in Asia.

Even the so-called "mixed" transition leaderships in Asia were not "pacts" between autonomous People Power movements from the streets and the regime. For instance, Freedom House describes the transition leadership in Indonesia as "mixed," because Megawati's "opposition party" won the most seats in the 1999 elections. But as we saw, the deep interpenetration of the authoritarian regime into all elements of the political elite makes it doubtful that it is accurate to call Megawati and her token party a social actor rather than a New Order actor. The truly unambiguous social actors – Rais and Sasono – were locked out of the process.

Asia is not unique in the predominance of transitions with involvement by the extant regime.[94] Rather, what is unique about Asia is that it has relatively more state-led transitions in the *simultaneous presence* of strong social mobilization. The reason, as the Asian Governance Model suggests, is that states and societies in Asia work in tandem. The dynamics of democratization in Asia are embedded in an accountability framework, in which states with a widely acknowledged authority pursue common good objectives through an ongoing process of social pressures and political contention. We might introduce the notion of a "responsive transition," which can be defined as a democratic transition led by existing regime actors responding to widespread social mobilization. Responsive transitions do not fit neatly into existing transition typologies, because these typologies are based on a regime *versus* society ontology (regime-led "elite transplacements," mixed "pacts," or society-led "overthrows"). The responsive transition is an elite-led transplacement that occurs through state-society interactions, reflecting a social rejection of the legitimacy of authoritarian governance. Modernization has worked in Asia because states have taken the initiative, often with the active participation of quasi-regime actors who voice social demands.

From the perspective of the ruling parties or elite groups, democracy does not need to be feared if it will normatively retain the essentials of nation and political order and if it will prudentially protect most key interests. Having what Slater and Wong call "the strength to concede" makes these groups responsive to social demands.[95] Again, it is not that such models are absent outside of Asia – they find that eighteen of the eighty-six authoritarian-era ruling parties that lost power elsewhere returned to power under democracy. Rather, it is that this model is the rule in Asia but the exception elsewhere. Future democratic transitions in China, Malaysia, Vietnam, Myanmar, and Singapore are likely to follow this model, too.

South Korea nicely illustrates the responsive transition. Like Indonesia, the transition to democracy in South Korea took place amidst a well-organized and powerful social movement that was led by students. Also, as in Indonesia, the leadership of the transition is described by Freedom House as "mixed." Yet if we peer behind the outward appearances, we find that the opposition sought only regime reform, not a break with the past. The transition leadership was "mixed" only if we consider regime-incorporated actors as belonging to "society" and ignore the fact that, as in Indonesia, the genuine "street" actors were left out in the cold.

Civil society played a key role in South Korean democratization, even though, in classic Asian form, it did not arise from the middle class but was composed primarily of students, teachers, women's groups, Christian clergy, and peasant activists.[96] Protests forced the resignation and exile of Korean War–era strongman Syngman Rhee in 1960 after police killed twenty-one students during a march in Seoul. The street actors (known as the *chaeya*, or "out in the fields," movement) also forged an alliance with the legal opposition party, Kim Young Sam's New Democratic Party, in 1979 to oppose the more repressive aspects of Park Chung-hee's "Revitalization" (*Yusin*) democracy. That alliance contributed to the tensions within the regime, and they were highlighted when Park was shot and killed by his intelligence director at a dinner party in 1980.

In 1987, civil society again rose up to press for democracy. The inaugural 1,400 "functional" members of the street movement formed that year were composed of 683 religious figures, 279 artists, writers, journalists, and lawyers, 171 peasant activists, 162 women's leaders, and only 100 middle-class or business representatives.[97] This street opposition was a moral one, not a class one, composed of "gentleman scholars ... [who] called for the *restoration* of morality and legitimacy in the ruling regime."[98] This remonstrative role of civil society in Asian politics is why religious leaders have figured so prominently in democratization processes in the region.[99] The "Great Labor Struggle" of 1987 that was observed by Marxist-inspired scholars was nothing more than a few wildcat strikes at some Hyundai factories. Economic growth in 1987, at 12.2 percent, was virtually unchanged from a year earlier, and exports surged that year.

The gentlemen street actors enjoyed the tacit support of the middle class, whose pro-democratic values sought democratic change to improve governance and maintain national unity.[100] At a certain point, the conflicted middle class threw its weight behind the street actors, and the regime responded. As Jones recounts: "As it became increasingly obvious that the military autocracy no longer guaranteed political certainty, middle class demonstrators demanded democracy to allay continuing uncertainty concerning orderly leadership transition." They "somewhat surreally took to the streets chanting the decidedly unrevolutionary slogan 'Order!'"[101] A village shopkeeper told the *Washington Post* that most rural folk wanted "stability and the blocking of left-leaning radicals."[102]

As elsewhere in Asia, despite massive social mobilization and hopes for a revolutionary change, the transition was regime-led, a responsive "reform from above." Korean students mimicked others in Asia in making "passionate patriotism" a core value, which allowed a chastened regime to reclaim leadership over the pace of change.[103] With the agreement to hold a direct presidential election in 1987 and new legislative elections in 1988, the "people's movement groups in civil society became incrementally marginalized" and "relatively inactive" in the transition process.[104] The united front between the "street" leader, Kim Dae Jung, and the "incorporated opposition" leader, Kim Young Sam, broke down – just as the flirtation between the regime-incorporated actors and the street actors ended in Indonesia once a transition began and momentum shifted back to the regime. In the 1987 presidential election, the authoritarian-era general Roh Tae Woo (the equivalent of the Habibie figure) came to power with 36 percent of the vote compared to Kim Young Sam's 28 percent and Kim Dae Jung's 27 percent. As Jones notes, South Koreans chose their "erstwhile oppressor" as their first democratic leader. A few South Korean newspapers sheepishly attributed this choice to the "sentimental" views of the citizenry. Students who took to the streets to contest the results found that "while a few bystanders cheered the protesters, most shouted at them to stop demonstrating."[105]

Most of Roh's first term of democratic government was taken up with struggles by the opposition to "liquidate the legacies" of the authoritarian past.[106] Street leader Kim Dae Jung's Party for Peace and Democracy, like Rais's party in Indonesia, was clobbered at the first legislative election in 1988. In the second presidential election of 1992, the formerly incorporated opposition figure, Kim Young Sam (the Megawati figure), won with 42 percent of the vote after merging his party with Roh's governing party and running on a campaign of stability and "no retaliation" against authoritarian-era politicians. It was not until 1997, a full ten years after the transition, that "the street" was briefly trusted with the wheel of the Korean state when Kim Dae Jung, the "Nelson Mandela of Asia" was elected president. It was as if the South African National Party's reform wing under F. W. de Klerk had won the first two post-apartheid elections, allowing Nelson Mandela to become president only ten years later for one term. After this brief tenure by the street, candidates rooted in the old order came back into power one after another. Symbolically, developmental dictator Park Chung-hee's daughter became president in 2012.

The state-led "responsive transition" is thus the default assumption for democratic movements in Asia. Street actors interacting with regime reformers will remonstrate for a long time until the consensus builds for change. Malaysia's *Reformasi* movement was formed in 1998 and won 47 percent of the vote in 2008, but it could not immediately overthrow the UMNO state. When this state-led "responsive" framework breaks down, social forces lack the means to reconstitute an authoritative state that can manage democracy. That is why the Philippines is by far the biggest underperformer in terms of democratic gains, having become only marginally more democratic than it had been under the Marcos era. Elsewhere in the world, society-led transitions deliver the biggest democratic gains. But in Asia, they spell trouble. People Power in the Philippines became entrenched in an overmobilized civil society and a weak and reactive state. The Filipino middle classes resorted to unconstitutional and illegal methods to protect their interests – first by ousting populist president Joseph Estrada in 2001 using a flimsy Constitutional Court ruling and then by defending president Gloria Arroyo in 2005 despite her obvious electoral fraud, which led to a brief suspension of democracy (Arroyo was arrested after leaving office).

In many ways, Indonesians should thank the Philippines for its timely reminder of the dangers of People Power in a state-dominant region. Rather than being a disadvantage, responsive transitions have been a blessing for South Korea, Indonesia, and Taiwan, and no doubt will be for Malaysia, Myanmar, Vietnam, and China. In Myanmar, for example, "the Buddhist street" is represented by young temple monks, as well as the so-called "88 Generation Students Group," both of which have always maintained their separation from the officially sanctioned opposition party, the National League for Democracy led by Aung San Suu Kyi, the daughter of modern Burma's revered founder. Like Megawati, Suu Kyi is an establishment figure more than a populist, but she is one who, like other elites, acts out the responsive transition. As she told reporters after being elected to parliament in 2012: "I want to be remembered as someone who did her duty."[107]

CONSOLIDATION WITHOUT KINGS

A democracy is consolidated when it is able to withstand the strains of political life without succumbing to the authoritarian temptation. Consolidation happens when pro-democratic values in society are robust, when important political actors all accept the democratic rules of the game, and when a dense set of institutions protects the system against backsliding. Only four of Asia's fourteen states – Japan, South Korea, Taiwan, and Indonesia – are consolidated democracies. In the two unconsolidated democracies – Thailand and the Philippines – politicians and elites still regularly resort to mass movements, dirty tricks, and thuggery to overthrow rivals. Cambodia, Malaysia, Myanmar, and Singapore have electoral regimes that fall short of democracy, while the remaining four are communist dictatorships.

From the standpoint of Asian politics, where democratic transitions follow modernization and are initiated by state actors, the most surprising failed consolidation is Thailand. This is a puzzle because Thailand had a responsive transition in 1992 that maintained the continuity of the state in the presence of strong social mobilization. This *should have* delivered rapid democratic consolidation. Moreover, with a marketized and prosperous middle-income economy, previous experiences with democratic rule, and a 1997 constitution with robust checks on power, Thailand had all the requisites for success. Indeed, between the 1992 transition and the overthrow of prime minister Thaksin Shinawatra by a military coup in 2006, it gained 2.5 points on the 7-point Freedom House scale to become an apparently consolidated liberal democracy, more or less as predicted.

What explains the Thai anomaly? Comparative evidence is useful here. Using a "split population survival" model to capture the intuition that some democracies are "cured" of authoritarianism while others have merely "not relapsed," Svolik finds that the key drivers of consolidation are higher development levels, the absence of a presidential system, and the absence of a military authoritarian past.[108] Unconsolidated democracies, he predicts, will last only fourteen years before succumbing to some crisis and then breaking down; this was exactly the length of Thailand's democratic run. Thailand is a middle-income country that adopted a parliamentary model, which suggests that the military factor in Thai politics is determinative. The 2006 coup, after all, was the eighteenth since the country adopted a constitutional monarchy in 1932.

But while the military factor is a good predictor (or correlate) of democratic breakdown, it cannot *explain* the troubled consolidation of Thai democracy, because theory and comparative Asian cases suggest that a military role per se is <u>not</u> a threat to consolidation. Blaming the Thai military is to beg the question of why, in a region and, indeed, a country that lacks a Latin American–style messianic view of the military, the Thai generals have been so active. In Taiwan, South Korea, Indonesia, and Myanmar, militaries remained neutral and uninvolved for the most part as power was handed over to civilian control. Even in the Philippines and Cambodia, attempts by rogue mid-ranking officers and remote regional commands to launch sporadic coups have been crushed. Thailand's redemocratization of 1992 indicated that its military, too, was content with democratization. One distinctive feature of Asian politics is that despite long episodes of militarized or military rule, the military has never replaced the civilian state as the default authority in any country. Militaries in Asia, notes Heiduk, "have led ministries and sometimes even governments, served as parliamentarians, bureaucrats and in the diplomatic service, built roads and schools, policed villages, run hotels, and owned TV stations, rice mills or airlines."[109] But nowhere have they assumed the mantle of legitimacy.

Traditional theories attribute military involvement to weak political institutions or domestic security threats. But neither factor is a very good explanation of the Thai case, because its institutions looked much like those elsewhere in the region where militaries were de-politicized. The Philippines banned active military officers from seeking elected or appointed office after 1986. China's military is no longer represented on the Communist Party's Politburo Standing Committee. Indonesia's military renounced its "dual role." In all of these cases, Asian militaries have accepted that whatever their functional role in the creation of the authoritarian developmental state, once the civilian leadership and broader social accountability pressures indicate that this role is over, there is no reclaiming it. The Asian Governance Model, in other words, has kept militaries in check everywhere – except Thailand. There must, therefore, be some *other* factor that explains military intervention in Thai politics, a factor that neutralizes the operation of the Asian Governance Model in unexpected ways. Much as astronomers predict the existence of an unknown body from deviations in the orbits of planets, an unschooled observer could predict that there is some additional element in Thai politics that has prevented what should have been a rapid democratic consolidation. What is it? The answer is obvious: Thailand's 775-year-old monarchy. Since ascending to the throne in 1946, Thailand's king has repeatedly intervened to sanction military assaults on democratic leaders and to allow narrow social demands (in particular, those of the Bangkok urban middle class) to trump broad social demands.[110] The absence of colonialism or Japanese invasion (Thailand was Japan's only Asian ally in World War II) and the king's quasi-deity status means that there has never been a formal break with traditional rule or the formation of a modern state. The "cataclysmic disruption of the ruling class" by modernizing elites that was so important to development and democracy elsewhere in Asia never occurred.[111] The traditional polity continues to exist despite modernization, built around what McCargo calls the "network monarchy," a royalist coalition that is separate from the social consensus, in which monarchic power is exercised through proxies. "Network monarchy is inherently illiberal, because it advocates reliance on 'good men', and the marginalization of formal political institutions or procedures. Low priority is given to democratic principles such as the rule of law and popular sovereignty."[112] In 1998, the Bureau of the Royal Household and the Office of His Majesty's Principal Private Secretary employed 2,300 staff (twice as many as the five departments of the British monarchy).[113] By identifying itself as a source of authority separate from the people, the Thai king has allowed the military to intervene in the name of social accountability. He has spawned an "elite coup culture" that is unusual in the Asian context.[114]

Thailand is an anomaly in that its better-educated and higher occupational status citizens have a *less* positive view of democracy than others do. Half the population of Bangkok in the mid-2000s supported a military intervention if "corrupt" politicians were elected to office.[115] Without the king, such views would be unmasked as self-serving. Under the king's patronage, they are rationalized as a principled stand. Thaksin's unpardonable sin, above all, was to attempt to disrupt this system in order to create a modern state (which will be discussed further in Chapter 5). The result was that anti-Thaksin forces wrapped themselves in royal patronage to launch a coup in 2006 and then to hound Thaksin's sister from office and launch another coup in 2014.

One of King Bhumibol Adulyadej's official monikers is "father of Thai democracy." In reality, he has done everything in his power since being crowned in 1950 to restore the feudal privileges of the absolute monarchy that were supposedly ended by reforms in 1932. The solution is probably not a republican revolution (Thais, after all, can be thankful for the stability of their monarchy, especially compared to their Indo-Chinese neighbors) but rather a constitutionalization of the monarch's power and a shift in political power to a modernizing populist – as Thaksin was. For Thais, the task is to remake their monarchy along the lines of the symbolic traditional rulers of Japan, Cambodia, and Malaysia. Bhumibol's old age may be a factor, for such an opportunity may arise once he passes away.

In a sense, then, the Thai case is reassuring for Asian politics, because no other Asian country has a feudal monarchic legacy unbroken by colonialism, occupation, or modernizing revolution. Democratic consolidation elsewhere does not face this same clog within its accountability mechanisms. The Philippines, meanwhile, will remain the only country whose democratic consolidation is plagued by the "original sin" of a popular democratic transition. Yet this, too, may be changing. One of the longstanding People Power street actors, the Catholic Bishops Conference, opted in 2005 not to voice an opinion when President Arroyo was under pressure to resign because of electoral fraud. This in turn may have prompted a more tolerant middle class that, as in Thailand, is always ready to abandon democracy when populists gain power. In the end, democracy in both countries will consolidate when society learns to recognize the prerogatives of the state and when the state, in turn, accepts its accountability to society.

THE RIGHTS OF THE MAJORITY

The concept of democracy is sufficiently expansive and flexible to admit of a variety of constitutional and institutional, not to mention ideological, possibilities. As with capitalism, it is the *varieties* of democracy that are the subject of debate in our contemporary world. Given that the motivations for democratic change in Asia center on improved governance, sustained development, and national integration, we would expect to see democracy institutionalized in ways that make these outcomes more likely.

Two features of the practice of democracy in Asia stand out: majoritarian political institutions and cooperative relationships between executives and legislatures. Both of these features reflect the ways that democracy in Asia has been institutionalized so as to minimize the demands of minority, sectarian, particularistic, or otherwise narrow interests. More broadly, they reflect the ways that democracy in Asia is conceived of as a means of strengthening the authority of the state, which is understood in Hegelian terms to embody the national purpose. Voting is seen as similar to shareholder rights in a corporation, a voice to advance common goals. The country, thus conceived, to use Oakeshott's terminology,[116] is a *universitas* with a shared purpose rather than a *societas* with different purposes and only shared rules. As Morlino and colleagues conclude based on a statistical analysis of the drivers of democratic satisfaction in the region: "Asian voters are happier with democracy when the executive is not scrutinized too closely, freedom of the press is lower, electoral turnout is lower, the gap between the largest and the second largest party is wider, and government is more effective."[117] These dual notions of majoritarianism and consensus that underlie democratic practice in Asia provide a basis for rethinking democracy everywhere.

Electoral systems are the starting point for majoritarianism in Asia. In general, voting systems are an attempt to balance the two principles of democracy – political equality and public control. Proportional systems, in which the proportion of votes cast is faithfully reflected in the proportion

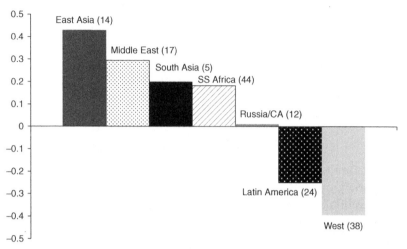

FIGURE 4.2. Disproportionality of electoral rules for legislatures by region.
Notes: Average degree of majoritarianism in electoral rules for national parliament (lower house), 1 = Most majoritarian, −1 = Least Majoritarian.
Source: Database of Political Institutions, 2009; Interparliamentary Union Parline, various. Plurality score minus proportional representation score.

of seats won, seek to maximize political equality. Majoritarian systems, in which the biggest vote-getters are given a majority of the seats, seek to maximize public control. While the global trend has shifted toward more proportional systems, Asia is an outlier in that it has maintained or strengthened majoritarian systems. The contrast with other regions is striking (see Figure 4.2). The results show that the largest parties in Asian legislatures tend to hold about 30 percent more seats than they would hold under strictly proportional systems (Table 4.1).

Asian countries (notably Japan, South Korea, Taiwan, Thailand, and Indonesia) have all adopted more majoritarian electoral institutions since the early 1990s, while Singapore and Malaysia have maintained their colonial-era majoritarian systems. The norm has been what Reilly calls "mixed-member majoritarian" systems, in which most seats are allocated through majoritarian winner-takes-all voting, while a small proportion are allocated through proportional voting.[118] Moreover, unlike in, say, Germany or New Zealand, the proportional seats in Asia are typically not used to "balance" the majoritarian results but are simply chosen in parallel, which often tends to reinforce the majoritarian results. The unusual tendency toward majoritarianism in Asian electoral systems even holds

TABLE 4.1. *Disproportionality of Legislative Seats in Asian Legislatures*

Country	Election System Type	Ratio of % Seats to % Votes[a] for Largest Party[b]	Year of Election
Japan	Mixed	1.74	2012
Singapore	Majoritarian	1.50	2011
Hong Kong[c]	Mixed	1.42	2012
Myanmar	Majoritarian	1.40	2010
Taiwan	Mixed	1.27	2012
Indonesia	Proportional	1.27	2009
Malaysia	Majoritarian	1.26	2013
South Korea	Mixed	1.18	2012
Cambodia	Proportional	1.12	2013
Thailand	Mixed	1.09	2011
Philippines	Mixed	0.99	2010

Notes: [a] For mixed systems, sum of total party votes in PR and plurality seats divided by sum of all votes cast for PR and plurality seats.
[b] includes parties running as a coordinated and explicit coalition.
[c] Pro-Beijing bloc share of all legislative seats and of popular vote in geographical constituencies.

true for the countries with systems that purport to be wholly or partially proportional. The reason is that every system also includes arcane rules of electoral system design that can create majorities, even if the seats are allocated proportionally.

The earliest and most important electoral rules change came in Japan in 1994, which created single-member, first-past-the-post constituencies for 300 of 500 seats and added another 200 seats by proportional representation in 11 large districts. While it was intended to prevent parties from breaking into factions, the redesign was also an opportunity to reaffirm and extend the country's commitment to majoritarianism. After socialists and communists won seats in a highly proportional system held under the American occupation in 1946, mainstream politicians pushed through a reduction in the number of seats per constituency from nine to four in 1947.[119] The 1994 reforms then continued Japan's postwar trend away from proportionality. In 2009, a small shift in voter opinion delivered a landslide victory for the opposition, which was then reversed by a small shift back that led to a landslide for the Liberal Democrats in 2012.

The embrace of majoritarianism is even more telling in Indonesia, because it has been accomplished under a formally proportional system that was adopted in 2003.[120] Much of the culling of small parties

takes place through rules that require parties to have branch offices in all
thirty-three provinces and in at least three-quarters of all cities in every
province, as well as in half of the districts in each city. As of 2014, parties
also need to win at least 3.5 percent of the *national* vote to be given a seat.
Moreover, except for the 3.5 percent national vote threshold, these criteria apply to provincial and local elections, as well, so that only national
parties can run for office, even at the local level. The proportional rules
are then applied in such a way as to bolster majoritarianism further. The
number of members per constituency (which can legally range from three
to ten) has been reduced in order to prevent small parties (disparaged
in the local lingo as *partai gurem*, or "flea parties") from winning seats.
In the 2009 election, the average number of members per constituency
was seven, compared to eighteen for the 1999 elections (meaning that
a party needed about 14 percent of the vote in a district to win a seat),
which means that usually only three to four parties won seats. Finally, to
nominate a presidential candidate, a party needs at least 25 percent of
the national vote or 20 percent of the legislative seats. As a result of all
these constraints, the "effective" number of parties in the Indonesian legislature (a measure of how concentrated the legislative seats are) declined
from seven in the 2004 elections to six in the 2009 elections (when thirty-
eight parties fielded candidates).

   In effect, rule from Jakarta is instantiated in the electoral rules that
have a majoritarian bias going back to the New Order, which sought
to discourage parochial or regional parties. While Indonesia's extreme
diversity and rapid politicization led to an explosion of new parties after
Suharto, the tourniquet of electoral institutions has been continually
tightened to keep the effective number of parties falling.[121] As one local
observer put it, there is "a commonly accepted understanding that reducing the number of parties in Indonesia is essential to creating an effective
government."[122] Or as another argued: "The extreme multiparty system
is considered as one culprit that inhibits the workings of the presidential
government and disrupts the quality of democracy."[123]

   The details of electoral systems take on a similar pattern elsewhere in
Asia. Singapore took the Anglo-American plurality system and made it
even more majoritarian by creating multimember constituencies in which
the winning party takes *all* the seats. The embarrassingly large majorities
that this creates in a country where only 60 percent of the people voted
for the ruling People's Action Party forced the government to introduce
token seats for non-PAP candidates in the form of "best loser" and "non-
party" functional seats. There is, as Reilly notes,[124] a "grand irony" in

the fact that Singapore and Malaysia, the two founts of communal Asian Values and of cautionary tales about the "polarizing" effects of Anglo-American democracy, have adopted those same polarizing institutions to keep their ruling parties in power.

Similar stories of electoral institutions being continually adjusted to ensure solid majorities can be seen in other countries in the region. Taiwan's 2008 legislative elections were conducted under a new majoritarian system, while at the same time, the total number of legislators was drastically cut from 225 to 113 and their terms extended from three to four years – all measures intended to improve efficiency by creating majoritarian and manageable legislative blocks. Cambodia, meanwhile, which had a proportional system imposed on it by the United Nations in 1993, has wriggled out of that straightjacket ever since. Reforms in 1997 reduced the average number of seats per constituency from six to five and adopted a formula for allocating seats that favored the biggest vote-getters over the smaller ones. That gave the ruling party three-quarters of the legislative seats with just half of the popular vote until 2013, when its share of the popular vote finally fell below 50 percent, which led to a large loss of seats.

Majoritarianism arguably contributed to the political crisis in Thailand, which in 1997 abandoned pure proportional representation for a mixed-member majoritarian system with a 5 percent national vote threshold for winning seats. This delivered a large majority for the populist Thaksin Shinawatra in the 2005 elections, causing royalist political elites to switch their views and argue *against* majoritarianism (because they were now in the minority). The chairman of a reform commission created after the crisis warned the pro-royalist elites to "accept the voting rights of the majority," adding: "Those who always campaign for voters to select 'good people' may need to adjust their thinking and give equal political opportunities to all."[125] As a result, Thailand introduced an only slightly more proportional system – 375 first-past-the-post seats and 125 proportional representation seats – that still delivered a narrow majority to the pro-Thaksin party in 2011. By then, Thai elites had abandoned democracy altogether, calling for an unelected "people's council" to govern the country. Again, the malign influence of its feudal monarchy in encouraging these views cannot be overstated.

The majoritarian flavor of electoral systems in Asia reflects the fact that Asian publics have taken public control (political power sanctioned by the people) more seriously than political equality (the primacy of the individual and their rights). As Choi puts it, even if political equality suffers, "there are other competing goals of electoral engineering such as stable and efficient government."[126] Dahl calls democracy "the steady appeasement of relatively small groups,"[127] but that is only true where institutions favor such a fragmented definition of "the public." In Asia, the concept of "the public" is still taken seriously as a unified, majoritarian ideal, and as a result, the corporatist and majoritarian flavor of democracy in the region is striking.

Asia challenges the notion that proportional systems create harmony and consensus, while majoritarian systems create faction and polarization. In Asia, the opposite has been true, and this may explain why majoritarian institutions in the United States and Britain have generated a remarkably stable system of rule that cleaves to the center. The dominant view in Asia has been that proportional systems encourage small parties with narrow agendas, thus making government less cooperative and consensual and more prone to extremes. In majoritarian systems led by large, catch-all parties, differences are worked out *within* the ruling party (where compromise is easier) rather than across parties (where compromise is more difficult).

This is a point that Inoue makes in order to justify Japan's electoral reforms.[128] Majoritarian systems, he argues, promote deliberation and accountability better than proportional systems because they empower a single party, constrained only by constitutional rights, that must govern well or face electoral failure. Although Japan's upper house, the House of Councilors, could throw up many obstacles to laws passed by the lower house, or Diet, in practice it has embraced what Inoue calls "critical democracy," a way of dealing with difference through internal, deliberative processes rather than cross-party horse trading. Majoritarianism strengthens the importance attached to governing justly and prompts parties to have extensive internal vetoes (i.e., to constrain themselves and their tendency to pander to their extreme wings) and to engage in substantive ex post deliberation about policies and how well they are working. This offers a clue about why majoritarianism has spread in Asia. As Croissant concluded: "A major motivation for electoral reform and institutional engineering in East Asia was to encourage political aggregation and to minimize the risk of political fragmentation by restricting the electoral prospects of small parties. This, so reformers hoped, would also promote more stable and cohesive political majorities, which in turn, would enhance the ability of party governments to govern."[129]

Unlike in Latin America, where attempts to create more majoritarian electoral institutions meet with fierce resistance, the arguments by political elites in Asia that such institutions will create more programmatic and stable parties are met with ready acceptance. In other words, there is both a bottom-up (social) as well as a top-down (institutional) reason for majoritarianism in Asia (paralleling the reasons for the developmental state, which include both bottom-up and top-down impetuses). As Reilly puts it, the change is "based on a historic compromise between mass constituents who have embraced the need for more programmatic and effective parties and elite politicians who favor restrictions on political fragmentation and the suppression of ethnic or regional movements."[130]

Even when institutions allow the emergence of small parties with narrow agendas, Asian publics tend to vote against them. This may be because conservative or right-wing movements are better able to create a united front than are radical or left-wing movements, which tend to splinter over minute ideological differences.[131] Thus, throughout Asia, where an essentially conservative middle class exists, majoritarian coalitions of the center-right can gain and hold power over long periods. The most enduring governments in Asia have been formed through electoral competition but always under the umbrella of a "grand conservative coalition" that sets itself up as an alternative to the splintering radicals and liberals – UMNO in Malaysia, the PAP in Singapore, the KMT in Taiwan, the CPP in Cambodia, and the New Order-era GOLKAR and Indonesia Democratic Party in Indonesia. Even the CCP in China and the VCP in Vietnam repositioned themselves as grand inclusive coalitions of the proletariat *and* capitalists alike, abandoning their earlier Robin Hood personas and spawning oppositions that grew up on the left. While Asian publics may briefly hand power to liberal or left-of-center parties – Kim Dae Jung in South Korea, Chen Shui-bian in Taiwan, or the Democratic Party in Japan – the "natural" conservative parties quickly come back to power. The hopes of leftists that democratization will lead to class-based Robin Hood politics have been constantly foiled, forcing intellectuals into increasingly obscure warrens of Marxist class analysis in order to explain the obvious: Most Asian citizens, including most "workers," do not think such policies would serve the general welfare.[132]

Empirically, the proportion of voters in Asian countries that identify themselves as "centrists" rather than people of the left or right is consistently higher (around 40–50 percent) than in other regions (20–30 percent), as is the proportion who reject close affiliation to any party.[133] This has led some scholars to conclude that the region's politics are "immature," "inchoate," or "underdeveloped" compared to the entrenched and agonistic polarizations of the traditional West, based on Marxist assumptions of "fundamental social conflicts."[134] But if we start with different assumptions, we may find that a fluid and fickle attachment to parties is a more mature and developed response to the challenge of politics than crude, unthinking attachments that assume that the common good is permanently lodged in one party or another, left or right. This is especially the case in a region where authoritarian developmental states led by dominant parties gave way to democracy precisely in order to free citizens and parties from fixed attachments.[135] The Asian experience reminds us that both left and right sensibilities appeal to reasonable and enduring concerns about political life and public policy. The common good may be located on the left at certain times and on the right at other times, something that Western thinkers in the classical liberal tradition, like Isaiah Berlin, Hannah Arendt, Bernard Crick, or John Rawls, understood well. For Asian publics, to permanently site one's political sympathies on only one side makes little sense.

This sociological basis of majoritarianism means that it is likely that majority center-right governments would be voted into office *even without* majoritarian electoral institutions, as Choi argues using statistical analysis.[136] According to this view, electoral systems are mainly a symbolic, rather than a substantive, choice. The real cause of majoritarian government is an underlying sociology of consensus reinforced by flexible and fluid electoral competition that brings out the strategically most broad-based party or candidate and allows political elites to coalesce around a majoritarian winner. The reason that the Philippines is an outlier (it is the only country whose ruling party received less seats than votes, as shown in Table 4.1) is "not because Philippine voters are less strategic compared to other nationals or because they are divided ethnolinguistically, but primarily because Philippine political elites are fragmented or divided," Choi argues.[137] This reminds us that looking only at rules and formal institutions will not yield the reasons for majoritarian democracy. In his study of Turkey, which operates much like Asia in this respect, Lord shows how democracy has become more majoritarian there, even as institutions have become less so.[138] The reason is that elites and mainstream society have coalesced around a more majoritarian vision of politics, which has changed the practice of democracy.

Asian parties and elections are also notable for the ways that this majoritarianism has not been based on *ethnic* majoritarianism. Singaporean and Chinese leaders regularly warn against "Han chauvinism." In Indonesia, there have been three attempts since independence to insert Islam into the constitution (usually in the form of the seven-word formulation "obligation of Muslims to practice Islamic law"), all of which have failed because priority was placed on national integration rather than ethnic zeal.[139] In Malaysia, majoritarianism was consciously crafted as a *cross-ethnic* concept under the National Front coalition, which incorporated the main Malay, Chinese, and Indian parties. The opposition, then, arose as a united front composed of multiple ethnic groups, as well. Moreover, the National Front, while certainly pursuing special assistance for the majority of Malays, is majoritarian in a much deeper sense – representing broadly socially conservative values and a middle-class developmental ideology. Former prime minister Mahathir Mohamad said in 2011: "In the East, it is considered civilized to defend the rights of the majority but in the West, the minority rights should be defended, no matter what."[140] In this respect, majoritarianism in Asia differs fundamentally from its variants in, say, Russia under Vladimir Putin's United Russia or Sri Lanka under the Sinhalese-nationalist People's Alliance or Turkey under the Islamic Justice and Development Party, all countries where the "rights of the majority" discourse was used in the 2000s to justify majoritarian chauvinism and the repression of ethnic, ideological, or religious minorities.

Conversely, majoritarianism is also intended to deter ethnic *minority* politics. Meisburger notes that proportionality often enlarges ethnic minority politics, because it gives candidates no incentives to reach beyond their particular groups.[141] It also gives winners an incentive to be accountable to the parties that made them candidates rather than to the constituents who voted for them. Majoritarian systems, by contrast, force candidates to reach across ethnic boundaries, especially when districts are drawn so as not to follow group boundaries. As Hicken and Kuhonta observe: "Asian governments exhibit a strong preference for political institutions that encourage aggregation and moderation across cleavage groups, rather than the articulation of those divisions.... As a result, even in divided societies ethnic parties are relatively rare."[142] Asian majoritarianism, then, provides an opportunity to rethink democracy, which since the French Revolution has steered toward political equality instead of public control and toward sterile, left-right cleavages rather than fluid contests for the public good. Institutions that both create a "public" and then empower that public with political control in the hands of broad-based parties may do more for social consensus than institutions designed to favor particularistic interests can. The Asian conception of the rights of the majority may be closer to democratic principles than the available alternatives are.

THE HOUSE OF ASPIRATIONS

A second notable institutional feature of Asian democracies that reflects a "rights of the majority" mentality is strong executives. While the *formal* powers given to legislatures in Asia line up predictably with their degree of democracy, their *actual* behavior and powers are significantly weaker. Life-and-death struggles between presidents and legislatures are rare, and they cause much consternation when they occur. Studies of legislatures in Asia have an underlying theme: namely, that they are *not* the center of political decision making and constantly struggle to maintain their relevance.[143] In a study of fifteen annual budget negotiations in South Korea between 1995 and 2009, for instance, Kim found that the legislature changed the president's budget by an average of only 0.55 percent each year.[144] The weakling prime minister's office was exiled to the barren new administrative capital of Sejong, 74.5 miles (120 kilometers) south of Seoul, in 2012 as part of a deconcentration plan, while the presidency and key ministries remained in Seoul.

A strong executive is more associated with presidential systems. Presidents can draw their cabinet from outside of parliament, they can veto parliamentary legislation, they are not accountable to a legislative caucus, and they can issue administrative or presidential orders that have the force of the law. Presidentialism also encourages parties to align themselves with a presidential candidate and to be more centrist by necessity. It is no surprise, then, that Asia's four main presidential democracies – South Korea, Taiwan, the Philippines, and Indonesia – have executive dominant governments.

Nor is it a surprise that executive dominance is the norm in the authoritarian parliamentary systems of Singapore and Cambodia. In Cambodia, for instance, the legislature has initiated no legislation since its inception in 1993. A USAID report noted that "legislation is proposed by the government and almost always moves through the parliament quickly with little opposition, debate or even discussion."[145] The executive issues "sub-decrees" without legislative approval that become part of the law.

The surprise, rather, is that executive-dominant government is also found in the three democratic parliamentary democracies – Japan, Thailand, and Malaysia. The "state dominance" tradition means that the executive and bureaucracy tend to be dominant even in these parliamentary systems. Legislatures are effective checks but are not entrenched obstacles to executive-led government. In all three cases, the prime minister's office and the party think tanks, along with the bureaucracy, conduct most of the policy research.

In Japan in the 2000s, the Japanese Diet passed on average one bill for every day it was in session, making it function as something of a rubber stamp.[146] This reflected a long postwar system in which the role of the legislature has been to support, not constrain, executive-led government. As one cabinet secretary recalled of the 1990s: "We only needed to seek approval from the powerful figures within the [bureaucratic] subcommittees and the party. The deliberation at the Diet was close to a ceremony."[147] The quest for "political reform" that would infuse this party and executive-led system with the *egalité* of civil society and parliamentary power has been an endless theme of liberal, Whiggish writing on the country.[148] But the system proves to be resilient even as these bottom-up forces become more complex and contentious. Opposition parties that use obstructionist techniques to block legislation – such as "cow walking," or going slowly to roll calls so that the allotted time for the vote expires – attract public censure. The main political battles continue to be fought among the executive, ruling party committees, and bureaucracy.

In Malaysia, the standing rules for parliament lay down strict, schoolroom-like procedures that make it virtually impossible for members to challenge the government. Questions to ministers, for example, in addition to a long list of subjects that have been deemed taboo, such as "the internal affairs of a foreign country" or "statements in the press," also cannot "contain any argument, interference, opinion, imputation, epithet or misleading, ironical or offensive expression" or anything that is "frivolous" or "trivial." Even if a question makes it past all of those barriers, a minister can simply refuse to answer on the grounds of "public interest."[149] Bills are introduced to parliament only a few days before being put to a vote, select committees are rare, and the preemptive closure of debates and questions is the norm.[150] Only two private members' bills have been introduced since independence (and neither passed).[151] The law expelling Singapore from the federation was rushed through parliament in four hours in 1965.[152] Ministerial accountability to parliament is emptied by the strong sanctions imposed on backbench MPs who dare to censure government incompetence. In 2004, regulations had to be passed to ensure that at least half of MPs would bother to show up for parliamentary sittings.

As in South Korea, executive dominance has become entrenched through a physical separation of executive and legislature. In the case of Malaysia, it is the executive that decamped from the capital, Kuala

Lumpur, to the new (and equally barren) federal capital of Putrajaya in 1999, along with every other institution and ministry. Only the legislature remained in Kuala Lumpur. The Prime Minister's Office known as Perdana Putra is now the visual focus of Malaysia's political capital. The system is described by two government researchers (admiringly) as one of "strong central government, executive dominance, and controlled democratic practices."[153]

Thailand, too, remains a country where, despite a parliamentary system, the legislature remains weak. In particular, the Thai constitution imposes severe restrictions on legislative power over the budget, limiting it to an up or down vote and prohibiting the addition of spending clauses. The parliamentary Scrutiny Committee that reviews the budget is headed by the Minister of Finance and dominated by the executive branch, which serves as its secretariat through the Bureau of the Budget.[154]

These "hard cases" give us a clue about the notional role of legislatures in Asian politics. But the most explicit description is found in democratic Indonesia, where the rules of procedure adopted by the legislature, known as the *Tatib*, prescribe in detail the notion of a cooperative legislature. The Tatib decision-making approach is called "deliberation and consensus" (*musyawarah dan mufakat*), which Sherlock calls "unique among democratic parliaments in the world."[155] Under this system, decisions are not considered final until there is a *unanimous* agreement. A vote is used only if such an agreement cannot be reached. The legislature's oversight functions relating to state agencies are described as "consultation and coordination." Legislators are expected to bring to the president any wishes expressed by their constituents through a "house of aspirations" (*rumah aspirasi*) located in each constituency – something we might take as a metaphor for Asian legislatures as a whole.[156] In 2010, it was agreed that parties would use their local branch offices as their houses of aspiration, strengthening the idea of parties as nonpartisan vehicles and of legislatures as aspirational, rather than adversarial, institutions.[157]

The principles of "deliberation and consensus" were drawn directly from the ideals of *Pancasila* that were propounded by Suharto in 1965 to restore harmony after his coup. These emphasized that democracy must be guided by the "inner wisdom" that arises out of deliberation among citizens, representatives, and leaders. The continuation and elaboration of these principles under democracy suggest they had deeper roots. The result is that most legislation in Indonesia is made in committees. This has caused alarm among liberals in the country, but it has not attracted wider public concern.[158] The legislature has adopted a political culture of consensus by using a practical method of debating bills only in closed-door committees rather than in open plenary sessions. In effect, by eschewing formal votes, factional leaders within the parliament can accede to the wishes of the executive and bureaucracy within committees, thus giving an appearance of "consensus" to decisions that are, in fact, executive-led.[159]

The result is that plenary sessions are poorly attended, and those present are often asleep. The amended constitution of 2002 required "joint approval" of laws by both president and legislature and gave the president the ability to pass regulations "in lieu of laws," as well as to implement regulations. In practice, while the legislature has "the authority to make laws," virtually all of the laws are executive-initiated. The Land Acquisition Bill, for instance, which allows the state to take over land deemed necessary for public infrastructure, took five years (from 2007 to 2012) to be formulated and implemented. But virtually all of that time was spent on technical, legal, economic, and political debates *within* the bureaucracy. The legislature passed it with only a few minor amendments in 2011.[160]

Even so, parties and legislatures are not endlessly pliant. Aspirational legislatures within an accountability framework that emphasizes good governance may morally remonstrate with leaders when those leaders have gone amiss. In 2010, for instance, three of the six parties in president Yudhoyono's governing coalition plus several members of his own party, voted for an opposition bill to launch a criminal investigation into the government's $716 million bailout in 2008 of the Jakarta-based Bank Century. The government lost the vote by 325 to 212. Political analysts decried the lack of "professionalism" shown by the parliament in its display of opposition.[161] *The Jakarta Post* editorialized that the vote caused a decline in public support for Yudhoyono, not because the public sided with parliament, but because it showed that "the executive branch would be very weak in dealing with the parliament."[162]

The Indonesian example shows that legislatures in Asia fulfill their functional roles in representing citizens and their interests, passing primary legislation, and exercising oversight over government. But initiative and leadership in the political system remain vested in the executive, ruling party, and bureaucracy (something we return to in Chapter 5). It is not so much a lack of formal power as a deeper, underlying assumption that policy capacity, like some phallic power, resides naturally in the executive, while legislatures should act as a remonstrative vox populi. The result, as Zeigenhain notes, is that "a parliament ... that is constitutionally powerful but institutionally weak is always in danger of being overruled by a better-informed and financially better-equipped executive."[163]

In a 1962 speech in London, Singapore's founding prime minister, Lee Kuan Yew, warned that "a government which is open to the vagaries of the ballot box is a government which is already weakened before it starts to govern."[164] For the next half century, as he moved from being prime minister to "senior minister" to "minister mentor" and finally to retired sage of Singapore, Lee repeatedly warned that democracy would cause social discord, economic decline, and political breakdown. At the height of the Asian Values debate in the mid-1990s, these views suddenly gained a wide following not just around Asia but also among many thinkers in the West.[165] In 1992, Lee told an audience in Tokyo: "With a few exceptions, democracy has not brought good government to new developing countries ... because the governments did not establish the stability and discipline necessary for development."[166] Lee's antidemocratic pronouncements have become known as the "Lee Hypothesis."

In general, the claim that democracy is bad for development or stability is empirically false: Democracy generally makes countries more stable, more peaceful, and more prosperous than they would be under some feasible authoritarian alternative, if that alternative even exists.[167] But the Lee Hypothesis was more particular to Asia. Democracy, Lee believed, would upset the state-dominant and majoritarian political foundations of the region by unleashing a torrent of narrow bottom-up demands. These fears were echoed by scholars like Pye, who warned of the "primitive power" lurking below the surface of Asian politics,[168] or Geertz, who interpreted cockfighting in Bali as a metaphor for the "animalistic demons" that could overturn social order at any time.[169] In other words, in a region where there is no self-governance tradition in civil society, democracy would spell disaster.

If Lee had been a keener student of Asian politics, however, he would have known that there are *social* foundations of governance in the region that do not depend on wise leaders or fears of discord alone. At the heart of those foundations is an accountability dynamic between state and society that rests on the fact that societies in Asia are remarkably well-ordered. Democracy, then, could in some cases strengthen, rather than undermine, the accountability on which stability, prosperity, and freedom depend. Around the region, countries have democratized without experiencing a decline in state strength or social order. Slater, for example, finds that democracy has *deepened* state power in Indonesia and Malaysia through the creation of broad-based parties, the incorporation into the political process of marginal populations, and the imposition of uniform political procedures on recalcitrant local elites.[170] In South Korea, democracy maintained political cohesion during a time of rapid social and economic stresses. This in turn made it easier for the state to meet complex governance challenges. As Kim wrote: "The Korean state seems to have become stronger in pushing for various reform measures which preceding authoritarian governments failed to implement."[171]

More generally, the Asian model seems to be one of "strong state democratization,"[172] wherein democracy is initiated by strong states and then contributes to their maintenance. People in countries as diverse as Japan and Cambodia never lost faith in democracy, because democracy was not associated with state weakness but with state building. Democracy usually has been what Friedman calls a "solidifying moment,"[173] rather than a moment of primitive power, in Asia.

In Indonesia, the only recent democratization that we can draw on for comparative data, democracy and stateness have moved forward hand in hand since 1998 (see Figure 4.3). While it is true that democracy has not dramatically improved stateness since before the democratic era, nor has it worsened it. Put another way, Indonesian citizens can now enjoy significantly wider freedoms without the state having been weakened. Indeed, throughout the region, the strongest states are also the most democratic ones. Lee's Hypothesis cannot yet be disproven in the cases of China, Vietnam, Malaysia, and Singapore, which have built relatively effective states, despite being authoritarian. If Lee's claim is that democratization in the very early stages of development might upend state building, he was probably right. The suspension of democracy in the 1950s and 1960s throughout Asia (and China's rejection of democratic change in 1989) may have been a rational response by societies to the social fragmentation and institutional weakness that democracy threatened to entrench in them. Asian leaders reasoned, as Baker puts it, that "state-building cannot be by-passed by political accommodation."[174] What is also true about Asia is that state building is able to proceed for much longer without democratic checks, resulting in cases like China, Malaysia, and Vietnam, where stateness far exceeds democracy in global comparison.

However, the resulting strong states and complex economies could not be governed by developmental dictators forever. The same accountability dynamic that sanctioned and empowered authoritarian regimes later

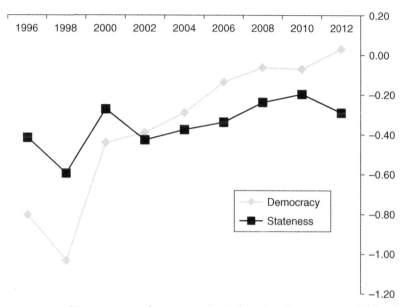

FIGURE 4.3. Democracy and stateness in Indonesia; Democracy = Voice & Accountability Indicator; Stateness = Government Effectiveness Indicator. *Source*: World Bank Governance Indicators (Scaled –2.5 to +2.5).

stripped them of their right to rule. If Lee's claim is that advanced state building would be threatened by democracy, he is plainly wrong. At a certain point, democracy becomes essential to state building in most of Asia. The main exceptions to this are tiny Singapore (which has an excess of stateness over democracy, even in the Asian context) and the Philippines (which has the opposite). In part, as with Cambodia, the case of the Philippines can be explained as a result of its low development levels. But unlike Cambodia and Indonesia, the absence of a state-led transition and the resulting collapse of institutions led to patronage-based government expansion. O'Dwyer calls this "runaway state-building" and finds parallels in some countries in Eastern Europe.[175] The state in the Philippines remains "contested" and thus unable to operate effectively.[176]

The Asian experience is a reminder of the Hamiltonian foundations of modern democracy. Because most democratic transitions include some involvement by existing power holders and are an attempt to relegitimate political power, states have often been strengthened by democratization. Democracy in Europe was not only a matter of Whiggish freedom but also a matter of Tory efforts to win the support of larger populations, so that they could be taxed (and sent to war) for the purposes of state strength.[177] Asia owes its democratic success to its long tradition of state dominance and majoritarian conceptions of the public good that have made it relatively easy to assimilate democracy.

What about economic growth? The conventional developmental state literature emphasized the key role of authoritarianism in ensuring good policy planning, public investment, and wage restraint. But from what we saw of developmental states in Asia in Chapter 3, contentious politics have been critical to growth. Properly constituted, then, democracy could be a means to strengthen the accountability pressures that drive Asian economic success. The "democratic developmental state," as Robinson and White call it,[178] needs precisely the legacies that developmental states inherited in Asia: state dominance, national integration, and effective programmatic parties. We should expect, then, that democracy would not threaten growth in Asia. Kong saw as early as 1995, for instance, that the transition from "relative autonomy to consensual development" in South Korea was likely to succeed.[179] In his seminal article on the "democratic developmental state," White argued that countries like Japan, which inherited an effective bureaucracy and corporatist politics, would grow rapidly under democracy.[180]

Using a sample that includes our fourteen core Asian states but also seven states on the periphery of the Asian core, and drawing on data going back to 1860, Knutsen found that democracy was not associated with slower growth.[181] While authoritarian regimes generally invested more in infrastructure, democracies invested more in education, and the two effects tended to cancel each other out. Chen also found that education investment, especially for the poor, improved with democracy in Asia.[182]

The most detailed work has been done by Rock, who finds that democracy has strengthened growth dynamics in Asia.[183] This is because the essential institutions of the developmental state – a leadership commitment to common good development goals, an effective bureaucracy, and social accountability mechanisms of self-constraint and self-correction – were carried over from one regime to the next. As he notes, this tends to reinforce the analytic importance of the factors that create developmental states (see Figure 3.3):

Those interested in the link between democracy/autocracy and development would probably be better served by asking questions such as does a given polity possess an effective governmental bureaucracy, does it adhere to the rule of law, is it developmentally oriented, does it have enough flexibility to change development policies when this is needed, and does it have enough capability to sustain policies when this is called for?[184]

Finally, has democracy in Asia delivered substantive equality and freedom? The Lee Hypothesis contended that excessive individualism and rent-seeking by the few would undermine freedom and equality for the many. Judging by the portrait of Asian democracies painted by Morlino and colleagues, Lee had no need to worry. Democracy, they write, is "continuously challenged by legacies of authoritarianism, technocratic developmentalism, and debates about a unique way of governance based on Asian cultural traits, values, and political thought.... Asian political systems remain reluctant to expand freedom and equality, particularly when they risk conflicting with collective aims articulated by the state, such as economic development, social harmony, or political stability."[185] In other words, as Scott argued as far back as 1968 about Malaysia,[186] freedom is only one value in the political system, not an overriding one, and it is adjusted accordingly as conditions require.

One statistical reminder of this is the gap between "political rights" and "civil rights" in Asian democracies. Whereas only 25 of 108 (23 percent) democracies outside of Asia tracked by Freedom House had worse civil liberties scores that political liberties scores in 2011, four out of five (80 percent) of Asian democracies (Japan, South Korea, Taiwan, and Indonesia but not the Philippines) did so. Electoral democracy, in other words, has not led to unconstrained liberties or rights claims in Asia. Rather, those liberties and rights have been expanded in ways that reflect competing values – in particular, political stability and social harmony. Human rights have been embraced as a concept but not as an ultimate value. Human rights commissions in Asia, where they exist, are notable for their lack of legal or constitutional powers over the state.[187]

More specifically, the claims made on behalf of particularistic groups – such as women, ethnic minorities, accused criminals, secessionists, journalists, protestors activists, asylum seekers, or unionists – are often circumscribed compared to Western liberal polities. Commentators who "vilify" political candidates in messages in online forums can be jailed for up to a year in South Korea. Social conservatism also limits sexual rights: Adultery remains a criminal offense in South Korea, for instance, while public lashing is the prescribed punishment for homosexuality under local *sharia* laws in Indonesia. Anticommunism, meanwhile, remains on the books to limit some rights in South Korea and Indonesia. In the former, it remains illegal to listen to North Korean radio broadcasts. In Indonesia, Law 27, prohibiting the propagation of communism and the formation of communist parties, remains in force with prison terms ranging from twelve to twenty years.

In these ways, rights claims have been taken not as absolute values but as political values that must compete against others and should never be put above politics. If liberalism is an ideology that, in Crick's words, wishes to "honour the fruit but not the tree,"[188] in Asia, preserving and sustaining the tree itself has remained paramount. Indonesia's ban on communism, for instance, is a legacy of the Indonesian Communist Party's participation in an antigovernment uprising in 1948 and the subsequent efforts by the Soviet Union and China to absorb Indonesia into an Asian communist bloc.[189] This very concrete threat to sovereignty was outlawed by Suharto but not formally codified until the democratic era in 1999. President Wahid's suggestion to end it contributed to his early downfall in 2001. Today, despite democratization, police still occasionally enforce the law, arresting artisans selling Karl Marx T-shirts and detaining little old ladies browsing in bookshops that carry *Das Kapital*.

If Lee Kuan Yew was worried about an explosion of human rights claims with democracy, then, he can rest assured. Asian democracies have found ways to expand freedoms in a manner that is consistent with more enduring values of state dominance, political and social stability, and majoritarian accountability. A more nuanced understanding of this evolving relationship between citizens and government must wait until Chapter 5.

THE CHINA WAVE

The spread of democracy, then, has been largely predictable, natural, and supportive of existing values and institutions in Asia. Of the remaining authoritarian regimes, none looms larger than China, which accounts for more than half of the entire world population living under authoritarianism. A democratization in China would affect as many people as each previous "wave" of democratization in world history. Democracy in China would profoundly affect political prospects in Vietnam, North Korea, Laos, and Singapore.

Like Indonesia, China experienced an anticolonial, nationalist revolution that brought to power a developmental dictatorship, although in this case it was organized around communist ideology and organization. Like Indonesia, it experienced a major political rupture between the first and second generation leaderships, in this case in 1976 with the death of Mao and the overthrow of the Gang of Four. Like Indonesia, this rupture ushered in a long period of rapid economic growth but also increasing social pressures for change. And just as Suharto's New Order survived its first serious economic and political crisis in the 1980s with a rapid liberalization program, China survived its 1989 Tiananmen crisis with a similar change. Deng Xiaoping's "reform or die" mantra propelled China for a generation after 1989.

With a GDP per capita of only about $1,500 in 1989, it is not surprising that attempts by students to dislodge the regime failed then. But as China's development levels approach $10,000 by 2020, the pressures for change will be immense. Wang, using survey data about social values, predicts that China's citizens will begin to demand democracy in large numbers between 2015 and 2020.[190] The "markets and modernization" that brought democratic change to the rest of Asia are well advanced in China.

Despite this, since the 2000s, China has been the subject of a vast proliferation of research on its "authoritarian resilience."[191] To be sure, China has some factors that will probably delay its democratization: its Leninist institutions, its superpower status, and its very deliberate efforts to prevent a "Gorbachev phenomenon." But the Asian experience tells us that such fin de siècle struggles will not prevent democratization once there is a paradigm shift on the streets.[192] China is as much embedded in the Asian Governance Model as other countries in the region are, and the acceptance of authoritarianism will have limits. The fundamental notions of accountability that have produced democracy elsewhere are present in China.

The Asian experience also tells us *how* democracy will likely come to China. The conflicted middle class is likely to be a late-stage participant in any democratic movement, which will instead emerge from a highly charged contention between street actors (students, intellectuals, *fenqing* – or angry male youths, monks, and peasants) and regime reformers. A responsive transition in China – one that is led by reformers within the Chinese Communist Party and that maintains a large continuity with the ancien regime – is to be expected despite significant social mobilization.

Because of its middle-income development levels and its success in eliminating the military from an active political role, democracy in China will have excellent prospects for consolidation. Without a chaotic Yeltsin era, China's people will not clamor for a Putin strongman, although its democratic leaders will be firmly drawn from the political elite of the communist past. The practice of democracy will strongly affirm the "rights of the majority" and prospects for succession in Tibet or Xinjiang, as well as Taiwan, will be dim. A strong executive working in cooperation with an aspirational legislature will replicate many aspects of the communist political system, not least its dominant party. Economic growth and government effectiveness will be inherited by China's new democracy and will not be threatened by it. Rather, democracy will reinvigorate China's political system and afford a much broader, but not unlimited, degree of freedom for China's people.

In all of these ways, democracy represents both change and continuity in Asian politics. There is no denying the immensity of institutionalizing the accountability mechanism through elections and political competition. At the same time, there is more to government than political competition. We turn to the questions of governance and public policy next.

5

Governance

The politics of compulsory land acquisition in post-Suharto Indonesia was contentious and complex. During the five-year period that led to the promulgation of a Land Procurement for Development in the Public Interest Law in 2012, the key political battles were waged not in public contests between the executive and the legislature, and much less in debates between civil society groups and the state, but rather in debates *within* the state, often in closed-door sequestrations of civil servants from various agencies. Once the law was passed by the legislature, further bureaucratic debates took place, leading to what was the most important part of the law, an implementing regulation called Presidential Regulation 71/2012 that laid down the specific rules governing the process. Thereafter, the politics of land acquisition moved into the field and sparked a contest between regulators in Jakarta, traditional *adat* land managers in the provinces, and the local courts that mediated compensation issues.

In studying politics in Asia or elsewhere, we are prone to look at legislative or electoral battles first. Yet the politics that matters often takes place *outside* of the limelight of the legislature and centers on bureaucrats, executives, courts, and local governments. A large part of politics involves how public policies are proposed, elaborated, implemented, and revised *within* the state. Legislatures typically pass only enabling statutes that leave the most important policy decisions to the administrative and regulatory functions of the bureaucracy and its governance networks. Indeed, often those statutes have been largely written by bureaucratic experts themselves, leaving very little scope for legislative influence.

In other words, much of politics – meaning the process of decision making that deploys state power on behalf of the political community – takes place *within* the state. Politics is less a battle between "state and society," and much less a struggle between "government and opposition," but primarily an iterative process of governmental decision making variously shaped or constrained by both social and global forces. Moreover, the everyday ways that citizens relate to the state is mainly a question of how they interact with "street-level bureaucrats" rather than with politicians or parties.

So far, we have examined the big questions of politics, namely how to create authority (Chapter 2), how to achieve development (Chapter 3), and how to tame political power (Chapter 4). What remains is perhaps the ultimate aim of politics: how to govern the complex polity that results. In a democratic age, questions about corporate governance, environmental protection, social policy effectiveness, public sector reform, administrative law, and local government capacity become paramount. These are the issues of governance (Chapter 5) and public policy (Chapter 6). What, if anything, is distinctive about governance and public policy in Asia?

The place to begin is the bureaucratic tradition of Asia. This tradition is long and complex, as the Malacca case reminds us. While the elevated status of the state was in part an inheritance from India, it is China where that ideal was manifested in a sophisticated bureaucracy. The early Chinese administrative state was built around several ideas: paternalistic authority based on rites, ethics, and obligations (*dezhi*, or rule of virtue); the supremacy of the virtuous ruler rather than of the law (*renzheng*, or governing through benevolence); and the organic relationship between governors and people (*hezhong gongji*, or working together harmoniously). After taking shape in the Western Zhou (1046–771 BC)[1] and Han (206 BC–220 AD)[2] dynasties, Chinese bureaucracy gradually became more institutionalized until the Tang dynasty (618–907 AD), when the office of the Controller of Administration made the momentous shift from the emperor's inner court to a new outer court of government called the *yamen*.[3] It was this highly ideational and institutionalized Tang system of bureaucracy that was transferred to Japan, where it reached its highest form under the *samurai* ("to serve") class in the Edo period (1603–1863).[4] Confucian virtues were "nationalized" by the state to serve the purposes of government effectiveness.[5]

In Southeast Asia, meanwhile, Confucian premises mixed with the Hindu-Indic tradition of the semidivine status of the state and the later

Malay-Islamic tradition of rule by custom (*adat*) to create bureaucracies that retained stronger reminiscences of the inner court. Even today in Thailand, the colleagues of a bureaucrat who passes away will, on behalf of the deceased, "ask his Majesty's permission to die."[6] A shared dimension of bureaucracy in Asia is that morality or virtue is deeply embedded in notions of governance. The word "governance" is translated in Thai as "ruling by justice" (*thammapiban*), while in China it is translated as "ruling by truth" (*zhili*) or "appropriate rule" (*shanzhi*). The thousand-year-old Buddhist *Ten Guiding Principles for a King* (still known by the Hindi term *Dhosapit Raja Dharma*) that were widely diffused throughout Asia prescribe rule by a virtuous and generous ruler who is persevering yet gentle, precepts that are very similar to those outlined much earlier by Confucius and then his follower Mencius (371–289 BC).

The modern bureaucracies of Asia were creations of either indigenous choices (China, Japan, Taiwan, Thailand, South Korea, North Korea, Vietnam, and Laos) or colonialism (Malaysia, Cambodia, Myanmar, Indonesia, the Philippines, and Singapore). Irrespective of these proximate origins, these bureaucracies have converged on common patterns that combine traditional notions of the virtue and authority of the state with a postcolonial drive for national uplift. Bureaucrats are not synonymous with the state, but as key agents of culturally and historically dominant states, they enjoy a privileged status. If there is one exception, it is the Philippines, whose three centuries of Spanish colonial rule until 1896 undermined the Malay cultural heritage and left deep legacies of state weakness and bureaucratic indifference.

Modern Asian administrative ideology emerged first in Japan, where a series of reforms in the 1920s and 1930s embraced a combination of Confucian moralism and German legalism. This new bureaucracy was given the label of "shepherds of the people" (*bokumin*), borrowing directly from the Chinese concept of "governance by shepherding" (*mumin zhonggao*) that originated in the 1300s, during the late Yuan and early Ming dynasties.[7] This was an early sign that Asian traditions would thrive under modernity and not "fall apart" as they did in Africa. As Brown writes: "Rather than proving incompatible with the political imperatives of modernity, the values of paternalistic supervision found in the Confucian ethics of *bokumin* continued to infuse the institution at the center of administering the new nation-state."[8] Japan's Home Ministry, the centerpiece of this new bureaucracy, won its independence in the 1932 Commission on the Guarantee of Officials' Status, which ensured that key personnel appointments to the ministry were beyond the reach of elected politicians. This was the modern rebirth of what would become the Asian bureaucratic tradition.

At about the same time, Thailand's new bureaucracy was constructed, following the reform of the absolute monarchy in 1932. The number of civil servants rose from 81,000 in 1920 to 100,000 by 1939, and the number of foreign "advisors" in charge of departments was slashed from fifty to four. Honorific titles for bureaucrats were replaced with administrative pay grades. Bureaucratic power grew because frequent changes of government under the fledgling democracy left de facto power in the hands of civil servants.[9] In Nationalist China (which later moved to Taiwan), a Committee for Studying Administrative Efficiency was established within the Ministry of Interior in 1934 and became the Committee for the Improvement of Administrative Efficiency within the executive office in 1937. In 1940, President Chiang Kai-shek articulated a "three stages" view of bureaucratic excellence that would integrate planning, implementation, and review.[10] Nationalist China was also notable in its creation of a separate branch of government for the civil service – the Examination Yuan – that had *equal* status to the executive, legislative, and judicial branches. After defeating the Nationalists in a civil war, China's Communist Party recruited somewhere between 40 and 80 percent of the state's new bureaucrats from the former Nationalist government.[11]

An informed thinker in the 1950s might have speculated that the emergence of powerful bureaucracies in Asia would, as in the Soviet Union, lead to sclerotic governance and widespread corruption. Weber had argued in 1915 that the Chinese bureaucratic tradition "prostrates rational management in administration, finance, and economic policy,"[12] because it was too embedded in personalistic relationships (*guanxi*), especially at the village level. Certainly, many scholars worried about the emergence of "neopatrimonial" states, where traditional authority armed with modern bureaucracy would be used to fleece the people, as had occurred in Africa and the Middle East. But while sclerotic rule emerged in other parts of the world that had long bureaucratic traditions – India and Russia come to mind – the deep and unique imperatives of the Asian Governance Model saved Asia, for this model requires not just that bureaucracies govern but that they govern well. As Berman, one of the very few scholars who study comparative public administration in Asia, summarizes: "East Asia is a group-based work culture that fosters committed, cooperative, courteous, and very hard working civil servants, driven and sustained by a sense of duty toward their groups, hierarchical relationships, preferences for harmony, and the advantages that these relationships bring."[13]

The traditional expectations and imperatives of the Asian administrative tradition were first captured in the notion of "development administration" that emerged in the 1950s to replace the colonial ideal of a politically neutral and noninterventionist bureaucracy. Bureaucrats were expected to be both politically motivated *and* development-oriented, not mere paper pushers, and much less amateurs. The bureaucracy was expected to spur national development through proactive planning, the spread of technical knowledge, and the extension of state (and ruling party) power throughout society. In 1966, Thailand created a National Institute of Development Administration, while Malaysia created a Development Administration Unit under the prime minister. The Burma Civil Service inherited from the British in 1948 was abolished in favor of a new politically loyal administrative system in 1972.[14] Taiwan introduced a Framework to Implement Political and Economic Efficiency in 1969 that was premised on the "scientific management" of society. In the Philippines, after two decades of personalistic rule by populist politicians, Ferdinand Marcos introduced an Integrated Reorganization Plan in 1972 that, among other things, created a constitutionally independent Civil Service Commission to oversee training and senior appointments and an independent Commission on Audit.[15] While the reforms in the Philippines foundered on the deep personalization and heroic myths of Filipino politics, elsewhere in the region they were a success. In short, the proactive bureaucratic management of society took Asia by storm.

While the two greatest despots of the period, Mao and Pol Pot, are remembered for their attacks on bureaucracy, such attacks were exceptional in the Asian context. The more typical authoritarian "revolutions" from above in Asia – Suharto's New Order, Marcos's New Society (*Bagong Lipunan*), Park Chung-hee's Revitalization (*Yusin*) Constitution, and Deng's Four Modernizations – involved the creation of powerful bureaucracies, which acted as lightning rods for modernization. Asian governance was often described in terms of a "bureaucratic polity," a concept used by Riggs in his study of Thailand,[16] borrowing an earlier formulation by Silberman in his study of Meiji Japan.[17] The bureaucratic polity was a political system run *by* bureaucrats (rather than nobles or populists) and *for* bureaucrats (who saw themselves as representing the forces of modernization and the national interest). Malaysia's longstanding ruling party, UMNO, for instance, was founded by civil servants in 1946. In the first general elections under British rule in 1955, 53 of the 103 Malay candidates were ex–civil servants (whom the British authorities had permitted to run in order to support this bureaucratic takeover).[18] Then, as now, leadership in Asian politics began in the bureaucracy.

The Asian development administration or bureaucratic polity generally served the region well during the period of rapid economic development. Arguably, China and Vietnam continue to reap its rewards. But elsewhere, the transition to middle-income economies and more democratic regimes created pressures for new forms of governance. The prime challenge for Asian bureaucracies since the 1990s has been how to maintain their pre-eminence at a time when governance challenges are more complex and expectations of public sector performance are higher. Given the centrality of bureaucracy in Asia, any plan for public sector reform has a significant bearing on politics, governance, and public policy. As a result, public sector reform became a major political issue itself. While this is not unique to Asia – countries with equally powerful bureaucratic traditions, such as Sweden or France, have faced the same challenge – it is more pervasive in Asia than in other regions.

Demands for improved public sector performance arose globally in the 1990s under the concept of "new public management" (NPM). Although varied in its prescriptions, NPM was an attempt to get the public sector to think and act more like the private sector. Internally, this meant setting measurable performance targets ("performance management"); evaluating bottom-line results ("managing for results"); focusing on innovation and leadership rather than rule-following and procedures ("new public leadership"); and being long-term and strategic in resource utilization and planning ("strategic management"). Externally, this meant giving up public services that could be better handled by the private sector ("downsizing, privatization, and competition"); devolving management to lower-level governments ("subsidiarity") or to networks made up of community and business leaders ("networked governance"); and treating citizens like customers or shareholders rather than supplicants ("citizen stakeholders"). The 1992 American book *Reinventing Government* and a 1997 sequel, *Banishing Bureaucracy*,[19] remain the bibles of the NPM movement, and they have been widely invoked in Asia in the cause of public sector reform.

At the same time, NPM in Asia has met with a long indigenous bureaucratic tradition, which means that it has been interpreted and implemented in distinctive ways. Whereas NPM was part of an effort to justify and relegitimate government in the West, in Asia, where there was a long state tradition, there was no need to "reinvent" government to justify it. The challenge, rather, was to *maintain* the legitimacy of the state through continuous self-improvement in the public sector and its capacity to govern. As Cheung and Scott note: "Building state capacity has been the predominant paradigm for public sector reform in Asia."[20] More broadly, as Cheung summarizes, administrative reform in Asia has not been driven by an antistate or "small government" agenda that attacks the bureaucracy. "The private sector oriented and neo-liberal connotations of current global reform ideas, such as NPM, do not sit logically with the rather statist and bureaucratic nature of many Asian administrative systems," he writes. As a result, "it is not surprising to observe that reform programs in Asia have not carried any overtly anti-public sector perspective, and do not seek to denigrate the bureaucracy *per se*. Administrative reforms remain essentially policy instruments to shore up an existing pro-state, and very often also pro-bureaucracy, regime."[21]

Understanding the politics of the NPM in Asia requires remembering the vigorous proto-NPM traditions that arose in the region *prior* to the 1990s. The "development administration," for instance, was always intended to be market-supporting, efficient, and strategic. More significantly, the Asian Governance Model and its manifestations in the Hegelian state prescribe a relationship between government and people that has many affinities with the socially embedded and consensus-based idea of networked governance. As Painter notes: "Asian administrative states ... are *already* relatively small and lean, and they have always been especially close to business."[22] Total public sector employment as a share of total employment, for instance, is much smaller in Japan (7 percent), South Korea (6 percent), and Thailand and Taiwan (5 percent each) than in the OECD (an average of 15 percent). The more narrowly defined "bureaucracy" (excluding policemen, teachers, and health workers) is also consistently smaller in Asia than elsewhere: 1.5 percent of the total population in each Japan and Taiwan and about 2 percent in each the Philippines and Thailand, according to International Labor Organization data for 2009. Only Malaysia, with its (relatively bloated) 3 percent level, has as many bureaucrats as the (relatively lean) U.S. government does and far fewer than most European countries, like Greece (3.5 percent), do.

In effect, what we see in Asia more than two decades after the NPM revolution is that the movement has transformed but not ended the Asian bureaucratic tradition. Some things *have* changed permanently, especially the amount of scrutiny now given to public sector performance.[23] On the other hand, as a broad doctrine with many prescriptions, it was inevitable that NPM would be selectively adopted and interpreted in Asia in a manner that was consonant with a bureaucratic tradition that long predates anything in the West. As Bowornwathana notes about Thailand: "Efforts to disperse political and administrative power, to introduce decentralization and foster strong civil society, and to downsize the central government are policies that run counter to Thai government traditions and culture."[24] There *is* a new public management in Asia. But it is a new public management that remains distinctively Asian.

Perhaps the most eager NPM devotee was Malaysian prime minister Mahathir Mohamad, who rebranded his country "Malaysia Incorporated" in 1983 and created a Malaysia Incorporated Officials Committee in 1996, in which private business would dictate reforms to the civil service. Under Malaysia's "Look East" policy, begun in 1982 to emulate Japanese economic efficiency, 3,000 Malaysian civil servants were trained in Japan. The Development Administration Unit was replaced by a new Malaysian Administrative Modernisation and Management Planning Unit. Mahathir became known for his obsession with "punch clocks, name tags, and quality circles" in the public service.[25] Even today, Malaysian public servants sport plastic name tags, the forerunner of the ubiquitous ID lanyard. Public sector employment (excluding police and army) has been steadily *reduced*, from 700,000 in 1990 to about 650,000 by 2005. ISO standards were introduced for all government departments in 1996, making Malaysia the first country to do so, and a cabinet position for bureaucratic performance was appointed in 2009.

The zeal for NPM in Malaysia has been driven in part by the need to counteract the threat of bureaucratic decline and communal patronage resulting from pro-Malay affirmative action policies introduced in 1971. Malays accounted for 77 percent of the civil service in 2005 and 85 percent of the elite Administrative and Diplomatic Service, despite constituting only 53 percent of the population.[26] The potential inefficiencies and corruption resulting from affirmative action encouraged Malaysia to join the region-wide drive for improved governance. In particular, living next door to superefficient Singapore has created nationalist incentives to prevent bureaucracy from becoming inefficient.[27] So strong was Mahathir's emphasis on bureaucratic efficiency that he was accused of trying to "transform Malays into Chinese."[28]

The distinctive direction that NPM takes in Asia is most notable in Japan, whose business practices partly inspired NPM itself. *Reinventing Government* praises Japan for its rigorous performance ranking of secondary schools and for its long-range urban planning.[29] To be sure, some NPM principles have long been embedded in Japanese administrative culture – the market-orientation and relative smallness of government, for instance, or the system of *ringi*, in which policy proposals are initiated by junior staff and trace a slow, spiraling "ring" as they move up the seniority pyramid.[30] But the state has never been seen as a mere extension of society in Asia; rather, it has been considered an autonomous and higher source of authority. As a result, and despite its role in inspiring NPM, "within the country itself, cultural barriers [to NPM] remain enormous and prohibitive."[31]

A similar story about the cultural limits of NPM can be seen in South Korea. Every Korean president since Roh Tae-Woo (1988 to 1993) has made bureaucratic reform a top priority. Both Kim Young Sam and Kim Dae Jung sought radical transformation of the bureaucracy as part of democratization, especially after the 1997 financial crisis. Reforms included "lateral entry" to senior positions, private sector secondment, and "performance pay" for high fliers. But in South Korea, as elsewhere in Asia, NPM-style reforms could only shape a traditional and hierarchical organization so much. For instance, most civil servants who were awarded merit bonuses distributed the money equally to everyone in their unit. The number of lateral entry positions to senior civil service positions hired through open recruitment was reduced from 30 percent to 15 percent, because the impact on group harmony had caused little uptake.

The ability of the bureaucracy to selectively resist the programs remained high, as well. The term *pockchi-pudong*, or "lying down and refusing to budge," reflects a bureaucracy that will not give up its central role in national political life. In 2012, for instance, the central bank's labor union successfully opposed the promotion of a private sector economist to senior deputy governor.[32] When the existing senior deputy governor stepped down that year, he assailed the U.S.-educated central bank governor for his promotion of youth and outsiders: "The values and rules that have been built up over the past 60 years were denied in a single day."[33] Two scholars concluded that: "The legacies of the traditional administrative culture make it difficult for the NPM reforms to fully take root in Korean soil."[34]

The reason that Asian governments were selective about NPM was not because of corruption but because Asian bureaucracy has its own indigenous sources of success. The main forces that make the bureaucracies in countries like South Korea, Japan, Indonesia, and Thailand successful are the *internal* mechanisms of "mutuality" (strong norms of mutual obligations to perform well) and "contrived randomness" (a culture of dynamism bred by the constant churning of the bureaucratic ranks as a result of executive demands).[35]

Not surprisingly, NPM has played into legitimation strategies of authoritarian regimes in Singapore, China (including Hong Kong), Vietnam, and Myanmar. It has offered a way to revitalize the roles of Asia's authoritarian states by shifting them from resource mobilization for development to public sector reform for good governance. Singapore exhorts its bureaucrats to be, in the words of the official scheme, "dynamic, progressive, and nimble" in order "to maintain Singapore's competitive advantage."[36] Every whiff of incompetence or laziness is met in Singapore with heroic civil service reforms – "NPM Fever," as one scholar has called it.[37] NPM reforms have become an alternative to democratization for Asia's authoritarian regimes. As Cheung puts it about Hong Kong: "Underneath the managerial rhetoric of NPM was a subtle legitimation agenda geared towards preserving public bureaucratic power in a new political context."[38]

The affinity between Asian-style NPM and authoritarianism is perhaps best exemplified by Myanmar, whose military junta established a Union Civil Service Board in 2010 to select senior civil servants to be trained in Japan, Singapore, and Thailand. Myanmar took over ASEAN's "Cooperation on Civil Service Matters" forum during 2013 and 2014, something that would have been unthinkable only a few years earlier. The fact that NPM has fit so neatly into the legitimation strategies of Asia's remaining authoritarian regimes tells us that its interpretation in the region has been acculturated through the state dominance paradigm in which democratization, if it comes at all, will be a state-led response to new governance demands. Democratization in Asia, then, can be seen as just one dimension of public sector reform for good governance within the Asian Governance Model framework.

The embrace of NPM has been more challenging for the communist authoritarian regimes in China, Vietnam, and Laos, because of their overt politicization of the civil service. In China, for instance, an attempt by the Shenzhen municipality in 2003 to introduce "administrative trifurcation" (*xingzheng sanfenzhi*), separating governance into policy making, implementation, and monitoring, was quashed by Beijing in 2011 because it threatened to weaken party leadership.[39] Just as Thailand's monarchy impedes democratic consolidation, communist politics impedes public sector performance in China, Vietnam, and Laos, and will someday in North Korea once it begins reforms. As Cheung observes: "In a sense the CCP reformers had tried to embrace Lenin, Confucius, Weber and Thatcher all at the same time."[40]

The fact that Asian bureaucracies are able to reform despite the weakness of pressures from legislatures, citizens, or the media presents a puzzle for standard theories, in which the strength of such external pressures are the key determinants of public service reform.[41] When external pressures are weak and the bureaucracy is relatively autonomous, reform must be either negotiated with the executive or self-initiated by the bureaucracy. The assumption is that neither approach will deliver much good. But in Asia, where *ideas* of good governance and *moral mechanisms* of accountability operate, such negotiated and self-initiated reforms have been more effective than those achieved through externally mandated reforms. As Painter notes, there is a "pervasive culture of administrative improvement" in the region that creates a robust *internal* capacity for bureaucratic reform.[42] The NPM notion of "continuous self-improvement" was already well-established in Asia long before *Reinventing Government*. Vogel referred to Singapore in a 1989 book as a "macho meritocracy" because of the unsettling gusto with which it pursued public sector reform,[43] and his term was subsequently embraced without irony by that country's public sector leaders.[44] The term is emblematic of an urgency that pervades Asian public administration as a whole.

NPM and its Asian interpretations have thus *strengthened* state capacity in an era when globalization, democratization, and economic liberalization were thought to be weakening it. A UN-sponsored program on "reinventing government in Asia" noted in a 2004 document that "the public sector should play as great a role as the private in the allocation of resources."[45] Functional measures of bureaucratic efficiency suggest that Asian governments generally out-perform their income peers elsewhere in the world. The World Bank "ease of doing business" indicator, for instance, shows that business regulation is better in Asia than it is in comparable countries globally (see Figure 5.1). A similar result is apparent from the United Nations' measure of e-government services and participation, which is a good way to capture innovation as well as public service delivery (see Figure 5.2). South Korea's astounding e-government capacity resulted from a top-down presidential initiative in 2001 that was pushed with vigor by the Ministry of Government and Home Affairs.[46]

What is particularly notable is that, in comparative perspective, the cliché of Japan as a sclerotic bureaucracy is wrong.[47] While its economic slowdown in the 1990s clearly reflected the slow pace of economic reform, broader governance and regulation remain excellent in Japan by

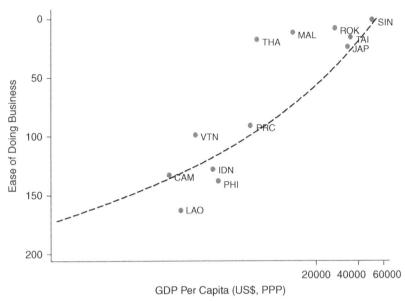

FIGURE 5.1. Ease of doing business in Asia vs. global averages.
Notes: n = 153, r² = 0.60.
Source: World Bank Ease of Doing Business Index, 2011.

any measure. Japan's rapid recovery from the 2011 East Sea earthquake and tsunami – the Tohoku Expressway was reopened within two weeks despite being damaged along more than half of its 419.4 mile (675 kilometer) length – was emblematic of this. One study of reform in maternal healthcare in Japan found that the country's decentralized governance, strong trust and cooperation between state and society, and professional and personal ethics are key factors driving bureaucratic excellence.[48] Another example of reform in Japan concerns private auto inspections. In the 1990s, a mandatory biannual inspection typically took *a week* and cost $2,000. More than a thousand central bureaucrats managed the system, which also employed hundreds of thousands of garages and workers. In 2002, a new, autonomoys National Agency of Vehicle Inspection was created to simplify the process with a staff (by 2012) of only 800. Inspection times were cut to fifteen minutes in local testing centers and cost $20 per vehicle. The number of complaints fell from about 600 a year to about 200 a year out of 30 million annual inspections.[49]

Likewise, the common refrain of the Philippines as "poorly governed" is at best a partial truth, and one that ignores how much its administrative culture has changed.[50] For a poor country, the Philippines bureaucracy

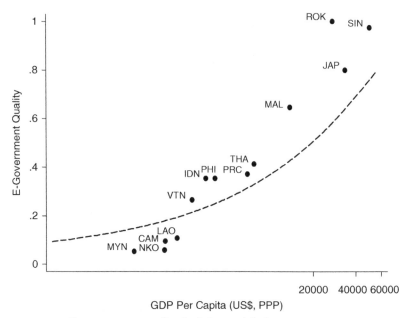

FIGURE 5.2. E-government quality in Asia vs. global averages.
Notes: n =157, r² = 0.52.
Source: United Nations Public Administration Network, *E-Government Development Survey*, 2012. Average of service quality and service participation scores.

performs about as expected and some of its agencies – the National Irrigation Agency and the Central Bank – have been cited as sites of excellence.[51] The Philippines budget process is among the most transparent and well-institutionalized in the world for a developing country, comparing favorably with those of richer countries like Argentina and Bulgaria.[52] Again, there is tantalizing evidence that the Philippines may be beginning to cast off its colonial legacy and "become Asian."

The resilience of effective bureaucracies in Asia may help explain the "Asian paradox" that public sector corruption seems to have enhanced rather than slowed economic growth.[53] The ability of the Asian bureaucratic polity to control corruption within its ranks is attributable to the comparatively strong internal capacity and internal norms that guide government in the region.[54] To the extent that corruption exists, it is more often efficiency-enhancing than it is destroying.[55]

Another consequence of the reaffirmation of the privileged status of the state in general and the bureaucracy in particular through NPM has been a continued rejection of the idea of public sector unionization and collective bargaining. The quid pro quo for social acceptance of the strong state has always been that the bureaucracy must act in a selfless, public-minded manner. Given that the bureaucracy embodies the state, the idea of bureaucrats organizing as a group *against* the state seems ridiculous, especially to bureaucrats themselves.[56] As a result, Asian countries have tended either to deny the right of civil servants to organize public sector unions or to allow them to do so but to strictly curtail their activities, usually by denying the right to strike or to other collective bargaining. Public sector labor rights remain highly curtailed in democratic Indonesia, Thailand, Taiwan, and Japan, in addition to in the authoritarian states, like Singapore, Malaysia, Cambodia, Vietnam, and China. An ILO report of 2009 said that public sector labor rights were "seriously underdeveloped in all East Asian countries."[57] A Japanese government report of 2007 concluded that there were no compelling reasons to amend the 1948 law that prohibits public sector unions and collective bargaining. Even in the populist Philippines, only one-third of public sector unions have the right to engage in collective bargaining, and fewer than 10 percent had actually done so by 2009.[58]

Only South Korea has extended unionization and collective bargaining (but not strike rights) to most civil servants, granting them first to teachers (1999) and then to other public servants (2006), in addition to those groups like postal and railroad workers who were grandfathered in because they were unionized prior to military rule. Yet there has been no labor unrest to speak of under the new arrangements. South Korean civil servants seem to understand that their privileged status depends on not being seen as a particularistic group but as representatives of the national purpose. As one South Korean civil service analyst puts it, the use of threats to "halt the functions of the nation ... may ruin the principles in which sovereign power resides with people" and "undermine trust between state and society."[59]

CEO GOVERNMENT

While the efficiency imperatives of NPM created new ways to reinvent state dominance in Asia, the accountability pressures brought by political liberalization and democratic deepening have made that dominance more complex. The bureaucratic polity has not shattered. But it has been fractured such that it is now held together less by its own singular authority than by its close relationships with other state institutions as well as social groups and citizens. Asia in the twenty-first century is a region where governance is upheld through a managed yet effective form of contention within and beyond the state.

Given the democratic expectations of global citizens everywhere, it was perhaps inevitable that Asian politics would evolve from a form of hierarchical state dominance to a new era of multi-institutional and multi-actor state dominance. Depending on the viewpoint, the subsuming of the bureaucratic polity into broader governance networks has made it more or less powerful. On the one hand, bureaucratic discretion and autonomy have clearly been reduced. On the other hand, sitting at the center of ever more complex networks that involve various state agencies, government ministers, private-sector businesses, local governments, courts, and social groups, bureaucracies have become "a direct and independent partici-pant in *both* government and business."[60] Morlino and colleagues, for instance, suggest that "the new emphasis on inter-institutional account-ability structures is in considerable part driven by notions of technocratic governance directed at mitigating the vagaries of an increasingly con-tentious political process."[61] Leadership from the middle may be more effective than leadership from the front.

Given that political executives sit at the formal head of state bureau-cracies, the most intimate place where the Asian bureaucratic polity has changed is in the executive-bureaucratic relationship. There is a strong tradition in Asia, notes Painter, "that the bureaucracy itself plays a major role in interpreting and implementing the public interest, *at the very most* sharing this role with the political executive but often viewing its quali-fications for the task to be superior, wielding real power and authority in the process."[62] Executives may have created powerful bureaucracies, but those executives often ended up subordinate to the bureaucracies in actual governance processes. Reforms since the 1990s have aimed to redress this imbalance, reminding us that public sector reform is about not just governance but also "deliberate attempts to manipulate power relations in the public sector," as Bowornwathana puts it.[63] Democratic executives demand more control over the rule making, budgeting, pol-icy formulation, and regulatory actions that occupy most government time. They have also engaged in "agencification," or carving out autono-mous agencies within bureaucracies to execute policy in order to disperse departmental power. The era of relatively autonomous bureaucracies has today transformed into one of *shared* executive-bureaucratic power. For instance, the passage of Administrative Procedure Acts (APAs) that put stricter demands on efficiency and transparency by bureaucrats originated, writes Baum, "in sitting executives' desire to prevent opposing politicians and recalcitrant bureaucrats from undermining policies."[64]

The symbolically most important place where the bureaucratic polity has been challenged by the executive is Thailand, whose prime minister from 2001 to 2006, Thaksin Shinawatra, made a point of clipping the prerogatives of the Thai bureaucracy and its shadowy royal patron (Thai bureaucrats are known as "royal servants," or *karachakan*). Thaksin expanded the number of ministries from fourteen to twenty to disperse and churn up bureaucratic power, appointed "CEO Governors" to run the seventy-six provinces in place of central bureaucrats, established an educational reform commission within the prime minister's office to wrest control of education from the Ministry of Education, put political appointees in charge of ministries, ended bureaucratic immunity from ministerial punishment, and transformed the budgeting process from one of intrabureaucratic negotiation to one of imposed budget performance agreements. As Painter observed: "Thaksin's aim was to break down existing forms of bureaucratic power, rather than merely to manage them for his own ends."[65]

Thaksin called himself the nation's "Super-CEO," hailing his own reforms as the first major shakeup of the Thai government since 1897. The reforms also achieved real results in areas like e-government, delivery times for citizen services, and budget management and strategy.[66] But they jilted the long-entrenched interests of the bureaucratic polity and its supporters in the palace – the king often portrayed himself as a humble agricultural extension officer. The 2006 coup that overthrew Thaksin was in many ways an attempt by the palace-centered bureaucratic polity to regain control. As Mansrisuk noted of Thaksin's supporters: "The possibility of the resurgence of bureaucratic authoritarianism was part of their concerns."[67] The landslide victory of his sister Yingluck's successor party in 2011 signaled that Thais by and large supported Thaksin's attempts to master the bureaucratic polity. One of Yingluck's first acts was to renew the Royal Decree on Good Governance that Thaksin had issued in 2003 as the framework for the reforms.

The other symbolically important country where executive control over the bureaucracy has been strengthened is Japan. In the normal course of things in Japan, notes Kikuchi, "because the legislation proposal process is dominated by the bureaucracy, the policy and legislative process is dominated by the bureaucracy."[68] The bureaucratic management of Japanese politics was variously challenged by prime ministers in the 1990s, but a book from that time concluded that the analysis of Japanese politics "does not support a strong prime ministerial theme."[69]

This began to change in 1999 when the system of "designated government members" (bureaucrats who took part in legislative sessions to answer questions directed at cabinet members) was replaced by a system of "deputy ministers," in which those questions were directed at governing party members in the legislature itself. In 2001, a separate Cabinet Office was created to serve as the center of policy formulation and administrative control, absorbing several bureaucratic agencies, most notably, the powerful Economic Planning Agency. The creation of the office by Prime Minister Junichiro Koizumi (who, like Thaksin, was in power from 2001 to 2006) had been suggested in 1962 but was shot down by senior bureaucrats. It was a long economic slump in the 1990s that discredited the high degree of autonomy held by Japan's bureaucratic polity and gave support to Koizumi's plan to empower the executive.

Under the Cabinet Office system, the Japanese prime minister began to have more control over not just policy making but also broader strategic direction. The Ministry of Finance lost considerable power over the budget process, which now begins in the Cabinet Office.[70] There are also now political appointees to staff senior vice minister and parliamentary secretary positions in each ministry. The intention has been one of "'bringing politics back in' to the policy making process."[71] The executive has sought new powers over personnel management within the bureaucracy. At the same time, fifty-two autonomous agencies were created in 2001 to reduce bureaucratic control. None of this has undermined bureaucratic power in Japan, but it has made bureaucracy more accountable to the executive.

In many ways, the reassertion of prime ministerial power in Japan is bringing it back to its prewar position. Under American tutelage, the prime minister's role was circumscribed in order, as Maki wrote in 1955, to "keep the power of the executive within reasonable limits."[72] But rather than creating legislative supremacy, the U.S. occupation unintentionally created a bureaucratic polity. The default rulers in Asian politics are not elected populists but courtly bureaucrats. To constrain executive power is to expand bureaucratic power.

While wresting more control from bureaucracies, political executives have at the same time had to maintain their privileged status vis-à-vis legislatures. The role of legislatures in the oversight of bureaucracies is well-established in Western democracies but remains a contested ideal in Asian politics. As with citizens and courts, as we shall see below, the question is how to integrate legislatures into an accountability system that is primarily remonstrative and supportive rather than adversarial and emasculating. Reforms are typically intended to keep legislatures in their rightful place as "houses of aspiration" rather than to make them powerful checks on executive-bureaucratic authority. This is perhaps no surprise, because a key motivation of the original "shepherds of the people" (*bokumin*) ideal for modern Asian bureaucrats was "reining in the power of the political parties and thereby securing their own administrative authority."[73]

In Malaysia, for instance, the opposition was given a deputy chair position in the legislature's Public Accounts Committee for the first time in 2008, bringing Malaysia in line with parliamentary practice in countries like Canada (although still not adopting the British model of giving the chair of this committee to the opposition, a model that was followed in Japan). But the powers of the committees remain deeply circumscribed in both Malaysia and Japan. In Malaysia, for instance, ministers and the heads of state companies regularly ignore summonses to appear before the committee (legally they are not obliged to), and the national anticorruption commission does not act on many reports that the committee sends to it for investigation. Under UMNO control, the committee has generally limited its inquiries to reports given to the legislature, such as the auditor general's annual report. Inquiries into scandals at state companies like Sime Darby and Port Klang in the late 2000s were rebuffed by prosecutors as "too sensitive."

In Taiwan, by contrast, historically based legislative powers to block even minor administrative reforms meant that public sector reform has involved clawing back authority from the legislature. For historical reasons, much of the Taiwanese bureaucracy operated under formal laws rather than administrative regulations, which meant that administrative reforms required legislative approval. In the 1990s, about a quarter of all laws sent to the legislature involved administrative reforms, which were either ignored or politicized. Taiwan's Government Reinvention Programme, begun in 1998 and continued under both parties, was an attempt to take away control of the bureaucracy from the legislature, which, while largely symbolic under authoritarianism, became a positive hindrance under democracy. New laws passed under the government reinvention rubric created broad standards, within which the executive could make changes to the bureaucracy without legislative approval. This included the creation of a new Central Personnel Administration to share control of the civil service with the Examination Yuan and the elimination of an entire level of government, the province. Most of the changes were finally passed into law between 2009 and 2011.

In Malaysia and Taiwan, as well as most other countries of the region, such as Japan, South Korea, China, and Indonesia, the alliance between executives and bureaucracies has preserved state dominance and the notion of a nonpartisan state that represents the interests of the nation as a whole. Hong Kong's post-1997 trajectory, for instance, has been an attempted "rebureaucratization" of politics after a brief period of legislative ascendance under the last British governor, Chris Patten (1992 to 1997).[74] But here there is a snag: While a bureaucratic polity was widely accepted by Hong Kongers under the British (whose pre-Patten governors styled themselves as refined Asian despots), it had less legitimacy under the tutelage of Beijing. No amount of NPM-style reforms to create a "macho meritocracy" under the effective leadership of a CEO Governor (the first post-1997 "chief executive" of the territory was a shipping magnate) could reconcile the population to what was, in effect, a form of alien rule. Most of the Hong Kong population fled from tyranny in China to live under British despotism. Antigovernment protest in China-ruled Hong Kong reflects not so much a desire for pluralist politics as a desire to domesticate the executive-bureaucratic polity by taking it away from the hands of Beijing.

In Thailand, where the bureaucratic polity is seen to represent the old guard that surrounds the monarchy, there is also more support to popularize and strengthen the executive. Thailand's 1997 constitution was a clear attempt to reassert bureaucratic power in the face of rising democratic pressures by creating a new autonomous commission to manage things like elections and audits.[75] Thaksin's efforts to assert executive control over the bureaucracy thus implied greater de facto legislative power, because Thailand is a parliamentary system. In both Hong Kong and Thailand, citizens duly wrap themselves in nationalist symbols and defer to the authority of the state, but the Asian Governance Model is troubled in both cases because of a lurking suspicion that the state has been seized by pretenders.

In the Philippines, finally, the executive-led bureaucracy of the Marcos era has come under sustained democratic attack since 1986, perhaps predictably, given the country's popular democratization. The World Bank called the Philippines bureaucracy "the most politicized in Asia" in a 2000 report, noting that there were no fewer than 8,400 political appointees.[76] Both presidents Estrada and Arroyo declared populist "war on bureaucracy" before having their plans cut short by political turmoil.

Under President Aquino after 2010, however, there were signs of the country trying to "become Asian" by slowly distancing itself from this populism. Aquino, the son of the "People Power" leader Cory Aquino, may have been the only person with the legitimacy to wean his country off of People Power. In 2012, he created an inter-agency task force on government performance that, unusually for the Philippines, did not include any civil society participation or political appointees. The aim, said a spokesman, was to "rescue government institutions from a culture of mediocrity."[77]

While political executives in Asia have used political-legal strategies to assert their control over bureaucracies and legislatures, the relationship with local governments is driven far more by economic and fiscal concerns. The retention of most fiscal powers, as well as national planning prerogatives by central governments throughout Asia, has allowed executives to devolve governance without losing authority. Provincial, local, and village governments play a larger role in governance today. But coordination with the central government remains imperative.

In Japan, where the principle of local autonomy was introduced during the American occupation, the Comprehensive Act on Decentralization of 1999 introduced changes designed to reduce the meddling of central bureaucrats in prefectural and municipal affairs. The old system, under which local government powers had been only informally delegated under administrative rules, was replaced by one in which those powers were formally delegated under statutory law. This unleashed a torrent of local government innovation. In Nagano prefecture, for example, the eighty-one municipalities created a system under which each government remains independent in order to bolster community involvement while at the same time pooling the provision of certain services, like water and transport.[78] Japan also shifted a huge proportion of its total bureaucracy away from the central level – from 25 percent of the total in 2000 to 15 percent by 2008.[79] In the past, the central government staffed local governments through the "descent from heaven" system (also used to put bureaucrats out to pasture in the private sector) that made local governments seem like branch offices of central ministries. After 1999, such secondments became permanent transfers, boosting local autonomy. By 2006, there were more prefectural officials on secondment to the central government than vice versa.[80] Local government revenues as a share of local spending rose from 50 percent to 60 percent by 2010.

However, in Japan, as elsewhere, recurrent budget instability at the local level and the force of national planning guidelines keep local governments in close line with central mandates. In a deeper sense, the centrality of "Tokyo" in the political and ideological imagination has been maintained, despite devolution and broader marketization of governance, because these things have been prescribed by and implemented by Tokyo bureaucrats as the latest "solution" to the country's national challenges. This reflects a broader theme in Asian politics that we have already seen with respect to development and democracy: Liberalization does not so much undermine so much as reconfigure state dominance.[81]

More broadly, devolution and decentralization throughout Asia since the 1990s has been widely practiced and yet accompanied by fiscal and institutional strategies that have retained the dominance of the center. In many ways, this trend mirrors the evolution of the bureaucratic polity itself from hierarchical leader to network leader. With the exception of the Philippines, where provincial-level "bosses" often rise to challenge central authority, it is remarkable how little one observes the rise of "provincial populists" in Asian politics, despite the wide devolution of governance powers to local governments. The reason is that running afoul of the central government pays no dividends when both hard power (fiscal and institutional) and soft power (authority and national identity) remain concentrated in the capital.

In Thailand, Thaksin's "CEO governors" idea for provincial chiefs was the latest of several ways to avoid democratizing the provincial level of government, a proposal that was rejected in 1992 during the country's democratization. In addition to retaining the power to appoint provincial governors, decentralization focused on the very lowest *tambon-* (subdistrict-) level of government, whose traditional leaders are even more likely to ally themselves with the Ministry of the Interior in Bangkok because of fiscal dependence. Local governments accounted for only 25 percent of government spending by 2007, far below the 35 percent target set out in 1999. A recurrent theme has involved attempts by Bangkok to reduce the number of urban *thesaban* and rural *tambon* governments, which stood at 5,700 in 2011, in order to make this relationship less unwieldy. Thaksin managed to cut the number down from 8,000, and he wanted it to reach 2,000. Likewise in South Korea, despite two decades of devolution, the 245 local governments (in this case all fully elected) accounted for only 26 percent of current (noncapital) spending in 2010.[82] Unusually, in global comparison, policing continues to be a wholly national function, making the South Korean police force one of the largest in the world.

If there is one country that best embodies this notion of "devolution of functions with recentralization of authority," it is Malaysia. Arguably, the entire postindependence trend in Malaysia has been toward the centralization and corporatization of the state. Despite formal federalism and a series of devolution reforms in the 2000s, the central government has used its administrative and fiscal powers to prevent state governments from becoming autonomous. The fact that opposition parties won five of the thirteen state governments in 2008 was far less threatening as a result. The 144 local governments, meanwhile, have gradually been reduced to service branches of the central government – first with the abolition of elections in 1971 and then in the 2000s with a series of national planning frameworks (National Physical Plan, National Urbanization Policy, and New Villages Master Plan) that made the central government the main player in local planning and infrastructure.

In light of these governance processes, it is no surprise that when it comes to *new* policies, the agenda setting, problem framing, and policy initiation are state-led, with little or no civil society or private sector involvement. Within the state, moreover, there is a tendency for bureaucratic actors (sometimes called "programmatic actors" to distinguish them from other policy actors within or outside the state) to take the lead. It is less common for, say, ambitious legislators or independent-minded executive cabinet members to act as "policy entrepreneurs" in the Asian context.

It is only as policies move from upstream initiation toward midstream formulation, selection, and legislation that other actors within the state become more prominent. The role of policy networks – state and non-state actors with a particular interest and expertise in public policy in a certain area – tends to be most prominent in the crafting of concrete laws and regulations for a chosen policy. Citizen involvement in public policy is mostly in the "downstream" phase of policy implementation and review.

Again, bureaucratic and more general state leadership over policy processes is not surprising in the authoritarian and semidemocratic countries. In Singapore, for example, attempts to build "public-private partnerships" for business policy making have become contests for policy initiative among new agencies.[83] In Malaysia, the Economic Planning Unit (EPU) of the PMO, combined with the leadership of the Malay-dominated elite Administrative and Diplomatic Service (PTD) – the elite service of generalists who staff top positions – essentially initiates all public policies. The EPU describes itself as "the principal government agency responsible for the preparation of development plans for the nation" and "the nerve center of the nation." Moreover, the EPU has become more powerful in recent years by absorbing implementation and evaluation functions that were once handled by another agency. Here, as elsewhere, with perhaps the exception of the Philippines, attempts to integrate legislators or civil society into the "upstream" end of the policy process have proven largely fruitless, not because of a lack of sincerity but because of an overwhelming authority vested in the state.[84]

It is instead in the more democratic cases, like South Korea, Taiwan, Japan, Indonesia, and Thailand, where the persistence of such processes confounds expectations of the emergence of participatory or truly networked policy making. In Japan, the bureaucracy-initiated policies are scrutinized by the policy affairs research commissions of the ruling party and by the executive – in particular, the Cabinet Office and Council of Economic and Fiscal Policy created in 2001. These bodies have claimed greater initiative at times when the bureaucracy is seen as vulnerable to concessions to so-called *zoku* (the Chinese character *zu*, meaning clan) politicians who specialize in adding pork for their constituents. But one result of this taming of the "corporatist" policy process of the developmental state era is that Japan's policy process has become less, not more, networked. Japan's labor policies, for instance, were long upheld by a powerful voice from the national labor federation. As electoral politics became more competitive and pressures for regulatory reform rose, the voice of labor in policy making became weaker.[85] Labor policy in Japan today is driven by executive and bureaucratic decisions shaped by globalization.[86]

Taiwan may be the only country in Asia where a plausible case can be made for some form of networked governance and participatory policy making. The "elected executives at the central and local levels and their political appointees have more say in the policy decision," write Huang and Tu, while "the public administration is more exposed to legislative oversight and interest group influence."[87] This, they note, has led the bureaucracy to engage in its own public opinion polling in order to maintain policy leadership.

In these ways, governance and policy making in Asia remain mostly state-led but under a condominium of executive and bureaucratic power, with occasional legislative, private sector, and civil society involvement. The public sector has changed significantly in Asia with the rise of more autonomous executives, legislatures, and local governments that now share real power with bureaucracies. But the bureaucratic polity has survived in most instances, and sometimes it has emerged stronger. Just as widespread expectations in the 1990s that globalization might lead to an "eclipse of the state" proved premature, so too have expectations that democratization would lead to an "eclipse of the bureaucracy" in Asia. Rather, Asia's strong states have found new ways to organize themselves in a new context.

THE TOKYO CONSENSUS

The matter of *how* Asian governments govern follows naturally from the questions of *who* governs within the public sector. The period of rapid economic development in which governments acted mainly through direct service provision, broad legislation, and ideological exhortation remains the dominant mode of governance in China, Vietnam, Laos, and Myanmar. But governance in other Asian countries is focused far more on regulating the polity than on transforming it. As a result, governments rule by setting regulations, monitoring behavior, and adjudicating disputes in specific policy areas.

In its ideal form, the regulatory state is one in which government functions are carried out by independent agencies that engage in a nondiscretionary manner to make and enforce rules and to coordinate nonstate actors who provide many public services. In the "Washington Consensus" version of the regulatory state, there is a strong preference for the privatization of services, a small and nondominating state, and limited intervention. The idealized alternative to the Washington Consensus has often been called the Beijing Consensus, in which regulation is under a heavy hand of the state – markets remain state-controlled, state provision of services and economic activity remain pervasive, and intervention is common.

Neither model captures the reality of the regulatory state in Asia. On the one hand, Asia is a region where a pro-market and pro-business orientation dominates – it is more Washington Consensus in this respect than the West is. In 2007, 22 percent of China's 208 water utilities were privately owned, while a further 11 percent had private sector investment.[88] The Philippines carried out the world's largest water privatization for Manila in 1998 with a surprising degree of social consensus.[89] While some European countries (notably the United Kingdom and France) have privatized water, others (notably Germany) have not, and in the United States, water privatization remains a nonstarter. The cartoonish picture of a market-driven West versus a market-limiting Asia does not stand up to scrutiny.

On the other hand, Asia is also a region where state regulation operates not as a pluralistic mediation of demands but through a state-led process that embodies what is seen as the highest demands of all – those of the bureaucracy. In this respect, the pervasive state of the Beijing Consensus is a more accurate account. For instance, in an effort to follow international best practice, the Thai government established twenty-nine "autonomous" government agencies between 1999 and 2010. The "agencification" of the regulatory state was supposed to give more autonomy to specialized, flexible, results-oriented bureaucrats and more power and coregulation to private actors. But rather than creating "unbundled" government, the Thai agencies reinforced and expanded "bundled" government – hierarchical, executive-led decision making.[90] Whereas the problems of agencies usually relate to their becoming too autonomous or too dysfunctional or both, in Asia the agency problem is mainly an issue of how agencies have become new sources of power for the executive-bureaucratic polity that are insulated from the modest accountability pressures of, say, legislative oversight. In the Thai case, senior bureaucrats and their executive allies came to dominate the agencies, reducing their autonomy and limiting private sector or civil society participation. The Thai Office of Knowledge Management and Development, the second largest of agencies by budget, is located within the prime minister's office and is heavily staffed with bureaucratic appointees.

A better way of understanding regulation in Asia, then, is to identify a third type of regulatory ethos that we might call the "Tokyo Consensus." This combines the pro-market and small-government principles of the Washington Consensus with the state-led discretionary regulation of the Beijing Consensus. Japan is the place to see this ethos because of its early adoption of this form of regulation in the 1990s. It is also fitting because it was the Japanese (not the Chinese) government that instigated the World Bank's 1993 book, *The East Asian Miracle*, which outlined the state-led markets model. Since then, Japan has experienced a shift away from the "interventionist" bureaucracy that had, in the words of one 1991 book, "authority without power,"[91] because it relied so much on informal mechanisms of control. Tokyo's new regulatory state has less authority but more power. In a case study of the failed bank merger between Sumitomo and United Financial of Japan in 2004, Taylor found that the previous informal but pervasive authority of the Ministry of Finance has been replaced by the formal and more powerful role of the Financial Service Authority, which is an agency.[92]

In another closely observed case study of financial regulation in Japan, Walter found:

The degree of regulatory discretion in Japan remains much deeper and more systematic compared to the major Anglo-Saxon countries and the gap between the appearance of imported "Western" regulatory frameworks and the reality of regulation is much greater.... Discretion, rather than the strict application of best practice rules, continued to be the overriding characteristic of government regulatory policy, suggesting considerable continuity with the past.[93]

Similar findings emerge from Wong and Painter's study of telecommunications regulation in Malaysia and Thailand. There, the creation of supposedly lean and rules-based regulatory agencies was the key to a *bigger* state role, because it gave those agencies the wherewithal to control through "soft power" regulation rather than "hard power" fiat. "The creation of an independent regulator under pro-competitive statutory guidelines is probably the key step in opening up the domestic market to 'top-down' influences."[94]

South Korea is another place to see this combination of pro-market and pro-state elements. On the one hand, South Korea is a global leader in neoliberal regulatory reform. South Korea's Regulatory Reform Commission, established in 1998, was given a mandate to review *all* regulatory efforts of *all* departments. The commission immediately axed an astounding 49 percent of the 11,000-odd national regulations on the books of the government at the time. South Korea then adopted an aggressive system of mandatory review and the sunsetting of all primary and secondary regulations. This review and sunsetting regime is shared by only seven other OECD countries (including the United Kingdom and Germany).[95] At the same time, South Korea has been more cautious than other jurisdictions about its regulatory culling. Sunset provisions have served not to make government irrelevant but to limit populist expansions of regulations with each new presidential administration, ensuring that the regulatory state is, above all, consistent.[96]

Although it is a shift away from the "interventionist state," the regulatory state in Asia has maintained state influence over both economy and society. In Malaysia, for example, while state ownership has declined, the government has taken a more active role in backstopping the private sector against financial stress, first through the asset management company Danaharta, which was set up under the central bank after the Asian Financial Crisis in 1998, and then through its successor agency owned by the Ministry of Finance, Prokhas, which was established in 2006. Operating with a high degree of autonomy from legislative oversight and with large budgets, both agencies expanded their original mandates to become agents of national corporate transformation. As a Prokhas statement notes: "We have transcended our own expectations and have broadened our services into various industries."[97] A similar trend is evident in South Korea, where, amidst popular demands for "economic democratization," governments since the 2000s have expanded the regulatory powers of the Fair Trade Commission to discipline the *chaebol* and their "labor aristocracy," as well as to bolster market competition generally. The Asian regulatory state has, in Bidin's words, "led to extensive discretionary powers given to the authorities under the name of transparency and accountability."[98]

Singapore, finally, is an indispensable case of the Asian regulatory ideal type, because it so starkly combines a radically pro-market approach with a muscular and often dominating state. The country's two gargantuan sovereign wealth funds, for example, whose assets were one-and-a-half times as large as the country's GDP in 2013, were corporatized and agencified in the 2000s, yet they remained highly directed by the Ministry of Finance, under close supervision by the PMO (the chief executive of one of the funds from 2002 was the wife of the prime minister, who was himself the son of Lee Kuan Yew). The ministry closely controls them to ensure they pursue the national interest alongside making good returns (the so-called "double bottom-line"). Yet when questions are asked in parliament about their operations, the ministry refuses to answer, calling such questions attempts to "politicize" their operations.[99] As Lin summarizes: "Governance in Singapore is primarily dominated by the executive, which is the ruling government, virtually unopposed in parliament and supported by a battalion of statutory boards to carry out the work of the regulatory state.[100]

In sum, the Tokyo Consensus of Asian regulation is one that combines a strong pro-market orientation with a supportive private network and an effective and dominant but not corrupt state. The regulatory state in Asia is not a rejection of globalization or neoliberalism but a selective adoption and adaptation of best practices of governance and regulation. Hsueh refers to China's regulatory state as "a new strategy for globalization" because it provided the state with a way to reinforce executive-bureaucratic goals in strategic sectors, whether through centralized control, as in telecommunications, or through decentralized control, as in textiles.[101]

The Tokyo Consensus shows how regulatory reform can reempower bureaucracies and executives in a complex governance era where companies depend on governments for things like intellectual property protection, fair market competition, and new product and labor standards amidst rapidly changing technologies and economics. In this context, the regulatory state in Asia was no mere convener of private sector networks but an active agent of pro-market economic transformation.

Asia's governance traditions make the region well-positioned to thrive in this context, one reason that the region continues to attract an outsized share of Western foreign investment.

Beeson argues that a Washington Consensus–type regulatory regime could never have taken root in Asia because of the traditions of state dominance and weak civil society there.[102] Jarvis concurs, arguing that Asian states lack the "soft institutional capacities," such as norms of fairness among key actors and a strong analytic capacity among civil society actors, that are needed for the state to disappear into the background of markets and self-governance by private actors.[103] As a result, while the scope of intervention has certainly fallen, in another sense the continuation of broad state dominance means that leadership exercised by the state remains pervasive. Asian governments have neither bowed to the Washington Consensus, nor have they "pushed back" with some socialist Beijing Consensus. Rather, they have selectively adapted the state dominance tradition to new governance needs, giving the regulatory state a distinctively Asian variant.

One hesitates, however, to push the Manichean East–West dichotomy too hard; as we have already seen with development and democracy, the Asian experience may provide a new baseline that is more evident elsewhere in the world, including in the West, than was previously realized. The regulatory state, after all, was *supposed* to be a compromise between market liberalism and state planning, between the Washington Consensus and the Beijing Consensus.[104] A close examination of the alleged "neoliberal" turn in European health care, for example, reveals that there, too, bureaucratic actors have used market-driven regulation to enhance rather than diminish the role of the state.[105] Asian governments are neither insincere nor inscrutable in creating regulatory norms that involve state discretion. Rather, they take seriously the possibility that the state, where it is subject to effective social accountability pressures and its own internal meritocracy norms, may often be indispensable to well-oiled markets – saving capitalism from the capitalists, so to speak. The Tokyo Consensus may thus hold promise for the complex, intractable, and chronic policy problems of contemporary governance, a preferred middle-ground of state-led market regulation that becomes the global standard.

JUDGE PAO AND THE DUAL STATE

In a 1976 ruling, Japan's supreme court forced the government to reapportion legislative districts to give urban voters a more equal voice with rural voters. This was arguably the first notable judicial challenge to a strong Asian state in the postwar era. Since then, courts have come to play an increasingly important role in governance in Asia. Courts have more power and authority in Asia today than ever before, and they have grown predictably as Asian countries have become richer, freer, and more integrated into the world.

In large part, there is nothing distinctive about the rule of law in Asia: The debates in each country follow quite predictably from general political and economic conditions – the question of whether the ruling party will limit its power within the rule of law in China and Vietnam; the overzealous invocation of the rule of law to repress dissent in illiberal democracies like Singapore and Malaysia; the struggle for constitutionalism in the new or unstable democracies of Indonesia, Thailand, the Philippines, and Cambodia; the debates about the politicization of law in the consolidated democracies of Taiwan and South Korea, as well as Hong Kong; and finally, the efforts to more deeply institutionalize the practice of law in a new social consensus in the lone mature democracy of Japan. The rule of law is developmental in Asia, as elsewhere, and it needs to be contextualized in each country. The issues confronted by China and Vietnam are fundamentally different from those confronted by Japan and South Korea, in part because they are poor and authoritarian. The real question, however, is how the trajectory in Asia compares to the trajectory in other regions.

To the extent that one can generalize, the exercise of judicial power in Asia remains constrained and "judicious," tending to defer to executives on policy matters and often used in a way that reflects a sensitivity to the Hegelian state. If courts in liberal states think of themselves as "countermajoritarian" institutions that uphold individual rights claims, courts in Asia think of themselves as defenders of the authority of the state against all comers – corrupt or inept officials, as well as unruly or selfish citizens. In Indonesia, for instance, "many of the newly enacted constitutional rights are more consistent with traditional conceptions of the role of the state in Asia than they are with the limited state of classical liberalism or even the most expansive social welfare state of Northern Europe," writes Peerenboom.[106]

Courts in Asia are agents of accountability, to be sure. But that agency is exercised in a limited, counselor-like fashion and does not challenge state dominance generally or executive authority in particular. The *legal culture* of Asia is one embedded in a more general *political culture* of state primacy and executive-bureaucratic authority. The practice of the rule of law in Asia is intricately tied up in normative conceptions of what kinds of democracies Asian countries want to become. Just as they favor majoritarian views of democracy, they also favor views of judicial role and interpretation that *do* promote liberal individualism but only alongside the importance of community, the state, morality, and public interest.

This is not to dismiss the rule of law as legalized Oriental despotism, which one group of scholars called "essentially administrative and penal … an instrument of governmental authority designed to maintain and perpetuate the existing political and social order within the context of a cosmic order."[107] Jones, too, often incisive in his Actonesque commentary, was probably too sweeping in claiming:

> The traditional Pacific Asian understandings of law … have little in common with Anglo-American jurisprudential thought and practice. *Fa* [law] cannot accommodate legal right or what Hayek terms the spontaneous extended order of the constitution of liberty. It provides instead for a precise regulation of duties through mechanically administered rules. East Asian law neither reflects a transcendental natural law nor proposes a contract with mutual obligations enforceable by an independent judiciary.… [Law] is essentially administrative and responds to the requirements of the technocratic planning of the latest growth plan and social cohesion.[108]

Rather, the rule of law has developed in a way that reflects attempts to variously *integrate* individual, liberal, and democratic values with older values. The common heritage of most of Asia is one in which law began as a tool of state power, not citizen rights. As a result, there is a common challenge of rebalancing the rights of citizens with the state. As Patapan concludes, courts in Asia have "successfully negotiated the contending demands of facilitating executive policy ambitions while defending the principles of rule of law and constitutionalism."[109]

The World Justice Project's Rule of Law Index examines multiple dimensions of the rule of law. The 2012 edition carried ten Asian cases and another eighty-six countries with populations of more than 500,000. Three of the dimensions measured – "order the security," "regulatory enforcement," and "criminal justice" – bear more on the state-dominance view of the rule of law, while three others – "fundamental rights," "open government," and "civil justice" – cleave more toward the citizen-centric view of the rule of law. Using a composite index of the pro-state measures and another of the pro-citizen ones, we find that the state dominance tradition remains clear. Nine of the ten Asian states (all except Cambodia) are above the levels of their income peers in terms of pro-state rule of law. However, this has not impeded the emergence of pro-citizen legal systems in some Asian countries: Six countries (Vietnam, the Philippines, Indonesia, Thailand, South Korea, and Japan) are above global averages in terms of pro-citizen rule of law, while four (Cambodia, China, Malaysia, and Singapore) are below global averages. State dominance, when it is embedded in a political sociology of accountability, is not necessarily inimical and may indeed be supportive of an expansion of citizen rights.

To some extent, this is no surprise, given that judges are state actors with a moral prestige often higher than that of the executive. Courts and judges have a unique edge as claimants to the mantle of state authority in Asia, because traditionally they *were* that authority. In prewar Japan, courts exercised power "in the name of the emperor." In the Chinese-influenced countries, the emblematic figure is Judge Pao (Bao Zheng, 999–1062) of the Northern Song dynasty who, as chief minister of the capital city Kaifeng, carried out both judicial and executive functions. He lives on in countless television dramas and dime-store novels as the embodiment of the upright and efficient state official.

Institutionally, Judge Pao worked within a legal code that was the most elaborate and sophisticated outside of Roman Law. The Tang Code of 624 was the first in a series of imperial legal codes that, in addition to criminal law, had extensive administrative law governing the bureaucracy. As we saw with Malacca, a similar legal culture grew up in the sultanates of Southeast Asia. Southeast Asia's first modern legal code was Thailand's Three Seal Code of 1805, which outlined the obligations of the king, as well as the status and roles of administrative officials. In the Malay and Javanese worlds of Southeast Asia, one counterpart to Judge Pao is the Cambodian Judge Rabbit, a regal hare who reprimands corrupt officials and metes out fair verdicts on everything from social to political affairs. In both subregions, law was primarily a means to administer an effective state and maintain social order.

Law, however, has always been "despotic" rather than tyrannical in Asia. Judges from South Korea to Indonesia view themselves as Confucian or courtly officials. They are *junzi*, or gentlemen. Some scholars use the term "Confucian constitutionalism" to describe the role of courts in modern Asian politics.[110] The role of a judge is to be a virtuous, nonpartisan generalist who remonstrates with rulers and seeks the truth in every case. Judges do not blindly follow procedures, nor do lawyers seek to advocate for clients heedless of the merits of the case. Sukarno, scorning the adversarial and procedural approach to law in the West, replaced the scales of justice with a banyan tree as the symbol of the Indonesian judiciary.[111]

This view of courts is most explicit in Singapore, which, by virtue of its development level and British heritage, has had to formalize the rights of the state. As a Singapore Court of Appeal judge put it in 2005, the jurisprudence of the Anglophone countries should be adapted "to the needs and mores of the society of which it is part."[112]

These traditional conceptions have often been described as similar to the German despotic conception of the "dual state," in which due process and the rights of citizens are balanced by the prerogatives of the virtuous sovereign, who uses law and courts to protect and advance the national interest when necessary.[113] Under the dual state, exceptions can be made to constitutional or legal constraints in order to protect sovereignty, which is understood as the maintenance of political order and the advance of the nation.[114] There is nothing particularly Asian about such "exceptionalism" in response to the constraints of constitutional or administrative law. Rather, it is *exceptionalism in the context of legitimate state dominance*, something less true of these other regions (although found to some degree in Putin's Russia[115]), that makes Asia unusual. The dual state is aimed at facilitating *both* the rule of law *and* the claims of the state. Such so-called "states of exception" are more enduring in Asia, even in the "least likely" countries, like Indonesia and Thailand, because of the confluence of state dominance and an effective accountability tradition.[116]

The resulting "soft constitutionalism" in Asia tends to strengthen both state power and social solidarity.[117] Constitutionalism has often emerged in democratic Asia bearing strong continuities with the constitutionalism of authoritarian pasts. Again, it is not that attempts to use constitutional law to reinforce state authority are unique to Asia. Rather, because it takes place in a context of state dominance and a political culture of state legitimacy, what is unique is how often it succeeds. Despite the "juridification" of politics (the expansion of laws and legal consciousness), there has not been a "judicialization" of politics (a shift of decision-making power toward courts). Courts administer the law and remonstrate with governments to do things properly, but they rarely insert themselves into political decision making. Courts have not sought a role in public policy as equals to the bureaucracy. Rather, they have sought a juridification of public policy to ensure that technocrats are rule-abiding, uncorrupt, rational, and deliberative.

While the U.S. Circuit Court for the District of Columbia regularly strikes down proposed new financial regulations from the U.S. Securities and Exchange Commission for "inadequate economic analysis," courts in Asia's leading financial markets of Japan, Hong Kong, and Singapore virtually never challenge new regulations or administrative actions by market regulators. The cautious attitude of courts against the judicial-ization of public policy means that virtually all administrative cases are quickly resolved in the first instance without a formal decision.[118] This approach to law, in Yeh's words, has "prevented the regulatory state from becoming a judicialized state or a legislative state."[119]

Thus, just as we saw with democratic transitions, "society" can almost never steal away the mantle of authority from the state in representing the public interest. "Public interest litigation" is oxymoronic in Asia, because it presumes that society can represent the public interest. A Buddhist nun who attempted – through a public interest case – to block a planned rail tunnel in South Korea to protect the local salamander population in 2003 was sentenced to six months in prison for "interfering with business."[120] Taiwan's relatively well-developed public interest litigation system is carefully controlled by an Administrative Litigation Act that forbids such suits unless they have been explicitly permitted by the relevant statutes.

Again, the contrast is stark with India, where courts grant standing to all but the feeblest public interest claimants and then actively micro-manage public policy through such cases. More broadly, courts are far more powerful and politics are more judicialized in India than they are anywhere else in Asia. For instance, even though Malaysia's legal system shares with India a British heritage, and its provisions on constitutional review to protect fundamental rights are borrowed explicitly from that of India, Malaysian courts exert none of the activism and intervention-ism of those of India with respect to administrative decisions, primary legislation, or the protection of individual rights. In nearly identical cases in which flight stewardesses for the national airlines, Air India and Malaysian Airlines, were fired after becoming pregnant, courts in India penalized the action as an "insult to womanhood" and to "gender equal-ity," but those in Malaysia upheld it on procedural grounds of bureau-cratic autonomy.

Along with public interest litigation, lay participation in courts is equally oxymoronic in the Asian context. In general, Asia has been averse to juries and lay judges. Japan in 1943, Singapore in 1969, and Malaysia in 1995 all abolished the lay participation in juries or on benches that they had inherited from colonial rulers. Singapore's Lee Kuan Yew, who as a young defense lawyer won several acquittals in jury trials in Singapore, said the experience left him with "grave doubts" about the system.[121] In 2009, Japan began a limited experiment with lay judges with the belief that this could improve justice. The so-called "Rashomon Effect," in which different people give differing accounts of the same event, is after all a term taken from Kurosawa's 1950 film, *Rashomon*. But early results suggest that the system has strengthened the already imperious role of judges, bureaucrats, and prosecutors in criminal trials because of the close control over the types of trials and in-court procedures that such "mixed benches" possess.[122] In effect, as in *Rashomon*, the complicated nature of deciding justice has enhanced the aura of the court.

The modern origins of this approach to law can be found in the "law building" periods of the developmental states, during which law came to be seen as an adjunct of virtuous state power.[123] Jayasuriya argues that administrative law in particular has "reconstituted" state dominance in Asia because of its ability to "facilitate a technocratic form of politics" through new forms of bureaucratic discretion and court enforcement.[124] Administrative law can ensure that bureaucracies follow procedures when they make decisions, are held to performance standards, and are liable for corruption – all of which are very helpful for an executive-led state. For instance, major new administrative laws passed in Japan in the 1990s and 2000s sought to codify bureaucratic interference and strengthen executive claims on this most traditional of bureaucratic polities. Most of the 2,000-odd administrative claims brought against the state per year in the 2000s related to bureaucratic-led infrastructure development (such as roads, airports, railways, and nuclear power plants).

The developmental state and soft constitutional law have gone hand in hand. Asia has developed without the sort of "comprehensive," liberal rule of law system often prescribed for developing areas – a system that includes human rights, competition law, property rights, minority share-holder rights, etc. The Anglo-model, which includes liberal rights, binding precedent, and contentious and activist courts that challenge executive authority, never fit Asia very well. Nor for that matter did the Napoleonic conception of law as codified, complete, and rational. Rather, Asian legal systems are mostly hybrids of civil and common law, and they embed limited liberal rights in a state-preserving legal code that aims to achieve substantive policy rationality.

Judges are better seen in this context as "faithful public servants" rather than "political lackeys."[125] The 100 career judges who manage the Secretariat of the Supreme Court in Japan ensure that rogue judges do not arise and maintain quality control over legal decisions. The idea of "judicial independence" means independence from populist or partisan political pressures but not from bureaucratic oversight. This idea, writes Upham, involves "a judiciary whose primary goal is moving cases through the system with little regard for anything else except regularly 'weeding the judicial garden' of any judges whose decisions might deviate from what its highly insular and bureaucratic leadership considers politically correct."[126] Malaysia's Federal Court remains the guardian of executive privilege there, frequently striking down High Court and Court of Appeal rulings it fears may undermine executive power. Chuan describes it as "more executive-minded than the executive," a description that could well stand for Asian courts as a whole.[127]

One sign of its less-judicialized politics (as well as economies and societies) is that the numbers of lawyers, prosecutors, and judges in Asia is systematically lower than in comparable jurisdictions – as a comparison of Japan, the United States, and Germany shows (see Figure 5.3). In 2011, the Japan Federation of Bar Associations had to publicly rescind proposals to expand the number of lawyers to 50,000, in light of the lack of work: "This job shortage itself may also be regarded as proof that the society has not created legal demand for attorneys as initially expected."[128]

In this context, activist courts who override executive decisions in the name of their own interpretation of the public interest are notable. The politicization of Thailand's Constitutional Court as an agent of anti-Thaksin forces between 2006 and 2011 led to a decline in its prestige and a surge of support for pro-Thaksin parties.[129] In a series of rulings in 2012, the court pulled back from its anti-Thaksin political agenda, reaffirming executive autonomy. However, the struggle by Thailand's monarch-backed bureaucratic polity to regain the upper hand over the executive continues. The country's administrative court, created in 2001, moved in 2011 to a grand new building, which had been built around the colonial-era Council of State audience chamber in Bangkok that hosted the kingly petition system established in 1874. By going over the head of the executive, the court seeks to rebuild the dominance of king and bureaucracy.[130] About 7,000 cases a year were heard by the court between 2002 and 2010, most of them against the Ministry of the Interior.[131]

Indonesia's constitutional court and supreme court were actively engaged in extending rights claims and getting involved in policy matters in the 2000s. The constitutional court's first bench of nine judges was nominated two days after the enabling legislation was passed in 2003, and the bench was sworn in one day later, reflecting the belief that the court could act like a committee of nobles committed to the truth and the common good. Yet its activist decisions on questions like broadcasting and energy policy led to a backlash. The court then became

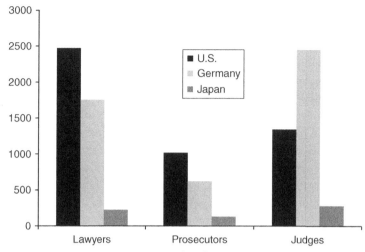

FIGURE 5.3. Lawyers, prosecutors, and judges per capita in Japan, the United States, and Germany.

Notes: Data for 2008 from national legal associations; Lawyers is per million population; Prosecutors and judges are per 100,000 population; Germany: Lawyers exclude notaries; Japan: Judges include summary court judges; United States: Judges includes administrative law judges, adjudicators, and hearing officers.

notably quieter under the Yudhoyono governments as the New Order was restored in democratic raiment.

By contrast, South Korea's constitutional court has treaded carefully in political cases from the start. When it was asked to decide the legality of a government plan to relocate the national capital to Sejong (named after an ultra-Confucian Korean king of the 1400s) in 2004, the court ruled that the move would require either a constitutional amendment or a national referendum. This allowed the political process to continue, resulting in a compromise in which most bureaucratic offices were moved in 2012, while the executive and legislature remained in Seoul. Earlier in 1996, when the legislature passed a special law allowing the government to prosecute two former presidents from the authoritarian period, the court ruled five to four that the act was unconstitutional, just short of the supermajority of six to three that was needed. As a result of this "remonstrance not remediation," the two men were tried and prosecuted but then immediately pardoned in 1997. In cases involving national security laws, meanwhile, South Korea's supreme court only admonishes the government to amend and narrow draconian laws through recommendations (so-called "non-conforming," rather than "unconstitutional," decisions).[132]

In other words, in normal times, Asian courts aim to provide remonstrative and administrative balance to executive power but not to replace it. Again, this may be more "normal" than the activist courts that have emerged within the unique cultural and historical conditions of the West. Jayasuriya may be too harsh in claiming that "the rule of law has been used ... as a mechanism to depoliticize society, and thereby legitimate the exercise of strong executive power."[133] But it is certainly true that the law has not been intended to *politicize* society and *delegitimate* the state. Singapore's attorney general in 1987 praised the fact that the "avoidance of examining the merits or substance of [an administrative] decision represents a self-conscious deference by judges towards the decisions of persons who have relatively greater technical and substantive experience and are consequently better equipped to decide."[134] This does not mean that governments in Asia are insincere or inscrutable in embracing constitutionalism and the rule of law. Instead, Asian governments have embraced courts, constitutionalism, and the rule of law as a means to continually reform the dynamic polity – as with NPM reforms – in order to serve the national purposes: prosperity, stability, integration, and democracy.

HARMONIOUS NETWORKS

Where does this leave the average citizen? It is easy to think that when it comes to matters of governance, the people of Asia remain more subjects than citizens. The general political culture of the region is one in which citizens are expected to be active yet compliant participants. Democracy has certainly ushered in a more pluralist civil society and has broken down some of the corporatist arrangements and institutions of the developmental state. But if the core question remains the role and salience of civil society in governance, far less has changed. Civil society groups remain embedded in the Hegelian assumptions of the state dominance tradition, improving governance from within, so to speak. Where they have cast off the state dominance tradition – in the Philippines ever since the ousting of Marcos, in Thailand during the anti-Thaksin era, and in occasional outbursts over issues like U.S. beef imports in South Korea – it has generally hurt rather than helped governance.[135] Asian publics associate pluralistic politics with episodes of national disaster – military rule and war in Japan, race riots in Malaysia and Indonesia, Pol Pot in Cambodia, and the Cultural Revolution in China.

As we saw in the discussion of economic development and of broader regulation, citizen participation is both central to Asian politics and yet also conceived of in fundamentally Hegelian terms. Democratic citizens have been forged not through social activism but through administrative procedures established by the state. Berman characterizes participation in Asia as based on "duty-based, consultative pragmatism,"[136] meaning that state actors seek broad engagement with society because of a duty-driven self-identity as "shepherds of the people." The relationship between bureaucracy and citizens has been weak in Asia compared to those between the executive and bureaucracy and between the executive and citizens.[137] Much governance reform in Asia in the 2000s and 2010s has strengthened the relative position of executives and bureaucracies vis-à-vis citizens.[138] As Oh argues, the absence of policy capacity within civil society and institutionalized mechanisms of civil society policy participation mean that attempts at "collaborative governance" more often fail than succeed.[139]

Still, the Asian approach to participation can, in some instances, be seen as a more robust form of citizenship than the agonistic pluralism or the formalized corporatism of many liberal democracies can. The "network governance" approach to which many governments now aspire is a governance mode characterized by egalitarian relationships among a plurality of state and non-state actors, decision making that is incremental and data-driven, and compliance that is based on trust and mutuality rather than legal or economic sanctions. While Asia clearly does not fit the pluralistic notion of the first principle, it is often better at the second and third. Some scholars argue that Asian notions of harmony, for instance, have a strong affinity with network governance.[140] This is because familism (modeling organizational behavior on the family) is normative (centered on shared values) and relational (built around personal relationships). Comparative evidence suggests that when governance networks are built on familial rather than pluralist ideals and operate according to consensus rather than negotiation or voting, they formulate and implement policy better. Rather than being a "structural constraint,"[141] the Asian tradition may be a structural advantage.

To the extent that the interaction between state and society is one that is grounded in a "deep institutionalization" of social consensus,[142] network governance could deliver legitimate and effective public policies.[143] In Asia, such deep institutionalization has become more common with democratization. The reason that governance networks have retained a hierarchical dimension is that citizenship in the region remains embedded in the assumptions of the Asian Governance Model. There is a strong sense of a patriarchal cultivation of citizens with the Hegelian aim of building up the strong community spirit that will meld with the effective state to make the nation more globally competitive. Citizenship, writes Turner, "was handed down by states that were involved in modernization and state-building projects."[144]

In the developmental state era, the role of the state was often described as "decide-announce-defend" (with the apt acronym DAD). But DAD has today given way to a more participatory approach that aims both to strengthen citizenship *and* to institutionalize the values and priorities of the state. Network governance in Asia, write Cheung and Scott, is "a means of strengthening approved values in the community through the mediation of the state."[145]

Probably the most developed participatory or network governance system is found in South Korea. The role of civil society in that country's democratization plus the loss of prestige of the central bureaucracy after the 1997 Asian Financial Crisis have combined to create more institutions and mechanisms of citizen engagement than anywhere else in Asia. Under Roh Moo-Hyun (2003–8), a "participatory government" was declared and a Senior Secretary to the President for Civil Society was appointed. At the local level, more than 400 "policy communities," in which citizen groups deliberate local issues, now exist in South Korea.

But the new mechanisms and institutions "have not succeeded in enlisting the active participation of the middle class, whose lukewarm attitudes have precluded the reshaping of society through reform," writes Kim.[146] While thirteen of the twenty members of the Regulatory Reform Commission that was established in 1998 came from outside of government, much of the groundwork, coordination, and consultation of the body was carried out by a thirty-member secretariat located in the prime minister's office.[147] The resulting governance reforms, writes Leung, "provided the state with an opportunity to re-align its own power position relative to business and labor."[148]

Meanwhile, a range of citizens' rights – including requesting an audit, participating in budget making, initiating a bill, and recalling an elected leader – have been deeply constrained by courts and central bureaucracies that treat them with caution. For instance, when citizens in the Seoul-area suburb of Hanam wanted to recall their mayor over a planned public crematorium in 2007, the court stepped in to annul the recall campaign on the grounds that not all the signatories to the petition had listed their reasons and "unlimited ability to recall without stating reasons would make local democracy unstable."[149] One expert believes that the role of civil society, which was mobilized as part of the democratization process, is now in decline in the country as the more traditional relationship between rulers and ruled returns.[150]

The closest model to South Korea is Taiwan, where the opposition DPP that held power from 2000 to 2008 was suspicious of the bureaucracy inherited from the KMT state and promoted bottom-up policy making. Environmental groups, for instance, which had previously participated only on an advisory committee, gained formal status in impact assessments and on the National Committee to Advance Sustainable Development. Citizen deliberative conferences were held on issues like surrogate motherhood, the Danshui River redevelopment, and the death penalty. The norm of network governance is now deeply institutionalized in Taiwan.

Japan, too, has advanced greatly to build citizen participation within harmonious governance networks. As Garon showed in his study of Japanese governance of religion, welfare, prostitution, gender equality, and savings prior to 1945, aptly titled *Molding Japanese Minds*, the Japanese state has always been successful in engaging citizens to take their proper role in public policies. This grows out of the notion of *kyōka*, or "moral suasion and guidance" (from the Chinese *jiaohua*, or "civilize the people through education," from an earlier expression *zhengjiao fenghua*, or "civilize the people in political and cultural decency"), which is provided by rulers to guide and improve the people through their own active participation in policy. Citizen participation was embedded in a larger national project of community improvement and national uplift. But this was not "state control" or a "Big State" project imposed on an unwilling or quiescent society. Rather, Japanese society was a willing and active participant whose role was indispensable in maintaining the accountability of the state: "Japanese officials and groups within society frequently interacted in formulating and implementing programs to manage society.... Common backgrounds and experiences contributed to the growth of close relationships between influential officials and the middle class activists who championed the modernization and Westernization of Japanese society."[151]

All forty-seven prefectural governments in Japan have policy advisory committees made up of citizens who join of their own accord. A Non-Profit Organizations Law of 1998 designated the legal status and tax breaks and other benefits for civil society groups acting in any activity that the government declared was a nonprofit area. The term *kyodo* is used to mean "equal partnership" between citizens and local governments, and deliberative "community councils" were established to advise the mayor *before* formal policy making began, a shift described as a "paradigm shift" by one scholar.[152] The city of Mitaka, a suburb of Tokyo, is renowned for its citizen-centric management, which includes citizen-led deliberations for the city plan.[153]

What is interesting is that the "Asian model" of participatory local government, to the extent that it emerges from Japan, is less focused on the agonistic working out of "compromise" than on the "harmonious" working out of shared responsibility and the shared production of public services. Decisions still tend to be initiated and shaped by the state – here the elected mayors – but when we recall that state dominance in Asia exists within an accountability framework that subsumes, or supervenes on, social preferences, this certainly should not make us declare the integrative Asian model as inferior to the pluralistic one.

In Thailand, the norm of including civic participation in the very early stages of national development planning was put into place in 1997 and then repeated and expanded by Thaksin in 2002. Civil society groups set the agenda and policy direction with their own People's Development Plan, which then became the basis for bureaucratic planning by the National Economic and Social Development Board. One work optimistically described a transition from bureaucratic polity to "liberal corporatism" in which social actors, while still co-opted by the state, had a stronger and more independent voice within the state-led model.[154] The military-written 2007 constitution was an attempt to reaffirm the powers of the bureaucracy. For instance, it stipulated that the appointment of commissioners to accountability institutions (elections, human rights, audit, anti-corruption, ombudsman, constitutional court, etc.), which had previously been done by the Senate, was to be placed in the hands of special committees composed of various judges, as well as the leader of the opposition in the legislature. "The upshot was that instead of empowering citizens, the transfer of the governance paradigm reinforced the monopoly of power by bureaucrats and politicians," wrote Bowornwathana.[155]

In the Philippines, decentralization in 1991 was largely driven by the political objective of de-Marcosifying government and raising political participation. That law included a bold provision that 25 percent of seats on local government development councils and health and school boards must be filled by local NGOs. At the national level, participatory reforms include the "alternative budget" that civil society groups are asked to submit to the budget process, and the Budget Call law that requires all agencies to consult with civil society prior to submitting their requests. The national constitution even mandates the government to "encourage non-governmental, community-based, or sectoral organizations to promote the welfare of the nation." But as Thompson notes, operating within a weak state system, Filipino civil society groups lack the institutional mechanisms to make their voices effective. The result can be a "culture of impunity" in which politicians ignore or subvert civil society efforts.[156]

Perhaps the "least likely" cases are those authoritarian governments where participation has expanded unexpectedly. China and Vietnam are notable in the area of governance not just for their public sector reforms but also for their embrace of participatory governance. While the legal and institutional basis for such participation remains limited, the norm of participatory policy making is now rooted in both countries. This is despite ideological strictures relating to the Leninist principles of democratic centralism and the mass line that should make such alternative channels superfluous, if not downright seditious. But these countries, as we have stressed throughout this book, are more embedded historically in the common imperatives of the Asian Governance Model than they are in the now-fading dalliance with Marxism-Leninism.

A far slicker and more limiting system than those in China and Vietnam is run in Singapore, where the government's Reaching Everyone for Active Citizenry at Home (REACH), a body headed by the health and labor minister, began operations in 2006 to go "beyond feedback." The body runs online and in-person policy workshops where citizens can contribute their views on sustainability, education, health, population, and the economy. At the same time, state bureaucrats carefully constrict the topics. A 2002 report on "best practices in political governance" by the bipartisan Political Development Feedback Group suggested a workshop on political reforms. The suggestion was ignored and the group was dissolved. By carefully managing both the agenda and process of citizen participation in this way, note Rodan and Jayasuriya, the result "is a compartmentalization of political issues and a disciplining of policy debate to choices and debates linked to the ruling party's agenda."[157] Nasir and Turner refer to the Asian model as "governance as gardening," because the role of government is to carefully cultivate a citizenry that consents to the legitimacy of the state and to weed out citizens who refuse to do the same.[158]

Singapore also provides perhaps the most paradigmatic case of the nature and limits of citizen participation in Asian governance in its decision to open two casinos in 2010. As a tightly run society, the

Singapore government had long banned casinos on the grounds that they undermined social values and hard work. But casinos were becoming a big part of global tourism, and Singaporeans gambled heavily on local horse races and at regional casinos. When the government announced that it was considering proposals for two casinos in 2004, an unprecedented opposition movement, Families Against the Casino Threat (FACTS), sprang to life. Muslim, Buddhist, Hindu, and Christian groups, along with social workers and the tiny opposition parties, joined the anticasino movement. Polls at the time showed that most Singaporeans opposed the plan. A petition with 19,000 names was submitted to the cabinet. The government, in typical fashion, congratulated itself for "moving its discussion of national issues up one notch."[159]

Despite the clear opposition inside the government and out, the cabinet pressed ahead with consultations with business leaders on concepts for the casinos. The key decision was probably made by Lee Kuan Yew, then Minister Mentor, who told a forum in early 2005 that he had changed his mind and now reluctantly supported the idea. A proposal by some backbench MPs for a free vote in parliament or a national referendum was rejected by the cabinet on the grounds that it would set a dangerous precedent for populist government. Police rejected an application for a public demonstration by the opposition on the grounds that it would disrupt civil order. In mid-2005, the prime minister told parliament that the government had decided to press ahead despite all of the opposition. His testimony to parliament is notable:

The public feedback showed clearly that some Singaporeans had strong views against the proposal. The Ministers themselves were evenly split.... I shared these doubts. I did not believe that ... we could be confident enough to proceed and override the reservations of a significant group of Singaporeans.... [But] the Government must maintain a secular and pragmatic approach. It cannot enforce the choices of one group on others, or make these choices the basis of national policy.... For the Government, the key consideration is what serves our national interest in the long term.... Some members of the public think that we had made up our minds right from the beginning, even before this whole process of public discussion. They are quite mistaken. In fact the Cabinet started off mostly against the [casinos]. The views of Ministers mirrored the spectrum of views among the public. Some were for, others against. As we discussed the matter among ourselves, and understood better what the [casinos] actually involved, our views gradually shifted.... I respect those who oppose the [casinos], and their views. We have decided to proceed, but not because we think those against the [casinos] are wrong, or their views unimportant. Their reservations are valid and shared by the ministers, even those who support the [casinos].... But now we are confronted by a new situation, and the overriding need to remake our city and our economy.[160]

Thus, despite popular preferences and an organized opposition, the government pressed ahead on the grounds that participatory governance is not the same as popular governance. There is a distinctive echo here of the views of English conservative Edmund Burke and the tradition of seeing the role of government not as parroting diverse wishes but as deliberating for the public good with the aid of public input: "Parliament is not a congress of ambassadors from different and hostile interests ... but Parliament is a deliberative assembly of one nation, with one interest, that of the whole," Burke told his Bristol constituents in 1774.[161]

The two casinos opened in 2010 and quickly begat many of the social problems that critics had feared, while generating the revenues for which the government had hoped. Citizen engagement certainly reshaped state policies: There are heavy entrance fees and the nanny state closely manages problem and poor gamblers. But ultimately it was the government, not society, that embodied the national interest.

The Singapore casinos debate is a reminder that the notion of the deferent and demobilized citizenry is flatly wrong in contemporary Asian politics. Even in Singapore, there was sufficient space and sufficient government interest for an active citizenry. On the other hand, citizen participation was largely confined within state-defined administrative structures, and when it developed into a nonsanctioned movement, the government dug in. The results were not the most popular outcome, but they may have been the most rational. If the old system of the developmental state was one of Decide-Announce-Defend (DAD), this updated participatory version of Asian governance might be described as Mobilize-Organize-Manage (MOM). Either way, the parents are still in charge.

Given this, there seems to be little basis for concerns about a weakening of the foundations of politics in Asia. Development, democracy, New Public Management, regulatory and legal strengthening, and network governance have all contributed to shifting patterns of governance. But politics in Asia maintains a remarkable degree of continuity with the normative underpinnings of accountable state dominance that were visible in the era of the Malacca Sultanate. Chapter 6 looks at the implications of this for public policy outcomes.

6

Public Policy

BIG, FAST RESULTS

In 2010, Malaysia launched a new public policy initiative that it called "Big, Fast Results." The idea was to turn public policy into a more entrepreneurial and strategic process that both served large constituencies (not small ones) and created immediate, visible results. As a government brochure put it: "It aims to rid the public of a ubiquitous concern – that the government simply is unable to execute and deliver on programs that otherwise sound great in theory. It's about ensuring that the initiatives put in place will do what they aim to do, and that they get done."[1] The program, formally known as the Economic Transformation Program, was managed by a new agency of government – the Performance Management and Delivery Unit (PEMANDU), under the prime minister – that initiated the strategic ("30,000-foot" level) public policy decisions and then handed them over to the implementing and management ("3-foot" level) departments. In its first two years of operations, the program committed $63 billion to various projects in infrastructure, finance, crime prevention, health, and education.

In Chapter 5, we looked at the processes of governance and policy making – the question of *how* government works. In this chapter, we turn to outcomes – the question of *what* government achieves. A key theme of the Big, Fast Results program was an emphasis on creating opportunities, services, and infrastructure for everyone rather than entitlements and spoils for particular claimant groups. And unlike most megalomaniacal Third World transformation projects, this one was carefully managed with a battery of scorecards, agreed-upon-procedures, and continual improvement panels that would make any management enthusiast squirm with joy. We have already seen in Chapter 4 how a "rights of the majority" discourse shapes democracy in Asia. It is no surprise that this translates into public policies that aim to have a broad impact. The nature of public policy in Asia is to favor inclusive, growth-oriented aims rather than exclusive, distributional aims. To borrow the terms used by philosopher John Rawls, it is the *expansion* of "primary social goods" – things that everyone could use in greater quantities, such as income, wealth, opportunity, social respect, and freedoms – rather than their *distribution* that motivates public policies. As Cheung puts it: "Developmentalism is still the foundation of East Asian public policy discourse."[2]

In addition to being broadly directed, a second, and often overlooked, dimension of public policy in Asia is that fiscal spending plays a comparatively smaller role than elsewhere. In the case of Malaysia's Big, Fast Results campaign, for instance, the government also used new regulations, public-private partnerships, information campaigns, norm creation (especially concerning the role of women), and new public accountability systems to achieve the desired outcomes. This helps explain an apparent paradox of public policy in Asia, namely that Asian governments, despite their dominant sociological status and their active involvement in delivering primary social goods, do not spend (or tax) as much as other countries at similar levels of development do. Government spending on public services in Asia is typically around 10–20 percent of the GDP, compared to around 20–40 percent in the rest of the world.[3] This may seem odd until we recall that, traditionally, the Asian state's dominant position in society is primarily cultural rather than fiscal or coercive.

Smaller government budgets in Asia reflect not so much a libertarian aversion to the state so much as the pragmatic idea (found in the principles of NPM) that, in general, the private sector is better than the public sector at putting savings to efficient use. The role of the state is enacted more through other public policy tools, like regulation, information, standard setting, prohibitions and sanctions, the rule of law, facilitation, public leadership, norm creation, and social mobilization. In the case of the Big, Fast Results campaign, for instance, the government whipped up a large public information campaign and sought to redirect private investment in its effort to "transform a nation." Public policy throughout the region involves national transformation more than it involves national taxation.

The corollary of this on the revenue side is that Asian governments do not engage in confiscatory or "progressive" taxations of personal incomes. The share of central government revenues in Asia accounted for by personal income taxes is vanishingly small, except in Taiwan. In South Korea, nearly half of all citizens paid no income taxes in 2000.[4] Revenues are drawn more efficiently from sales and property taxes, as well as investment income, because the state does not need to establish its legitimacy through taxation. Spending is intended to serve everyone, not just taxpayers, while legitimacy is not based on a fiscal contract but on a moral imperative.

In this context, fiscal spending in Asia is generally subject to a high degree of scrutiny. The "budgeting for results" principle of the NPM sought to allocate budgets based on the benefits that various policies were generating, shifting budget decisions from the "value allocations" of political leaders to the "market and citizen" allocations of society. Consistent with this principle, public sector spending in Asia is remarkably efficient. In one study of public sector efficiency in five-year periods between 1980 and 2000,[5] Asia as a region was by far the most efficient in using public resources: Japan, South Korea, Thailand, and Malaysia had positive growth effects from government spending in *all* periods covered, while Indonesia (which saw positive growth effects from government spending in one of two periods covered) and the Philippines (which saw positive growth effects in only one of three periods covered) were somewhat less successful. This relative ranking is confirmed by another study for the 1986 to 2007 period that found that the most efficient spenders in Asia were Japan, South Korea, and Singapore, while Taiwan, Thailand, and Malaysia were less so.[6] But relative to the rest of the world, even Asia's poor performers had robust positive effects from government spending in both studies. In the former study, government spending had positive growth effects in only 15 percent (one in seven) of the five-year periods for the fifty-eight non-Asian countries on average. In other words, Asia's *worst* performing state was better at generating positive benefits from government spending than the rest of the world was on average. In a separate study, Malaysia's public spending was found sometimes to have an even higher effect on economic growth than private sector investment had.[7]

While it is commonly assumed that democratization leads to a rise in spending, widening deficits, and increased outlays for special interests, the public finance strategies adopted by the strong bureaucracies of Asia embedded in a social consensus have averted this threat. The accountability dynamic in Asia's politics created a norm of "budgeting for results" long before it was discovered by management consultants in the West.

There is no debate about "the role of government" in Asia, because public policy is experienced as a natural part of social life rather than an intrusion into it. In a region where development, transformation, and "Big, Fast Results" have been the norm for two generations, the debates center instead on how to improve public policy.

Coming back to our earlier discussion of "Oriental despotism" versus "Asian dynamism," fiscal policy in Asia reflects both the imperatives of the dominant state and the imperatives of dynamic societies. The state keeps spending in check in order to encourage private savings and work initiatives, to keep corporate taxes low and to avoid crowding out private investment. But what it does spend it spends in a strong-state manner to deliver primary social goods, like infrastructure, crime control, social safety nets, and education, not heeding the claims of interest groups. The call for "economic democratization" that began in South Korea in the 2010s, despite its populist ring, was an appeal to reaffirm the nonpartisan role of the state after two decades in which *chaebols* had capitalized on democratization to transform their corporatist role under the developmental state into a rent-seeking one under the free-for-all of democracy. Indeed, a common theme of public policy in contemporary Asia is the way that the developmental state has reinvented itself in the era of globalization and democracy as a defender of the *public* in public policies. In this chapter, we will see how this particular ethos of public policy informs four main areas of public concern – social welfare, public works, the environment, and regional relations.

PRODUCTIVIST WELFARE

The biggest item of public spending in Asia, as elsewhere, is social or welfare spending, including health, housing, pensions, income support, employment benefits, and social services. Given its importance to governments and societies everywhere, social spending is an aspect of public policy that is pulled in many directions. This has led to multiple interpretations of the "fundamental nature" of social spending in Asia. On the one hand, there is what we might call the "welfare universalist" view that rejects the salience of Asia as a variable in explaining the variations and evolution of social spending in Asian countries. According to this view, welfare policies in Asia can be easily deduced from the degrees of development, democracy, and globalization in each country. In particular, since the early 2000s, Asia has been undergoing a dramatic transformation of welfare that looks much like similar transformations

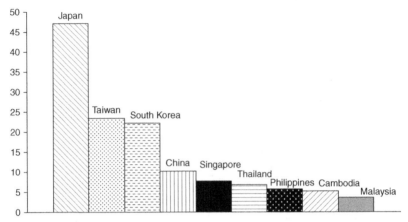

FIGURE 6.1. Welfare spending as percent of total government spending.
Source: Asian Development Bank, *Spending on Social Security and Health*, 2010 and 2011.

in other modernizing regions. The idea of an Asian welfare model has become difficult to sustain, because several of the region's countries have "graduated" into welfare policies that share features with those of other advanced industrial states.[8] The changes have been spurred not just by long-term trends like development, democratization, globalization, and demographics (Asia's population over the age of sixty was only 7 percent of the total population in 1975 but is expected to be 15 percent by 2025) but also by the more immediate effects of two major economic recessions. As *The Economist* put it in a 2012 survey: "Asia's tigerish economies are turning marsupial, carrying their dependents along with them as they prowl."[9]

Japan is most clearly similar in its welfare policies to developed Western states, which is why it is often cited as the proof that there is no distinctive Asian model of welfare policy. Japan spends far more on social security and health and covers a far greater proportion of its disadvantaged population than any other Asian country does (see Figures 6.1 and 6.2). As one moves into the newer democracies like Taiwan, Thailand, South Korea, and Indonesia, there is evidence of a similar expansion of welfare spending, such that when compared to a cross section of states elsewhere, Asia does not appear to be distinctive in matters of welfare policy. As Kasza puts it: "For an East Asian welfare model to exist, the countries of the region must embrace a similar set of welfare policies, and that set of policies must differ from welfare systems elsewhere in

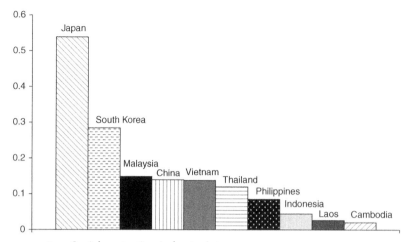

FIGURE 6.2. Social protection index in Asia.
Notes: Social Protection Index = Government spending per person in the total target population (including poor, disabled, elderly, sick, disaster-stricken, etc.) as a proportion of the poverty line income (defined as one-quarter of GDP per capita).
Source: Asian Development Bank, *The Social Protection Index* (Manila: ADB, 2013).

the world. No matter how one defines Asia or East Asia, neither of these conditions holds true."[10]

The other view, which we might call "welfare Orientalism," is that there is a distinctive "Asian factor" that shapes the universalistic evolution of welfare spending in the region. Specifically, it is argued, Asian countries tie social spending closely to employment and productivity, designing programs with an eye to avoiding welfare dependency and introducing programs on the basis of economic logic rather than social rights. Holliday coined the term "productivist welfare" to describe this system.[11] Noting national variations and global patterns, Aspalter also found a "great degree of unity within the East Asian welfare state systems," which he summarized as a "clear focus on productive investment in social and in particular human capital development" and a relatively broad/universal and nonredistributive type of provision.[12]

In some instances, this debate arises because analysts look at different aspects of welfare policy. For instance, the scope and size of unemployment insurance is systematically lower in Asia than in any other region of the world.[13] Japan's unemployment system remains smaller, less extensive, and more work-oriented than others in the OECD. It is more "welfare through work" than "welfare without work."[14] Combined public spending on health, too, is just 2–4 percent of the GDP in all Asian countries except for Japan, compared to 5–10 percent in most lower-middle- to upper-income countries. On the other hand, pension and elderly care funding in Asia looks more similar to comparable states in other parts of the world.

Probably more of the debate is explained by the difference between formal rules and regulations, which often look indistinguishable from those elsewhere, and the context and management of the policies, which appear to take on distinctive Asian characteristics. In the area of workfare, for instance, where governments provide unemployment benefits in return for community service or participation in government-run training and work schemes, program managers in Asia are notably more draconian in their application and management of schemes. Japan's government, for instance, sets numerical targets for the proportion of disabled, homeless, and single mothers who should return to work within a five-year period. "The combination of strong administrative-led governments and coercive workfare strategies has made social assistance in such polities involve highly stigmatizing schemes that help to suppress wages and maintain minimal welfare systems," writes Chan.[15]

Public housing, too, has long been managed to support the middle class, as well as the poor, and to serve private savings and economic development needs.[16] While housing in Western welfare states is often nationalized and centered on poor rental housing, public housing in Asian countries has been commodified and centered on middle-class owner-occupiers. The aim has been to foster self-reliant and family-based welfare. In the 2000s, middle-income households were "graduated" from public housing subsidies in the region and encouraged to purchase their homes. Public housing in the region since then has focused on keeping house prices affordable for the middle class, making fewer concessions to low-income housing.[17] "This kind of welfare regime," write Ronald and Doling, "concerns itself with expanding property ownership rather than citizenship rights, marking a move away from egalitarian redistributive welfare models towards a system in which market-determined changes in the value of property affect the opportunities and life chances of households."[18]

This debate tends to miss two additional questions of public policy: how it is justified and brought about politically; and what its outcomes are. By focusing only on the *content* of policies and ignoring their *causes* and *consequences*, we may easily overlook additional distinctive features of social policy in Asia.

Firstly, despite the variety of public policies adopted in Asia, one thing they hold in common is a particular type of political *justification* or motivation that is critical to understanding how they come into being and are maintained and reformed. Cheung argues that "welfare developmentalism" is the best description, because, while welfare provisions have expanded, they continue to be justified with an eye to development rather than rights. Welfare in Asia is notable because policy changes come from bureaucratic initiative, not popular demands (through unions or social democratic parties), to boost growth, and they are thus called "developmental welfare."[19] In their study of the expansion of policies to support working women in South Korea in the 2000s, for instance, Peng and Wong argue that an "instrumental logic of social investment," rather than an intrinsic logic of equal opportunity, was the main motivation: "These bureaucrats were neither pro-women nor pro-welfare. They were pro-economic reform policy makers, many of whom had come from what was the Economic Planning Board and all of whom saw liberal market reform as the way to move Korea's economy in line with the global economy."[20] Some scholars believe that the Asian model of tying social entitlements to economic growth and resources is better suited to a world of constant economic volatility.[21]

Secondly, and relatedly, the *outcomes* of public welfare policies in Asia differ systematically from those in the rest of the world. For whatever reasons, welfare policies *work differently* in Asia than the same policies do elsewhere.[22] For instance, the elderly are more likely to live with extended families in Asia than the elderly elsewhere are, and single mothers are more likely to be permanently employed in the advanced economies of Japan and South Korea than single mothers in advanced economies elsewhere are. By accepting welfare policies as justified by a productivist, instrumental logic, Asian citizens have tended to respond in kind, by building up or maintaining their fitness for work. As they are administered by an ethos of "security without entitlement," to borrow Vogel's phrase in his study of Japan,[23] welfare recipients maintain a positive attitude toward the programs and seek to remain in the active labor force.

The evidence suggests that in the realm of social policy, Asian governments compel their citizens to make choices that are paternalistically better for themselves (whether in the realm of long-term savings, investment in education, employment, or health and social services) than they would otherwise make in the absence of such "nudges" from the state. Families, for instance, are encouraged to remain critical components of

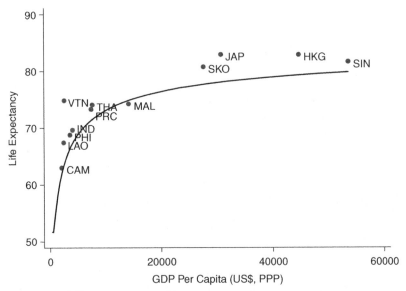

FIGURE 6.3. Life expectancy and income per capita.
Notes: n = 154, r² = 0.62.
Source: World Bank.

welfare provision alongside the market and the state because they, too, deliver better outcomes.[24] Again, rather than seeing this as distinctly Asian, we should see it as a more prevalent emphasis in Asia that can be learned elsewhere, as recent debates on the "new paternalism" in the West suggest.[25]

When all is said and done, social policy in Asia seems to deliver better outcomes at all levels of development, as measured by life expectancy. Ten of the twelve Asian countries measured have life expectancies above what would be predicted by their development levels, while the other two, Malaysia and Cambodia, have life expectancies exactly as predicted (see Figure 6.3). While formal laws and regulations have evolved in Asia in a predictable manner, the practice of social policy remains embedded in distinctive cultures and ideologies that help explain differential outcomes.

THE *GIRI* OF PUBLIC WORKS

In Chapter 2, we canvassed the theories of the German scholar Karl Wittfogel concerning the centrality of public, large-scale irrigation projects (canals, reservoirs, embankments, etc.) to the Asian strong state. We found that this public works theory cannot replace culture in explaining state dominance in Asia. Rather, as with the rise of the fiscal state, large-scale public works are mainly a *result* of that state dominance. Now is the place to come back to this idea that large and effective public works are a notable outcome of Asian politics.

Public works include a wide variety of areas – industrial zones, water, energy, communications, transportation, recreation, waste, and much else. As the emblematic example of "primary social goods," public works are obviously a high priority of Asian states. Anyone who has whisked through the region's impressive airports and ridden its flashy urban subways would know this. Again, by comparing Asian countries to other countries at similar income levels, we see a region-wide tendency for infrastructure, as measured, for instance, by the World Bank's trade and transport infrastructure index to be much better than average. Japan, China, Malaysia, and Thailand stand out for their infrastructure, while the cluster of the Philippines, Vietnam, and Indonesia are also comfortably above their income-peer averages. Good infrastructure built in a fast and cost-effective manner has been a key reason for Asia's economic growth.[26] The political question is: How do Asian countries get the public policies to serve this end?

Unlike in India, where public works are used to bolster incomes and employment, especially in rural constituencies controlled by the ruling party, in Asia public works are seen as a genuinely public undertaking with an aim to bolster broad growth rather than particular incomes. In Chapter 3, we saw how port development in South Korea has been managed in a way that is both rational and prudent on the one hand and yet contentious and competitive on the other hand. To generalize, the politics of public works in Asia has become more complex and contentious with development, democracy, and globalization. Yet state dominance and good governance still ensure that public works are rarely stalled or ended by legal or political opposition. The Asian Governance Model generally delivers positive outcomes when it comes to public works. Yet we need to recall that this model is not simply a model of a domineering state imposing its will on society but is rather a contentious model in which state authority is linked to underlying accountability systems that relate to moral obligation, or *giri*, to use the widely invoked Japanese term. Neither a rational developmental state nor political accountability alone explains Asian success: Rather, it is the confluence of the two that is critical.

Public works often involve land, and the politics of compulsory land acquisition and land use in Asia are contentious, as they are elsewhere. These conflicts have taken on unique features in the former communist economies of China and Vietnam, because private property rights there were never assumed in the first place, making government actions more prone to high-handedness and corruption.[27] China's "tough nails" (*dingzi hu*) who resist state expropriation are notable because of their lone cries against the use of state power to seize land. For the most part, and again in stark contrast to India, squatter areas that occupy land that the state needs do not stand a chance in Asia, much less enjoy some semiformal status. In less draconian Asian states, the more common strategy is to limit outright freehold ownership in favor of long-term leases. In Singapore, for instance, the government can unilaterally alter the terms of a land lease as long as it compensates the holder. In other cases, Asian governments achieve public policy aims by regulating land use, often without compensating owners. Courts in Asia have generally rejected the concept of "regulatory taking" used in the United States and Europe, under which heavy regulation is declared to be legally equivalent to compulsory acquisition and thus must be compensated.[28]

When states are forced to expropriate private land for public works (also known as eminent domain, compulsory acquisition, or compulsory purchase), they generally face few legal or political obstacles. In Taiwan, according to Kotaka and colleagues writing in 2001, "proving need is easy for the state, and constitutional protection has become secondary at best.... When the [central] government is looking for land to appropriate, landowners, local government agencies and other affected landowners get little to no chance to speak. As a result, until recently, almost all land appropriations have been approved."[29] In South Korea, 92 percent of land acreage acquired by the state between 1975 and 2001 for public works was purchased with the agreement of landowners, while only 8 percent was acquired by expropriation or court order.[30]

The practice of eminent domain acquisitions in Asia has, however, conformed to Montesquieu's view that such confiscations would be carefully exercised because rulers know there are no courts (or civil society or media or legislatures) to check this power. In other words, while the right (even duty) of the Asian state to acquire and use land for public purposes is rarely constrained by individualistic or private claims, the practice *is* constrained by genuine public good interests (that need to be shown and justified) and by a tradition of adequate (often generous) compensation. More often than not, the issues of state land acquisition in Asia center on the amount of compensation rather than on the act itself.

This "good governance" claim is most strained in China and Vietnam, where the state has often expropriated land merely to resell it to industrial or commercial interests, pocketing the revenues and leaving peasants landless and in poverty. Yet even in these cases, the expectations of state benevolence explain why villagers engage in a "rightful resistance" that invokes the policies and commitments of the state itself in defense of their interests.[31] This deferential style of resistance, blaming local officials and not the state itself, again separates Asia from India, where peasants more often engage in dissenting resistance supported by social activists and a Gandhian tradition that sees the state as the enemy.

Perhaps the most long-running, dramatic, and high-stakes battle against land acquisition for public works by an Asian developmental state began in 1965 when Japan's government decided to build a new airport near the city of Narita, east of Tokyo, to relieve the overstretched Haneda airport on Tokyo Bay. Farmers at the initial site protested bitterly, forcing the government to choose another site nearby. The new site was less heavily populated and would work just as well. While the government and imperial household already owned about 30 percent of the 1,000-hectare site, the remaining 70 percent was privately owned by 357 households.

At first, land acquisition went well. By 1969, about 90 percent of the private land had been acquired by agreement. Surveys showed that more than half of the local population supported the airport. But in making the alternative siting decision, the government in Tokyo had not gone through the normal processes of consultation with local farmers and local governments. The reason was that politicians, bureaucrats, and the imperial household were in disagreement themselves in Tokyo, so when a new Minister of Transport was appointed in 1969, he moved quickly to begin construction in order to avert deadlock. "So concerned was he with political problems at the top that he ignored political problems at the bottom," wrote Apter and Sawa in their classic study of the movement. The public meeting where the decision was announced to locals lasted only five minutes. "Many farmers saw the airport affair as a breach in obligation (*giri*).... It was the treatment they received, compounded by coercion, which seemed to them to break the social contract."[32] Or, as a journalist later wrote: "At the root of it all is a single, unforgivable breach of etiquette."[33]

As a result, the landowners who had not yet sold dug in their heels and were quickly joined by students, union radicals, and members of the Japan Communist Party, and they formed an antiairport movement. Between 1969 and 1978, the airport site was a carnival of protest. The protestors built a system of tunnels below the land, complete with futon bunk beds, plentiful supplies of *sake*, and bamboo tubing for ventilation. Forcible expropriations in 1971 constituted the most violent phase of the airport movement. But opening day in 1978 was hardly a success either, as recounted by *Time* magazine:

The 14,000 police spread across the terminal were caught by surprise as hel-meted students in steel-plated trucks battered down the terminal gates. Tossing fire bombs and swinging metal rods, demonstrators swarmed wildly through the sprawling airport complex. The central battle took place in the administration building. There, a band of 20 radicals emerged from the storm-drain sewer and attacked the nerve center of the airport. In a running skirmish with security forces, ten of the radicals made it to the elevators leading to the control tower 16 floors above. They disembarked at the 14th floor, climbed up a huge parabolic antenna, beating it with hammers as they went, and smashed the slanted windows of the tower. Six rioters shinnied through the broken windows and proceeded to batter radar and communications consoles. Five frightened technicians who had been in the tower fled to the roof, from which they were evacuated by a police helicopter. The swift demonstration paralyzed Narita. Casualties numbered 34 police and 20 demonstrators injured, including one youth who was severely burned when a fire bomb exploded prematurely in his hand.[34]

Once the airport opened, the protest movement declined, splitting into factions in 1983, and then losing public sympathy thereafter. An extended second runway was opened in 2009 after the last of the "hold-out farms" were bought. In 2012, the original "protest huts" at the airport were finally demolished by court order.

The Narita movement has sometimes been seen as a populist uprising against the development state, a sign that the development state is noth-ing more than an illegitimate imposition on Asian societies rather than a genuine manifestation of them. But Apter and Sawa argue that the land-owners (as opposed to the radicals and the Marxist scholars who wrote about the landowners) were neither antidevelopmental nor antistate. Some landowners, mostly those who had served in Japan's World War II army, were actually motivated by fears that the airport would be used to host U.S. Air Force planes. Their opposition was motivated by remnant nationalism. For most, "one of the crucial factors in the entire airport struggle was the way the government offended the farmers' dignity by its failure to consult and by ignoring their initial constitutionally appropri-ate attempts to protest." The farmers generally supported development and would have been happy to move to the new farming lands that were offered or to take the money and retire. But the high-handedness of the decision making, failure to consult farmers and local governments, and the general lack of cooperative spirit that infused the project led to a protest of principle against the lack of due process. The *giri* owed to farmers was particularly highly valued as Japanese society lost touch with its rural roots. Filmmaker Shinsuke Ogawa's two epic documentaries on the movement – *The Battle Front for the Liberation of Japan* (1968) and *Peasants of the Second Fortress* (1971) – lodged its sympathies in an idealized portrait of the farmers rather than with the self-absorbed students who were constantly trampling the crops on their way to another night of ideological schism. The movement was not a matter of development or government so much as a matter of lost innocence and an attempt to rebuild social fabric. Never did the landowners engage in terrorism, for to do so would have placed them "in a war against their own society," wrote Apter and Sawa. Nor did they reject compromise, for to do so would have been "to turn one's back on the legitimacy of the state itself." The self-interest of landowners was "almost trivial."[35] Obligation and courtesy were key.

Understanding the massive rollout of public works in Asia, then, requires understanding the balance between the dominant, rational state and the strong moral obligations (*giri*) that it entails. The Narita airport was a rational piece of public policy, and government officials were right about its public benefits. Today, Narita regularly tops global rankings as one of the world's most efficient airports. But the protest arising from the violation of *giri* had important effects on this and future projects. The size of Narita itself was scaled back and a rethink began about the costs and benefits of land acquisitions. More broadly, the importance of reaffirming the social obligations of prudence and consultation in a context of state dominance was healthily affirmed by the Narita movement. In a sense, it ensured that future public works projects in Japan remained "on track," in the sense that they were developed by bureaucrats who had a keen, even fearful, sense of the need to get it right and achieve harmonious governance. The next major airport project in Japan, at Kansai, which opened in 1994, was built on an artificial island after initial consultations led to the conclusion that reclaiming yet more farmland would not make sense. *Giri*, in other words, is not just a matter of procedure but also a matter of making public policies better.

This same dynamic is most evident today in power and electricity policies in Asia. Electricity demand in Asia has soared with economic development, putting intense pressures on the government to increase capacity. By 2010, Asia accounted for 32 percent of global electricity consumption, up from 13 percent in 1971.[36] China's share of the Asian total was more than 60 percent, compared to 20 percent in 1971. Given the low levels of electrification in Asia, the region will likely account for more than 40 percent of global electricity consumption by 2030. The result is a rash of new power projects.

In the early decades of development in Asia, electricity supply was largely provided by state-owned utilities. But beginning in the 1990s, public policies on electricity production shifted in favor of private supply with public regulation. Public policies encouraged, planned, oversaw, and regulated private power production. The state's authority has been regulative rather than fiscal. Not only has the need for electricity grown, but the complexity of the policy problems have grown, as well, because of the private ownership approach and because these issues are being played out in political systems that are more democratic than they had been. Here is a test case of whether the "Tokyo Consensus," a pro-market yet state-dominant regulatory model, actually works.

Compared to Narita-era struggles, the dynamics of *giri* in Asian electricity no longer involve valiant students and farmers climbing out of sewer pipes; instead, they involve remonstrative courts and political parties that are engaged in political contention when *giri* has been violated. Public works remain a key manifestation of the developmental state, enacted through mostly rational planning not subject to boondoggles. Political contention arising from a failure of the obligation to consult is more intense the more that this obligation taps into a broader accountability problem – namely that the policy itself is flawed. Public protest arises not when there are self-interest or antidevelopmental urges but when good public policy is called into question.

Indonesia since democratization has been a classic example of the strong state trying to deliver effective public policies to improve electricity supply through pro-market tools and public policies being nudged in the right direction by "rightful" or *giri*-based protest. In the Suharto era, electricity prices were about half of what they needed to be to cover costs.[37] The result was that supply was inadequate and unreliable. Reforms in the 1990s allowed private producers to sell their power to the state utility, PLN. The Asian Financial Crisis, however, revealed the dangers of partial reforms, because PLN was left with contract obligations and debts that it could not service. A 1998 white paper on reform proposed moving to a fully competitive market system. Under a 2002 electricity law, PLN was given a monopoly over only transmission and distribution, while a free-wheeling market of private generators began competing to sell it power.

This plan led to general worries in the population that a rash of new private sector producers would overwhelm the new regulatory state, because private sector profit aims would take precedence over the public interest of affordable and reliable electricity. Indeed, those in charge of the sector's new regulatory bodies were themselves often uncertain about who was in charge. As with Narita, the 2002 bill was also rushed through the legislature with little or no consultations with society, little knowledge of how the regulatory structure would operate, and no study of the environmental and social impacts.[38] Fears of corruption, unequal access to power, and inefficient power production rose. "In few countries in the world would the technical business of the electricity sector so occupy the mass media or the populace, let alone exercise such a central place in the political life of the nation," wrote Jarvis.[39]

There were good reasons, in other words, for supposing that the Indonesian state was mismanaging public policy by creating competition in the sector long before it had the ability to manage it for the public good. The "regulatory risk" was severe not just for Indonesian citizens and their government but, indeed, also for the few private producers who dared to enter the sector, because they could find themselves sideswiped by populist protest if the government mismanaged.[40]

The failure to harmonize society on this issue led to a corrective in the form of popular opposition. Rather than a Narita-style offensive, however, opponents lodged a constitutional court challenge, which was easy to win because the country's socialist-era constitution still held that "sectors of production which are important for the country and affect the life of the people shall be under the powers of the state." The electricity law was overturned in 2004, and the state had to go back to the drawing board as budget subsidies and periodic blackouts worsened.

What finally resulted in a 2009 revision to the law was a far more viable (and constitutional) public policy. Efforts were recentered on transforming PLN into an efficient public sector utility. Private investment was shifted into build, operate, and transfer schemes, under which ownership would revert to PLN after a fixed period (a $3 billion investment was signed with a Japanese consortium in 2011). Local governments won far more control over planning and tariff rates. The pragmatic policy eschewed ideological orientations (such as pro-market or antimarket views) in favor of what would work in the context of a complex country at a complex stage of political and economic development. Not incidentally, this policy allowed the government to move ahead with the price increases needed to free up budgetary resources for other worthwhile spending. Despite the remonstrative protests, the new policy reforms were largely shaped by discussions between the executive, the bureaucracy, international donors, and the Indonesian power sector lobby.[41] The *giri*-based contention in this case led to revisions to electricity sector reforms that delivered better outcomes.

Indonesia, like much of Asia, will be facing an energy crunch in the coming decades as demand soars while costs and environmental concerns rise. The country's first nuclear power plant will likely be built. Coal development will become increasingly contentious. Local governments and communities, as well as international organizations and companies, will want their say in the country's energy policies. At the center of these debates will be the state – dominant, democratic, and deliberative. Achieving a smooth landing to this public policy challenge will require all of these qualities in equal measure.

KNOWLEDGE FOR NATURE

Public policies to protect and rebuild the environment in Asia represent one area where a genuine argument can be made that public policy is a failure. The dominant themes of research on environmental policy in Asia center on the weakness of civil society organizations, the environmental insensitivity of the growth-oriented state, the absence of international or regional pressures for environmental protection, and the failure of political parties and legislatures to set an environmental agenda. As with social welfare, the "productivist" approach to public policy in this area means that the environment always comes second and serves only the aim of sustaining and boosting growth. Moreover, Asia is caught in a perfect storm of the confluence of several environmentally degrading processes: urbanization, democratization, population growth, and industrialization.

Looking at the depressing spectacle of environmental destruction in Asia – lost rain forests in Indonesia, toxic rivers and air in China, the depletion of fisheries in the Philippines – it is hard not to conclude that whatever else Asian politics has achieved, the one thing it has signally failed to do is protect the environment, which at the end of the day may render all other achievements moot. Japan and South Korea have relocated polluting industries to Southeast Asia. Thailand has encouraged devastating hydro projects in Laos and Myanmar to ensure "clean energy." The traditional use of fallow fields utilizing field rotation in

TABLE 6.1. *Negative Environmental Impact by Country*

Country	Rank by Relative Impact (Rank by Absolute Impact)
Singapore	1 (131)
South Korea	2 (23)
Japan	5 (5)
Thailand	6 (16)
Malaysia	8 (13)
Philippines	9 (17)
Indonesia	13 (4)
China	17 (3)
North Korea	21 (46)
Cambodia	26 (68)
Vietnam	31 (43)
Myanmar	35 (14)
Laos	77 (54)

Southeast Asia has given way to industrial annual cropping, which has had severe consequences on greenhouse gas emissions and biodiversity.[42] These problems will only worsen with continued rapid growth and with the fact that, by 2020, most Asians will for the first time be living in cities rather than the countryside. Ironically, the same ports that we looked at as models of the developmental state in Chapter 3 are also major contributors to air and water pollution in the region.[43] As five Chinese academics wrote in one paper in 2013: "In China, the planned economy and strong demands on GDP growth have led to rapid resource depletion and striking environmental degradation. With astonishing economic growth, the costs are immense. China has been suffering severe consequences from its typical resource export dependent economy that significantly counteracts the great economic achievements."[44]

Most measures of environmental performance are problematic in not taking into account a country's performance relative to the amount of environment it has to degrade (number of species, area of land, amount of fresh water, etc.). The Proportional Environmental Impact Index controls for these factors, and the results offer a stunning indictment of Asian countries (see Table 6.1).[45] Across the board, there is a tendency for Asian countries to be the worst environmental impacters in the world. Furthermore, China, Indonesia, Japan, Malaysia, Thailand, the Philippines, and South Korea have the dubious distinction of being among the top twenty-five global polluters in both absolute *and* relative terms.

The only other countries that are "top twenty-five" on both measures are Peru and Ecuador. As with economic growth, such a clear regional clustering is highly improbable unless there is some common factor at work among the countries. The factor must be the politics and policy of the environment in Asia.

Does the Asian Governance Model predict the environmental catastrophe of Asia? By combining a *proactive* state with an accountability system that seeks to deliver primary *social* goods, the Asian Governance Model has a double weakness for the environment. Asian states are obsessed with social (not environmental) uplift and have a structural tendency to crowd out, ignore, or repress transformational agendas that come from outside the state – either from domestic or international society. The environment and its nonhuman stakeholders have no advocate in this system, and they suffer grievously as a result. While the so-called "environmental Kuznet's curve" (in which development causes degradation to worsen at first and then to improve) holds true for socially visible pollution, like air and water quality, the socially invisible forms of pollution, like greenhouse gas emissions and species decline, show only linear and continuous destruction in Asia.[46] Because it lacks the moral agency required for accountability to work within the Asian Governance Model, the environment suffers.

Asia's environmental problems are fundamentally governance problems rather than problems of economic growth or population. While it is easy to observe this in visibly polluted countries, like China, Indonesia, and Cambodia, a more searching inquiry can be made by looking at the "green city" of Singapore. Singapore is notable because its reputation for being a "green city" obscures severe environmental destruction. In addition to having the world's worst impact relative to its environment, Singapore's ecological deficit – the gap between its ecological footprint and the carrying capacity of its natural environment – is the fifth largest among the 152 countries studied in 2010 by the Global Footprint Network (South Korea and Japan are not far behind).[47] Singapore is a classic example of the brutal logic of economic nationalism that underpins governance in much of Asia. It insists that Indonesia controls its forest burning, because the burning causes haze in the city-state, and that Malaysia protects its water resources, on which its economy depends. But in turn, Singapore rejects greenhouse gas emissions limits for itself on the grounds that they would raise manufacturing costs, and it turns a blind eye to the importation of pillaged sand from Southeast Asia for its land reclamation projects.[48]

Wong shows how the macho meritocracy of Singapore has tried to embrace a climate change agenda with policies that focus on industrial upgrading and green growth. Given this framing of environmental concerns in productivist terms, however, Singapore is creating new environmental problems. For instance, by building new "eco towns" of low-energy buildings, precious land is lost to development. By emphasizing bio-fuels, agricultural impacts are exported to the rest of Southeast Asia. Energy efficiency is leading to increased energy use. "Environmental protection is only valid when it fits within the modernization agenda," Wong writes.[49] In this sense, Singapore's present is Asia's future, unless some fundamental tenets of the Asian Governance Model can be changed.

There is little hope of this, however. The problem with expecting an "ecological transition" toward sustainable living in Asia, concludes Wong, is that it "fails to capture the politics of environmental reform in the region, which is deeply embedded in the vastly different historical trajectories of industrial development, as well as the pre-existing structures of state domination."[50] "Green growth" becomes just another state-led developmental project, so the environment itself gets lost in the shuffle. The 2012 Singapore Green Plan, for instance, pledges to protect sensitive and biodiverse nature areas on land and sea "for as long as possible," a policy the government touts to "represent the balance struck between nature conservation and our other land use needs."[51]

What, if anything, might improve the effectiveness of public policies for the environment in Asia? The two obvious candidates are regional mechanisms and bottom-up civil society pressures linked to democratization. But from what we know of politics and governance in Asia, there is little hope that either of these will work. Environmental regionalism in Asia is weak and largely state-orchestrated – a kind of state-led forum for state-led polities. As with other forms of regionalism (see the next section), it has little chance of making a difference. Likewise, the hopes for grassroots environmental activism, or "people-centered" environmentalism, in Asia is no less forlorn. Contentious politics has often been effective in Asia in remonstrating with the state to correct its policies on issues that the state itself has made a priority. Harmonious networks help the state do its job better. But social movements do not set agendas, at least in the short term, much less constrain state behavior on their own. Democratization has paradoxically led to *weaker* environmental civil society in places like Taiwan and Indonesia because of the unlinking of the environment from the socially compelling issue of regime change.

As a result, a consensus has emerged that state dominance will be reinforced by the rise of environmental politics and that any solution will have to be found through state-led initiatives.[52] Governments and their macho meritocracies will need to embrace environmental protection as part of their own rational policy making rubrics. This in turn requires a widening of what is meant by social goods – the environmental basis of social goods, perhaps – as well as a continued change in what is meant by state dominance – harmonious networked governance that includes environmental groups.

Some scholars argue, for instance, that the Asian developmental state could transform itself into the "Asian environmental state," or Green Asian Capitalism. This is because growth itself may depend on a "green transition," given the resource scarcity, the costs of environmental damage, and the shifting global demands for "green" products. Considering what is at stake for the global environment, the siting of the United Nations Green Climate Fund and of the intergovernmental Global Green Growth Institute in South Korea (which has led the "green growth" thinking in the region) makes sense. But the ecological transition being advocated by governments in the region so far is heavily developmental.[53]

To truly embrace environmental policy requires an acceptance of environmental costs when there is <u>no</u> benefit to the national uplift (such as saving sand in Cambodia or slowing global warming). To do so, Asian states need to unlink their notion of national uplift from their desire for growth. Rather than social movements, the hope must lie in transformed social values that filter through into public policy through the accountability mechanisms of the Asian Governance Model. One reason for the rise of Thaksin in Thailand, for instance, was that he promised to steward the environment in rural areas, an issue that concerned farmers. In cities, new middle-class citizens are more concerned about environmental values, too. Just as the "paradigm shift" that was necessary for democracy began in the streets, the paradigm shift that is necessary for environmental salvation will require a green transition in society first and then a preemptive and rational embrace by the state.

For a long time, Asians lived quite happily and productively in the region's often hot and humid climate through a combination of traditional building structures that increased shade and air flows and a warmer conceptualization of comfort. The developmental state's emphasis on widespread air conditioning – which accounts for about a quarter of the region's greenhouse gas emissions[54] – replaced this tradition for the purposes of economic growth. Restaurants throughout the region often provide patrons with blankets against the chill of modern "comfort." As one Singaporean journalist wrote: "If Singaporeans were told that there's some secret statutory board working on how to air-condition the whole country, I really think that revelation would be a vote-winner."[55] To overcome this impasse – productivist states supported by modernist societies – will require a rethinking of what it means to be modern.

Two long-time forest advocates in southwestern China argue that reframing policy using traditional Chinese notions of a harmony between people and the natural environment (heaven and human oneness, or *tian-ren heyi*) could do more to motivate change within state policies than any number of international or political mandates could: "A renewed emphasis on Chinese values from multiple traditions that place humans in partnership with the land could strengthen overall support for science-based conservation practice."[56] The so-called "ecological turn" in contemporary Confucianism links expanded knowledge about environmental destruction to changes in personal and political behavior.[57] Environmental advocates across Asia will need to discover similar indigenous sources of paradigm change if the regional, and the global, environment is to be saved.

TOWARD EASTPHALIA?

This book has considered the nature of Asian politics as a primarily domestic phenomenon that is variously shaped by regional and global influences. The international politics among Asian states operates at a different level of analysis. However, it is worth asking to what extent the domestic politics of Asia has been "externalized" within the region and even the world. Regions are nothing more than aggregates of states – regionalism in Asia, as elsewhere, is nothing more than the extension of domestic political processes to the regional level.[58] During the Cold War, the important domestic sources of Asia's international politics were often obscured by the unremitting focus on the superpowers. For instance, while often seen as a U.S. proxy in Asia, Japan carved out a distinctive regional voice through participation in the conference of the nonaligned movement held in Bandung, Indonesia, in 1955 and through its leading role in the creation of the developmental and inclusive Asian Development Bank of 1966. Today, international relations scholars who focus excessively on the rise of China and its challenge to the United States easily overlook the ways in which China is an Asian nation that fits the Asian model and is thus a natural leader in the region's politics.

This book began by justifying Asia as a region (comprised of Southeast Asia and Northeast Asia) based on its geography, intensity of interactions, and emerging identity. The fact that Asia is an ocean-based geography has tended to strengthen both the intensity of its interactions and its identity, because oceans increase trade and communication, and they blur the strict lines of sovereignty that define land-based regions.[59] The strong and sovereignty-conscious states of Asia have been forced by necessity to develop a regional approach to many public policy issues. As a result, there is now a regional politics of Asia that is not reducible to Sino-U.S. rivalry.

The notion of a distinctive Asian approach to international politics has often been discussed under the heading of "Eastphalia,"[60] a play on words relating to the dominant Western mode of international politics that can be traced to the 1648 Peace of Westphalia. When China's premier proclaimed the "rejuvenation of Oriental civilization" in 2011, he was repeating an age-old belief that at some point in world history, the precolonial glory of Asia would be restored. For the world, there is always a temptation to heed the advice offered in 1894 by the young French Prince Henri d'Orléans: "Be Asiatic, there lies the future!"[61]

There are various external dimensions of public policy that are included in the idea of Eastphalia: trade, security, environment, regulation, and much else. In all of these areas, Asian governments have pursued policies that reflect the imperatives of the Asian Governance Model. More narrowly, they have pursued external policies consistent with the public policy aims of "Big, Fast Results." Asian economic integration policies, for instance, have been based on piecemeal, quick deals and often unilateral liberalization in the interests of national economic development. Japanese-led initiatives to build Asian economic integration that date back to World War II and continue today under the rubric of the Regional Comprehensive Economic Partnership also reflect distinctive Asian policy approaches. These include weak intellectual property provisions, protections for states against foreign investor claims, support for state-backed enterprises, and the protection of agriculture from imports. Meanwhile, both Japanese and Chinese aid to Africa reflects developmental approaches that emphasize infrastructure, resources, and education. The debate is whether this "new aid paradigm" might deliver better results for these countries.[62]

At the most general level, Asia is a region populated by dominant and authoritative states, which means it is no surprise to find that external policies that undermine or surrender state dominance are nonstarters. There is, for instance, a widespread Asian rejection of international refugee law, because it would complicate sovereign noninterference among Asian nations.[63] Asian states have also interpreted the "responsibility to protect" doctrine, under which the international community may intervene to save lives, in a way that is largely focused on the reinforcement of state sovereignty.[64]

Sovereignty is not simply a rhetorical principle in Asia (which is more true of *weak* state regions like Africa) but also a matter of practice. There is, simply put, little room for the seedlings of cosmopolitanism to grown in a region of dominant and effective states. Regionalism has never been allowed to accelerate state weakness in places like Myanmar, Cambodia, or North Korea. The Association of Southeast Asian Nations (ASEAN), which sits at the center of Asian regionalism, condemned and continually opposed Vietnam's intervention in Cambodia in 1979, insisting that the brutal Khmer Rouge regime hold Cambodia's UN seat until 1992. China vetoed and Indonesia abstained from a U.S. attempt to censure Myanmar in the UN Security Council in 2007, a watershed moment that led to the Asian-style "Bangkok Process" of inclusion and diplomacy, which was vindicated by Myanmar's subsequent decision to initiate political reforms. There are no institutions like a human rights court, a regional parliament, or a regional monetary union that might compete with domestic institutions. Asian regional institutions have sought to enhance state capacity, not undermine it.

The state-led nature of foreign policy making in Asia can be observed by comparing the number of civil society groups from each country that are accredited to the United Nations Economic and Social Council, the UN body that deliberates on nonsecurity issues. Countries that are richer, more democratic, and have larger populations generally have more civil society groups represented at the body, and this is true of Asian states, as well. Yet when we compare Asian states with non-Asian states that are roughly similar in terms of population, regime, and development, we find a consistently lower level of civil society participation from Asia, with the perennial exception of the Philippines (see Figure 6.4). Cosmopolitan and confident Singapore, with fifteen groups registered, barely pips the insular and tyrannical United Arab Emirates, with fourteen, thanks to a membership roll that includes the World Toilet Organization and the Restroom Association of Singapore. Within Asia, meanwhile, attempts to create a civil society–led regionalism founder because of the inability of states to refrain from structuring and co-opting civil society participation.[65]

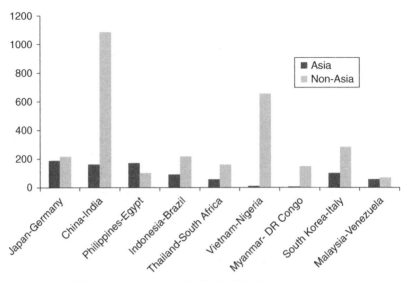

FIGURE 6.4. Civil society groups at the United Nations.
Source: United Nations Economic and Social Council.

In this sense, Eastphalia reinforces a core principle of Westphalia that was often seen as under threat in the post–Cold War era – the formal sovereignty of the state. Indeed, some believe that the international politics of Asia is a throwback to Western modernity, when conceptions like the state, democracy, economic performance, and integrative nationalism were the coin of the realm.[66] The main difference is that domestic accountability pressures push leaders to adopt developmental and peace-building policies in Asia rather than aggressive or destructive ones. Given its population, economic growth, multiple territorial disputes, and many cultural differences, Asia should be bristling with conflict. Moreover, the region's governments are not all democratic, and there are no effective collective security institutions that operate at the regional level. Nonetheless, since the end of the Vietnam wars in 1979, the region has been an unexpected zone of peace. Battle deaths have declined precipitously, even faster than they have elsewhere.[67]

The role of the United States as an external guarantor of stability cannot be ignored. Tough security issues, like the situation of North Korea, continue to be managed with a strong U.S. role, and Asian nations are nearly united in their belief that the U.S. presence is indispensable.[68] But domestic imperatives also constrain aggressive behavior, even when tensions and stakes are high. Just as democracy is deliberative and majoritarian in domestic policy, so, too, is external policy more easily unlinked from minority, hard-line voices. The border dispute between Thailand and Cambodia over the eleventh-century Hindu Preah Vihear temple is a classic case: The dispute is laced with nationalist and territorial interests but remains peaceful even in the absence of any U.S. or regional intervention and despite the presence in government on both sides of political parties with war-mongering constituencies. Simply put, Asian governments were built on political survival strategies of growth and development.[69] The creation of modern states under colonialism redirected super-legitimated rulers toward development, creating an external "foreign policy shift" away from dangerous and aggressive nationalism. As a result, while major interstate war is not unthinkable in Asia, the probabilities and likely magnitudes of such conflicts are reduced.

Asian notions of external order are also less anarchic and more hierarchical. The origins of this may lie in the "hierarchical stability" of the Chinese tributary system,[70] as well as the various *mandala* tributary systems of Southeast Asia.[71] Asian notions of external order map their notions of internal order – they are based on relationships, on assumptions of hierarchy, and on majoritarian or network inclusion as organizing principles.[72] Sovereignty, as in the domestic case, is not based on "hard power" attributes of wealth and arms but rather on "soft power" attributes of legitimacy, culture, and developmental attainments. A common theme of studies of Asian regional politics, especially compared to regionalism elsewhere, is its heavy reliance on socialization and enmeshment of the "less civilized" by the "more civilized." As such, there is every reason for less-developed or admired states to accept the leadership of those that are better-developed or admired.

This domination of great powers based on cultural attainments was seen not just in the Chinese tributary systems but also in Japan's World War II Greater East Asia Co-Prosperity Sphere. Japan's 1942 document *Matters Concerning Policy Towards Thailand*, its lone Asian ally, vowed to "pay heed to the present sovereignty of the Thai people," while at the same time ensuring that "Thailand will be truly guided by Japan" and enjoy "alignment with the ideals" of the Japanese empire.[73]

Because these fundamental reasons for the Asian peace are domestic, scholars who scour the region for systemic explanations beyond the U.S. role usually come up empty-handed. Formal structures of collective security are absent in the region. Attempts by the United States to create a collective security organization for Asia (known as SEATO) fell apart in 1977 after two decades of tepid interest. The most that can be observed is the operation of informal processes of communication and consensus building within the region, which have often been called "the ASEAN Way."[74]

It remains an open question whether this Eastphalian system is sufficient to meet the complex governance challenges of Asia in the twenty-first century. Some analysts believe that Asia will require binding collective action through formal mechanisms of supranational sovereignty.[75] But grand, new regional and international institutions have not proven the most effective remedy for many of these problems. Instead, informal and ad hoc state-led responses, in concert with like-minded states, have proven more effective. As with democracy, regionalism can be embraced by strong Asia states without losing their identity or power. Asian states, for example, have endorsed limited actions of "intervention" in the cases of postindependence peacekeeping forces in East Timor in 1999 and a regional humanitarian task force for Myanmar after Cyclone Nargis in 2008. They have worked toward the establishment of a regional human rights forum that would provide resources for shared goals in areas like human trafficking, education, and criminal procedures. But the global governance agenda and new institutions have been adopted and interpreted in a manner that is consistent with Asian notions of formal sovereignty wed to informal hierarchy.

As with the challenge of the environment, creating public policies that ensure external security, a well-regulated regional economy, and shared governance norms is something that Asian governments have yet to solve. But a bias for hope about the region is well-justified. The quasi-religious political orders that were transformed into modern states throughout Asia were once thought unlikely to develop, unlikely to democratize, unlikely to reform their public sectors, and unlikely to expand welfare. All of those predictions have proven false. Improved global governance in the twenty-first century will not only depend on Asia but will also have much to learn from it.

Notes

Preface

1. "Strengthen Good-Neighborly Relations and Deepen Mutually Beneficial Cooperation: Speech by Premier Wen Jiabao at Balai Kartini," *Xinhua News Agency*, April 30, 2011.
2. Pierre Leroy-Beaulieu and Richard Davey, *The Awakening of the East: Siberia – Japan – China* (New York: McClure, Phillips & Co., 1900); Kakuzo Okakura, *The Awakening of Japan* (New York: Century, 1904); Robert P. Porter, *Japan: The Rise of a Modern Power* (Oxford: Clarendon Press, 1918); Henry Mayers Hyndman, *The Awakening of Asia* (London: Cassell, 1919).

1. Introduction

1. The founding date of the Malacca Sultanate is in some dispute. In 2011, a group of Malaysian historians claimed new evidence that it had been founded in 1262.
2. This section draws heavily on Kernial Singh Sandhu, Paul Wheatley, and Ton Abdul Aziz bin Mat, *Melaka: The Transformation of a Malay Capital, c. 1400–1980*, 2 vols. (New York: Oxford University Press, 1983).
3. Craig A. Lockard, "'The Sea Common to All': Maritime Frontiers, Port Cities, and Chinese Traders in the Southeast Asian Age of Commerce, ca. 1400–1750," *Journal of World History* 21, no. 2 (2010): 219–47, 229.
4. Ibid., 230.
5. Craig A. Lockard, *Southeast Asia in World History* (Oxford: Oxford University Press, 2009), 52.
6. Benjamin J. Cohen and Eric M. P. Chiu, *Power in a Changing World Economy: Lessons from East Asia* (New York: Routledge, 2013).
7. R. O. Whyte, "The Ecological Setting," in *Melaka: The Transformation of a Malay Capital*, ed. Sandhu, Wheatley, and Abdul Aziz bin Mat, 70–97, 74.

8. Liaw Yock Fang, "The Undang-Undang Melaka," in *Melaka: The Transformation of a Malay Capital*, ed. Sandhu, Wheatley, and Abdul Aziz bin Mat, 180–94, 192.

9. Zinal Abidin bin Abdul Wahid, "Power and Authority in the Melaka Sultanate," in *Melaka: The Transformation of a Malay Capital*, ed. Sandhu, Wheatley, and Abdul Aziz bin Mat, 101–12, 103.

10. Kenneth R. Hall, *A History of Early Southeast Asia: Maritime Trade and Societal Development, 100–1500* (Lanham, MD: Rowman & Littlefield), 309.

11. Ibid., 339.

12. J. Kathirithamby-Wells, "Introduction," in *The Southeast Asian Port and Polity: Rise and Demise*, ed. J. Kathirithamby-Wells and John Villiers, 1–16 (Singapore: National University of Singapore Press, 1990), 13.

13. Angela Schottenhammer, *Trading Networks in Early Modern East Asia* (Wiesbaden: Harrassowitz, 2011).

14. Lockard, "'The Sea Common to All,'" 221.

15. Kernial Singh Sandhu, Paul Wheatley, and Ton Abdul Aziz bin Mat, "From Capital to Municipality," in *Melaka: The Transformation of a Malay Capital*, ed. Sandhu, Wheatley, and Abdul Aziz bin Mat, 495–597, 547.

16. Donald F. Lach and Edwin J. Van Kley, *Asia in the Making of Europe* (Chicago: University of Chicago Press, 1965), 287.

17. Barbara Watson Andaya, "Melaka under the Dutch, 1641–1795," in *Melaka: The Transformation of a Malay Capital*, ed. Sandhu, Wheatley, and Abdul Aziz bin Mat, 193–241.

18. Hugo Grotius, *The Freedom of the Seas, or, the Right Which Belongs to the Dutch to Take Part in the East Indian Trade* (1633). On this, see Martine Julia van Ittersum, *Profit and Principle: Hugo Grotius, Natural Rights Theories and the Rise of Dutch Power in the East Indies, 1595–1615* (Leiden: Brill, 2006); Peter Borschberg, *The Singapore and Melaka Straits: Violence, Security, and Diplomacy in the 17th Century* (Singapore: National University of Singapore Press, 2010).

19. Sandhu, Wheatley, and Abdul Aziz bin Mat, "From Capital to Municipality," 517.

20. Andaya, "Melaka under the Dutch, 1641–1795," 221.

21. C. M. Turnbull, "Melaka under British Colonial Rule," in *Melaka: The Transformation of a Malay Capital*, ed. Sandhu, Wheatley, and Abdul Aziz bin Mat, 242–96.

22. Graham Irwin, "Melaka Fort," in *Melaka: The Transformation of a Malay Capital*, ed. Sandhu, Wheatley, and Abdul Aziz bin Mat, 782–805, 802.

23. Anne Booth, "Night Watchman, Extractive, or Developmental States? Some Evidence from Late Colonial South-East Asia," *Economic History Review* 60, no. 2 (2007): 241–66.

24. Henry Norman, *The Peoples and Politics of the Far East; Travels and Studies in the British, French, Spanish and Portuguese Colonies, Siberia, China, Japan, Korea, Siam and Malaya* (London: T. F. Unwin, 1900), 44.

25. Tjoa Hock Guan, "The Social and Political Ideas of Tun Datuk Sir Tan Cheng Lock," in *Melaka: The Transformation of a Malay Capital*, ed. Sandhu, Wheatley, and Abdul Aziz bin Mat, 299–323.

26. Yoji Akashi, "The Japanese Occupation of Melaka," in *Melaka: The Transformation of a Malay Capital*, ed. Sandhu, Wheatley, and Abdul Aziz bin Mat, 311–87.

27. "Melaka Government to Develop Aviation Sports," *Bernama Daily Malaysian News*, June 11, 2011.

28. United Nations Educational, Scientific, and Cultural Organization (UNESCO) World Heritage List, "Description: Melaka and George Town, Historic Cities of the Straits of Malacca," http://whc.unesco.org/en/list/1223/.

29. Joel S. Kahn and Francis Kok-Wah Loh, *Fragmented Vision: Culture and Politics in Contemporary Malaysia* (Honolulu: University of Hawaii Press, 1992).

30. Ismail Abdul Hamid, "The Monarchy and Party Politics in Malaysia in the Era of Abdullah Ahmad Badawi (2003–09): The Resurgence of the Role of Protector," *Asian Survey* 52, no. 5 (2012): 900–23.

31. Nigel Worden, "'Where It All Began': The Representation of Malaysian Heritage in Melaka," *International Journal of Heritage Studies* 7, no. 3 (2001): 199–218, 202–3.

32. Kenneth Hall, "The Roots of ASEAN: Regional Identities in the Strait of Melaka Region circa 1500 C.E.," *Asian Journal of Social Science* 29, no. 1 (2001): 87–119.

33. Clifford Geertz, *The Interpretation of Cultures: Selected Essays* (New York: Basic Books, 1973).

34. James C. Scott, *Domination and the Arts of Resistance: Hidden Transcripts* (New Haven: Yale University Press, 1990).

35. Samuel P. Huntington, *The Clash of Civilizations and the Remaking of World Order* (New York: Simon & Schuster, 1996).

36. Shintaro Hamanaka, "Is Trade in Asia Really Integrating?" *ADB Working Papers on Regional Integration*, no. 91 (2012).

37. Asian Development Bank, "Progress in Regional Cooperation and Integration," *Asian Economic Integration Monitor* (October 2013): 15–17.

38. Asian Development Bank, *Financial Integration in Emerging Asia* (Manila: Asian Development Bank, 2011); Giovanni Capannelli, Jong-Wha Lee, and Peter A. Petri, "Economic Interdependence in Asia: Developing Indicators for Regional Integration and Cooperation," *Singapore Economic Review* 55, no. 1 (2010): 125–61.

39. World Tourism Organization, *Yearbook of Tourism Statistics: 2005–2009* (Madrid: World Tourism Organization, 2011); Capannelli, Lee, and Petri, "Economic Interdependence in Asia," 139, fig. 9.

40. John M. Steadman, *The Myth of Asia* (New York: Simon & Schuster, 1969).

41. Reinhard Bendix, *Max Weber An Intellectual Portrait*, 1st ed. (Garden City, NY: Doubleday, 1960), 117.

42. Dan Slater, *Ordering Power: Contentious Politics and Authoritarian Leviathans in Southeast Asia* (Cambridge: Cambridge University Press, 2011); T. V. Paul, *South Asia's Weak States: Understanding the Regional Insecurity Predicament* (University Press: Stanford Security Studies, 2011).

43. George McTurnan Kahin and Harold C. Hinton, *Major Governments of Asia* (Ithaca: Cornell University Press, 1958); Roy C. Macridis and Robert Edward Ward, *Modern Political Systems: Asia* (Englewood Cliffs, NJ: Prentice Hall, 1963).

44. Key works include C. I. Eugene Kim and Lawrence Ziring, *An Introduction to Asian Politics* (Englewood Cliffs, NJ: Prentice Hall, 1977); James C. F. Wang, *Comparative Asian Politics: Power, Policy, and Change* (Englewood Cliffs, NJ: Prentice Hall, 1994); Vera Simone, *The Asian Pacific: Political and Economic Development in a Global Context*, 2nd ed. (New York: Longman; 2001); Xiaoming Huang, *Politics in Pacific Asia: An Introduction* (New York: Palgrave Macmillan, 2009); Peter Ferdinand, *Governance in Pacific Asia Political Economy and Development from Japan to Burma* (London: Continuum, 2012).

45. Francis Fukuyama, *Trust: The Social Virtues and the Creation of Prosperity* (New York: Free Press, 1995).

46. Selig S. Harrison, *The Widening Gulf: Asian Nationalism and American Policy* (New York: Free Press, 1978).

47. Evan A. Feigenbaum and Robert A. Manning, "The United States in the New Asia," in *Council Special Reports* (New York: Council on Foreign Relations, 2009), 10.

48. David Martin Jones, *Political Development in Pacific Asia* (Cambridge: Polity Press, 1997).

49. Yumei Zhang, *Pacific Asia: The Politics of Development* (New York: Routledge, 2003).

50. A good summary is Joseph A. Camilleri, *States, Markets, and Civil Society in Asia-Pacific* (Cheltenham: Edward Elgar, 2000), 359.

51. Confucius, *Analects* (13.9).

52. Richard Boyd and Tak-Wing Ngo, *State Making in Asia* (London: Routledge, 2006); Kullada Kesboonchoo Mead, *The Rise and Decline of Thai Absolutism*, 1st ed. (New York: RoutledgeCurzon, 2004).

53. Susan Carpenter, *Special Corporations and the Bureaucracy: Why Japan Can't Reform* (New York: Palgrave Macmillan, 2003).

54. Staffan Burenstam Linder, *The Pacific Century: Economic and Political Consequences of Asian-Pacific Dynamism* (Stanford: Stanford University Press, 1986); Steve Chan, *East Asian Dynamism: Growth, Order, and Security in the Pacific Region*, Dilemmas in World Politics (Boulder: Westview Press, 1990); A. J. H. Latham and Heita Kawakatsu, *Asia Pacific Dynamism, 1550–2000* (London: Routledge, 2000); Jeffrey Henderson, *East Asian Transformation: On the Political Economy of Dynamism, Governance and Crisis* (London: Routledge, 2011).

55. Frank-Jürgen Richter, *The East Asian Development Model: Economic Growth, Institutional Failure, and the Aftermath of the Crisis* (New York: St. Martin's Press, 2000); David Anthony Hollingsworth, *The Rise, the Fall, and the Recovery of Southeast Asia's Minidragons* (Lanham, MD: Lexington Books, 2007).

56. Francis Doré, *Les régimes politiques en Asie* (Paris: Presses universitaires de France, 1973), 17.

2. State and Society

1. Henry Norman, *The Peoples and Politics of the Far East; Travels and Studies in the British, French, Spanish and Portuguese Colonies, Siberia, China, Japan, Korea, Siam and Malaya* (London: T. F. Unwin, 1900), 229–30.
2. Sangmin Bae, "Is the Death Penalty an Asian Value?," *Asian Affairs* 39, no. 1 (2008): 47–56.
3. The following figures are from David T. Johnson and Franklin E. Zimring, *The Next Frontier: National Development, Political Change, and the Death Penalty in Asia* (Oxford: Oxford University Press, 2009), 108, 60, 64, 403, 312.
4. Ibid., 317. See also Roger Hood and Surya Deva, *Confronting Capital Punishment in Asia: Human Rights, Politics and Public Opinion* (Oxford: Oxford University Press, 2014).
5. Johnson and Zimring, *The Next Frontier: National Development, Political Change, and the Death Penalty in Asia*, 304.
6. Ibid., 111.
7. Ibid., 406.
8. Ibid., 89.
9. Ibid., 86.
10. Fort Fu-Te Liao, "The Abolition of the Death Penalty in Taiwan: Why a De Facto Moratorium Was Established and Lost," *Asia-Pacific Journal on Human Rights & the Law* 11, no. 1 (2010): 1–22.
11. N. Ganesan and Sung Chull Kim, *State Violence in East Asia* (Lexington: University Press of Kentucky, 2013).
12. "A Matter of Life and Death," *The Economist*, March 27, 2010, 50, italics added.
13. Confucius, *Analects: With Selection from Traditional Commentaries*, ed. Edward G. Slingerland (Indianapolis, IN: Hackett Publishing Company, 2003), 144.
14. Jongwoo Han, *Power, Place, and State-Society Relations in Korea: Neo-Confucian and Geomantic Reconstruction of Developmental State and Democratization* (Lanham, MD: Lexington Books, 2013).
15. Aristotle, *The Politics* (Oxford: Oxford University Press, 2009), secs. 85a:21, 27b:24–30.
16. Michael Curtis, *Orientalism and Islam: European Thinkers on Oriental Despotism in the Middle East and India* (Cambridge: Cambridge University Press, 2009).
17. Charles de Secondat Montesquieu, *De l'esprit des lois* (Paris: Editions Garnier Fréres, 1962), vol. 1, 68.
18. Perry Anderson, *Lineages of the Absolutist State* (London: New Left Books, 1974), 414.
19. Ibid., 397–400, 72.
20. Benedict R. O'G. Anderson, "The Idea of Power in Javanese Culture," in *Culture and Politics in Indonesia*, ed. Claire Holt, 1–69 (Ithaca, NY: Cornell University Press, 1972), 24–25.
21. Curtis, *Orientalism and Islam: European Thinkers on Oriental Despotism in the Middle East and India*, 53.

22. Etienne de Silhouette, *Idée générale du gouvernement et de la morale des Chinois* (Paris: G.-F. Quillau, 1729); Francois Quesnay, *Despotism in China*, ed. Lewis A. Maverick and George Dognini (San Antonio, TX: P. Anderson, 1767 [1946]).
23. Jean-Baptiste Du Halde, *The General History of China. Containing a Geographical, Historical, Chronological, Political and Physical Description of the Empire of China, Chinese-Tartary, Corea, and Thibet. Including an Exact and Particular Account of Their Customs, Manners, Ceremonies, Religion, Arts and Sciences*, 3rd ed. (London: J. Watts, 1736).
24. Xiaoming Huang, *Politics in Pacific Asia: An Introduction* (New York: Palgrave Macmillan, 2009), 61.
25. Anthony B. Cheung, "Executive-Led Governance or Executive Power 'Hollowed-out' – The Political Quagmire of Hong Kong," *Asian Journal of Political Science* 15, no. 1 (2007): 17–38.
26. Claudia Derichs and Thomas Heberer, *The Power of Ideas: Intellectual Input and Political Change in East and Southeast Asia* (Copenhagen: Nordic Institute of Asian Studies, 2006).
27. Anderson, "The Idea of Power in Javanese Culture," 18, 19, 52.
28. Joji Watanuki, "State Formation and Nation-Building in East Asia," *International Social Science Journal* 23, no. 3 (1971): 421–36.
29. William Case, "Sayonara to the Strong State: From Government to Governance in the Asia-Pacific," in *Governance in the Asia-Pacific*, ed. R. A. Maidment, David Goldblatt, and Jeremy Mitchell, 250–74 (London: Routledge, 1998), 272.
30. Julia C. Strauss, *Strong Institutions in Weak Polities: State Building in Republican China, 1927–1940* (Oxford: Oxford University Press, 1998).
31. Amy Blitz, "The Philippines: The Contested State," in *Nation Building, State Building, and Economic Development: Case Studies and Comparisons*, ed. S. C. M. Paine, 48–65 (New York: M. E. Sharpe, 2009); P. N. Abinales and Donna J. Amoroso, *State and Society in the Philippines* (Lanham, MD: Rowman & Littlefield Publishers, 2005).
32. Gloria Macapagal-Arroyo, *Strong Republic: Selected Speeches of President Gloria Macapagal-Arroyo* (Manila: Philippine Information Agency, 2002).
33. Erik Martinez Kuhonta, "Studying States in Southeast Asia," in *Southeast Asia in Political Science: Theory, Region, and Qualitative Analysis*, ed. Erik Martinez Kuhonta, Dan Slater, and Tuong Vu, 30–54 (Stanford, CA: Stanford University Press, 2008), 31.
34. Milton J. Esman, *Administration and Development in Malaysia; Institution Building and Reform in a Plural Society* (Ithaca, NY: Cornell University Press, 1972).
35. Fred Warren Riggs, *Thailand: The Modernization of a Bureaucratic Polity* (Honolulu, HI: East-West Center Press, 1966).
36. Andrew J. MacIntyre, *Business and Politics in Indonesia*, Southeast Asia Publications Series (North Sydney: Allen & Unwin, 1991).
37. Kuhonta, "Studying States in Southeast Asia," 39.
38. Ibid.

39. William Case, "Semi-Democracy and Minimalist Federalism in Malaysia," in *Federalism in Asia*, ed. Baogang He, Brian Galligan, and Takashi Inoguchi, 124–43 (Cheltenham: Edward Elgar, 2007).

40. Lorenz Blume and Stefan Voigt, "Federalism and Decentralization – A Critical Survey of Frequently Used Indicators," *Constitutional Political Economy* 22, no. 1 (2011), tab. 1.

41. Baogang He, Brian Galligan, and Takashi Inoguchi, *Federalism in Asia* (Cheltenham: Edward Elgar, 2007).

42. Marco Bünte, "Decentralization and Democratic Governance in Southeast Asia: Theoretical Views, Conceptual Pitfalls and Empirical Ambiguities," in *Critical Studies of the Asia-Pacific*, ed. Aurel Croissant and Marco Bünte (New York: Palgrave Macmillan, 2011); Paul J. Smoke, Eduardo J. Gómez, and George E. Peterson, *Decentralization in Asia and Latin America: Towards a Comparative Interdisciplinary Perspective* (Cheltenham: Edward Elgar, 2006).

43. Maribeth Erb, Priyambudi Sulistiyanto, and Carole Faucher, *Regionalism in Post-Suharto Indonesia* (London: RoutledgeCurzon, 2005); Syaikhu Usman, *Indonesia's Decentralization Policy: Initial Experiences and Emerging Problems* (Jakarta: SMERU Research Institute, 2001); Coen Holtzappel and Martin Ramstedt, *Decentralization and Regional Autonomy in Indonesia: Implementation and Challenges* (Singapore: Institute of Southeast Asian Studies, 2009).

44. Blume and Voigt, "Federalism and Decentralization – A Critical Survey of Frequently Used Indicators."

45. Vedi R. Hadiz, *Localising Power in Post-Authoritarian Indonesia: A Southeast Asia Perspective* (Stanford, CA: Stanford University Press, 2011); Mark Turner, *Central-Local Relations in Asia-Pacific: Convergence or Divergence?*, International Political Economy Series (New York: St. Martin's Press, 1999).

46. Jürgen Rüland, "Governance, Decentralisation and Democratisation in Southeast Asia," *European Journal of East Asian Studies* 11, no. 1 (2012): 5–16.

47. Kai Kaiser, Daan Pattinasarany, and Gunter Schulze, "Decentralization, Governance, and Public Services in Indonesia," in *Decentralization in Asia and Latin America: Towards a Comparative Interdisciplinary Perspective*, ed. Paul J. Smoke, Eduardo J. Gómez, and George E. Peterson, 164–207 (Cheltenham: Edward Elgar, 2006), 168.

48. Syarif Hidayat and Hans Antlov, "Decentralization and Regional Autonomy in Indonesia," in *Decentralization, Democratic Governance, and Civil Society in Comparative Perspective: Africa, Asia, and Latin America*, ed. Philip Oxhorn, Joseph S. Tulchin, and Andrew D. Selee, 266–91 (Washington, DC: Woodrow Wilson Center Press, 2004), 279.

49. "Megawati against the Federal State Concept," *Jakarta Post*, July 17, 2000.

50. "People's Welfare Improvement yet To Be Seen in Regional Autonomy," *Antara News Agency*, April 26, 2011.

51. Peter Blunt and Mark Turner, "Decentralisation, Democracy and Development in a Post-Conflict Society: Commune Councils in Cambodia," *Public Administration and Development* 25, no. 1 (2005): 75–87.

52. Huang, *Politics in Pacific Asia: An Introduction*, 57.

53. Aristotle, *The Politics*, sec. III.ix.3.

54. Margaret Levi, *Of Rule and Revenue* (Berkeley: University of California Press, 1988).

55. Ray Huang, *Taxation and Governmental Finance in Sixteenth-Century Ming China* (London: Cambridge University Press, 1974).

56. Wenxian Zhang, "The Yellow Register Archives of Imperial Ming China," *Libraries & the Cultural Record* 43, no. 2 (2008): 148–75.

57. Madeleine Zelin, *The Magistrate's Tael: Rationalizing Fiscal Reform in Eighteenth-Century Qing China* (Berkeley: University of California Press, 1984).

58. Bartolomé Yun Casalilla and Patrick Karl O'Brien, *The Rise of Fiscal States: A Global History, 1500–1914* (New York: Cambridge University Press, 2012).

59. TransResearch Consortium, "Relative Political Extraction."

60. Ja Ian Chong, *External Intervention and the Politics of State Formation: China, Indonesia, and Thailand, 1893–1952* (Cambridge: Cambridge University Press, 2012).

61. Tuong Vu, "Studying the State through State Formation," *World Politics* 62, no. 1 (2010): 148–75.

62. Yung-myung Kim, "Understanding East Asian Political Systems," *Sungkyun Journal of East Asian Studies* 3, no. 1 (2003): 45–78, 55–56.

63. Vince Boudreau, "Interpreting State Violence in Asian Settings," in *State Violence in East Asia*, ed. N. Ganesan and Sung Chull Kim, 19–46 (Lexington: University Press of Kentucky, 2013).

64. Mary P. Callahan, *Making Enemies: War and State Building in Burma* (Ithaca, NY: Cornell University Press, 2003).

65. Karl August Wittfogel, *Oriental Despotism: A Comparative Study of Total Power* (New York: Vintage, 1957 [1981]), 21.

66. Ibid., 200.

67. Ibid., 49, 50.

68. Ibid., 17, 18.

69. Aristotle, *The Politics*, secs. 85.a.21, 27.b.24–30.

70. Nicolas Antoine Boulanger, *Recherches sur l'origine du despotisme Oriental* [*Research into the Origins of Oriental Despotism*] (Amsterdam, 1764).

71. Max Weber, *Economy and Society: An Outline of Interpretive Sociology*, ed. Guenther Roth and Claus Wittich, 2 vols. (Berkeley: University of California Press, 1922 [1978]), vol. 2, 629, 508, 507, 508.

72. Max Weber, *The Religion of China: Confucianism and Taoism* (Glencoe: Free Press, 1951), 215, 63, 27, 135.

73. Robert Heine-Geldern, *Conceptions of State and Kingship in Southeast Asia* (Ithaca, NY: Southeast Asia Program, Dept. of Far Eastern Studies, Cornell University, 1956).

74. Anderson, "The Idea of Power in Javanese Culture," 25.

75. Benjamin Schwartz, "The Primacy of Political Order in East Asian Societies," in *China and Other Matters*, 114–24 (Cambridge, MA: Harvard University Press, 1996), 115, 117.

76. Confucius, *Analects* 12:7.
77. Stephen McCarthy, *The Political Theory of Tyranny in Singapore and Burma: Aristotle and the Rhetoric of Benevolent Despotism* (New York: Routledge, 2006).
78. Montesquieu, *De l'esprit des lois*, bk. 8, sec. 11.
79. George McTurnan Kahin, "Indonesia," in *Major Governments of Asia*, ed. George McTurnan Kahin and Harold C. Hinton, 535–689 (Ithaca, NY: Cornell University Press, 1963), 540–41.
80. Lucian W. Pye, *Asian Power and Politics: The Cultural Dimensions of Authority* (Cambridge, MA: Belknap Press, 1985), 285, 320, 321, 329, 329, 339.
81. Yang Zhong, "Legitimacy Crisis and Legitimation in China," *Journal of Contemporary Asia* 26, no. 2 (1996): 201–20; X. L. Ding, *The Decline of Communism in China: Legitimacy Crisis, 1977–1989* (Cambridge; New York: Cambridge University Press, 1994).
82. Muthiah Alagappa, ed., *Political Legitimacy in Southeast Asia: The Quest for Moral Authority* (Palo Alto, CA: Stanford University Press, 1995).
83. Robert W. Compton, "Reconstructing Political Legitimacy in Asia: Globalization and Political Development," *International Journal on World Peace* 17, no. 4 (2000): 19–39, 29, 20, 31, 36.
84. John Kane, Hui-Chieh Loy, and Haig Patapan, "Introduction to the Special Issue: The Search for Legitimacy in Asia," *Politics & Policy* 38, no. 3 (2010): 381–94.
85. Bruce Gilley, "Legitimacy and Institutional Change: The Case of China," *Comparative Political Studies* 41, no. 3 (2008): 259–84; Thomas Heberer and Gunter Schubert, *Regime Legitimacy in Contemporary China: Institutional Change and Stability* (New York: Routledge, 2009); Yongnian Zheng, *The Chinese Communist Party as Organizational Emperor: Culture, Reproduction and Transformation* (New York: Routledge, 2010).
86. Greg Barton, "Indonesia: Legitimacy, Secular Democracy, and Islam," *Politics & Policy* 38, no. 3 (2010): 471–96; Marcus Mietzner, "Indonesia in 2009: Electoral Contestation and Economic Resilience," *Asian Survey* 50, no. 1 (2010): 185–94.
87. Leonardo Morlino, Björn Dressel, and Riccardo Pelizzo, "The Quality of Democracy in Asia-Pacific: Issues and Findings," *International Political Science Review* 32, no. 5 (2011): 491–511, 505.
88. Bruce Gilley, "The Meaning and Measure of State Legitimacy: Results for 72 Countries," *European Journal of Political Research* 45, no. 3 (2006): 499–525; Bruce Gilley, "State Legitimacy: An Updated Dataset for 52 Countries," *European Journal of Political Research* 51, no. 3 (2012): 693–99.
89. Blunt and Turner, "Decentralisation, Democracy and Development in a Post-Conflict Society: Commune Councils in Cambodia," 77–78.
90. G. Carter Bentley, "Indigenous States of Southeast Asia," *Annual Review of Anthropology* 15 (1986): 275–305.
91. Ian Charles Harris, *Buddhism, Power and Political Order* (New York: Routledge, 2007); Ruiping Fan, *The Renaissance of Confucianism in Contemporary China*, 1st ed. (New York: Springer, 2010).

92. Pye, *Asian Power and Politics: The Cultural Dimensions of Authority*, 47.
93. Yoshiko Ashiwa and David L. Wank, *Making Religion, Making the State: The Politics of Religion in Modern China* (Stanford, CA: Stanford University Press, 2009); Jinhua Chen, *Legend and Legitimation: The Formation of Tendai Esoteric Buddhism in Japan* (Brussels: Institut belge des hautes études chinoises, 2009); Harris, *Buddhism, Power and Political Order*; Suksamran Somboon, *Buddhism and Political Legitimacy* (Bangkok: Chulalongkorn University Press, 1993).
94. B. L. Putnam Weale, *The Fight for the Republic in China* (New York: Dodd, Mead and Company, 1917).
95. Adrian Chan, "Confucianism and Development in East Asia," *Journal of Contemporary Asia* 26, no. 1 (1996): 28–45, 37.
96. Yaoji Jin, *Chinese Society and Politics* (New York: Oxford University Press, 2005); Zhenglai Deng and Sujian Guo, *Reviving Legitimacy: Lessons for and from China* (Lanham, MD: Lexington Books, 2010); Fan, *The Renaissance of Confucianism in Contemporary China*; Xiaoqin Guo, *State and Society in China's Democratic Transition: Confucianism, Leninism, and Economic Development* (New York: Routledge, 2003).
97. Chan, "Confucianism and Development in East Asia," 32.
98. Anthony Reid, *Southeast Asia in the Early Modern Era: Trade, Power, and Belief*, Asia, East by South (Ithaca, NY: Cornell University Press, 1993); Bardwell L. Smith, *Religion and Legitimation of Power in Thailand, Laos, and Burma* (Chambersburg, PA: Anima Books, 1978).
99. Joseph Kitigawa, "Buddhism and Asian Politics," *Asian Survey* 2, no. 5 (1962): 1–11, 5.
100. Yoneo Ishii, "Thai Muslims and the Royal Patronage of Religion," *Law & Society Review* 28, no. 3 (1994): 453–60.
101. Adam D. Tyson, *Decentralization and Adat Revivalism in Indonesia: The Politics of Becoming Indigenous* (London; New York: Routledge, 2010); Michael Francis Laffan, *The Makings of Indonesian Islam: Orientalism and the Narration of a Sufi Past* (Princeton, NJ: Princeton University Press, 2013).
102. Charles F. Keyes, Laurel Kendall, and Helen Hardacre, "Introduction: Contested Visions of Community in East and Southeast Asia," in *Asian Visions of Authority: Religion and the Modern States of East and Southeast Asia*, ed. Charles F. Keyes, Laurel Kendall, and Helen Hardacre, 1–16 (Honolulu: University of Hawaii Press, 1994), 1.
103. Ibid., 4–5.
104. Charles F. Keyes, "Buddhists Confront the State," in *Buddhism, Modernity, and the State in Asia*, ed. Pattana Kitiarsa and John Whalen-Bridge, 17–40 (New York: Palgrave, 2013).
105. David Martin Jones, *Political Development in Pacific Asia* (Cambridge: Polity Press, 1997), 13.
106. Pye, *Asian Power and Politics: The Cultural Dimensions of Authority*, 35.
107. Chae-hak Ham and Daniel Bell, *The Politics of Affective Relations: East Asia and Beyond*, Global Encounters (Lanham, MD: Lexington Books, 2004).

108. Shlomo Avineri, *Hegel's Theory of the Modern State* (London: Cambridge University Press, 1972).

109. Georg Wilhelm Friedrich Hegel, *Outlines of the Philosophy of Right* (Oxford: Oxford University Press, 1821 [2008]), sec. 258.

110. Ibid., sec. 268.

111. Ibid., sec. 124.

112. Georg Wilhelm Friedrich Hegel, *The Philosophy of History* (New York: Dover Publications, 1825 [1956]), 452.

113. Terence Chong, "Embodying Society's Best: Hegel and the Singapore State," *Journal of Contemporary Asia* 36, no. 3 (2006): 283–304, 297.

114. Bruce Cumings, "Civil Society in East and West," in *Korean Society: Civil Society, Democracy, and the State*, ed. Charles K. Armstrong, 11–35 (London: Routledge, 2002), 25.

115. Herbert Spencer, *The Principles of Ethics* (New York: D. Appleton & Company, 1892).

116. Herbert Spencer, *An Autobiography* (New York: D. Appleton & Company, 1904).

117. Yamashita Shigekazu, "Herbert Spencer and Meiji Japan," in *Japan in Transition: Thought and Action in the Meiji Era, 1868–1912*, ed. Hilary Conroy, Sandra T. W. Davis, and Wayne Patterson, 77–95 (Rutherford, NJ: Fairleigh Dickinson University Press, 1984).

118. Douglas Howland, "Society Reified: Herbert Spencer and Political Theory in Early Meiji Japan," *Comparative Studies in Society & History* 42, no. 1 (2000): 67–87, 76.

119. Hiroshi Unoura, "Samurai Darwinism: Hiroyuki Kato and the Reception of Darwin's Theory in Modern Japan from the 1880s to the 1900s," *History and Anthropology* 11, no. 2/3 (1999): 235–54, 241.

120. Stephan Schmidt, "Mou Zongsan, Hegel, and Kant: The Quest for Confucian Modernity," *Philosophy East & West* 61, no. 2 (2011): 260–302; Daniel Bell and Chae-bong Ham, *Confucianism for the Modern World* (Cambridge; New York: Cambridge University Press, 2003).

121. Michael D. Barr, "Lee Kuan Yew and the 'Asian Values' Debate," *Asian Studies Review* 24, no. 3 (2000): 309–35.

122. Beng Huat Chua, "Disrupting Hegemonic Liberalism in East Asia," *Boundary* 37, no. 2 (2010): 199–216.

123. Kanishka Jayasuriya, "Understanding 'Asian Values' as a Form of Reactionary Modernization," *Contemporary Politics* 4, no. 1 (1998): 77–93; Jeffrey Herf, *Reactionary Modernism: Technology, Culture, and Politics in Weimar and the Third Reich* (New York: Cambridge University Press, 1984), 2.

124. W. Macmahon Ball, *Nationalism and Communism in East Asia* ([Carlton]: Melbourne University Press, 1952), 5.

125. Anderson, "The Idea of Power in Javanese Culture," 24–25.

126. Claudia Derichs and Thomas Heberer, "Diversity of Nation-Building in East and Southeast Asia," *European Journal of East Asian Studies* 5, no. 1 (2006): 1–13, 8.

127. Kia Soong Kua, *May 13: Declassified Documents on the Malaysian Riots of 1969* (Petaling Jaya, Selangor: SUARAM, 2007).

128. Michael O'Shannassy, "More Talk than Walk? Umno, 'New Politics' and Legitimation in Contemporary Malaysia," *Journal of Contemporary Asia* 43, no. 3 (2013): 428–51.

129. Jacques Bertrand and André Laliberté, *Multination States in Asia: Accommodation or Resistance* (New York: Cambridge University Press, 2011).

130. Jacob Bercovitch and Mikio Oishi, "Management of the Rivalry across the Taiwan Strait: Addressing the Transformation from Ideological Rivalry to Ethnic Conflict," in *International Conflict in the Asia-Pacific: Patterns, Consequences, and Management*, 77–100 (Milton Park: Routledge, 2010).

131. Chaiwat Satha-Anand, "When Autonomy Is Not an Option?: Governing Violence in Southern Thailand," in *Autonomy and Ethnic Conflict in South and South-East Asia*, ed. Rajat Ganguly, 138–55 (New York: Routledge, 2012); Ian Storey, "Southern Discomfort: Separatist Conflict in the Kingdom of Thailand," *Asian Affairs: An American Review* 35, no. 1 (2008): 31–52; Duncan McCargo, "Autonomy for Southern Thailand: Thinking the Unthinkable?," *Pacific Affairs* 83, no. 2 (2010): 261–81.

132. Christopher Joll, "Religion and Conflict in Southern Thailand: Beyond Rounding Up the Usual Suspects," *Contemporary Southeast Asia* 32, no. 2 (2010): 258–79, 262.

133. McCargo, "Autonomy for Southern Thailand: Thinking the Unthinkable?," 266.

134. Marc Askew, "Insurgency and the Market for Violence in Southern Thailand: 'Neither War nor Peace,'" *Asian Survey* 50, no. 6 (2010): 1107–134, 1134.

135. Michael Jerryson, "Appropriating a Space for Violence: State Buddhism in Southern Thailand," *Journal of Southeast Asian Studies* 40, no. 1 (2009): 33–57.

136. Charles Fisher, "Southeast Asia: The Balkans of the Orient?," in *Man, State, and Society in Contemporary Southeast Asia*, ed. Robert O. Tilman, 55–71 (New York: Praeger, 1969).

137. Jacques Bertrand, *Nationalism and Ethnic Conflict in Indonesia* (New York: Cambridge University Press, 2004).

138. Zachary Abuza, *Conspiracy of Silence: The Insurgency in Southern Thailand* (Washington, DC: United States Institute of Peace Press, 2009).

139. Askew, "Insurgency and the Market for Violence in Southern Thailand: 'Neither War nor Peace,'" 1117.

140. Derichs and Heberer, "Diversity of Nation-Building in East and Southeast Asia," 9.

141. Cemil Aydin, *The Politics of Anti-Westernism in Asia: Visions of World Order in Pan-Islamic and Pan-Asian Thought* (New York: Columbia University Press, 2007).

142. Maung Maung, *Burma in the Family of Nations* (Amsterdam: Djambatan, 1956), 34.

143. See Bruce Gilley, *The Right to Rule: How States Win and Lose Legitimacy* (New York: Columbia University Press, 2009), ch. 5.

3. Development

1. This section draws on Chin-shing Huang, *Banshi jidei fendou: Wu Huoshi xiansheng koushu zhuanji [Doing Business and Struggle: An Oral History of Mr. Wu Ho-Su]* (Taipei: Yunchen Cultural Enterprises, 1996); Chin-Shing Huang and Hoyt Cleveland Tillman, *Business as a Vocation: The Autobiography of Wu Ho-Su* (Cambridge, MA: Harvard University Press, 2002).

2. Kuo-hsing Hsieh, *Wu Xiuqi xiansheng fangwen jilu [An Interview with Mr. Wu Hsiu-Chi]* (Taipei: Academia Sinica, 1992), 191.

3. Huang and Tillman, *Business as a Vocation: The Autobiography of Wu Ho-Su*, 114.

4. Ibid., 116, 115.

5. Ibid., 134.

6. Ibid., 145.

7. Gilles Guiheux, *Les grands entrepreneurs privés à Taiwan: La main visible de la prospérité*, Collection Asie Orientale (Paris: CNRS Editions, 2002), 89.

8. Peter B. Evans, *Embedded Autonomy: States and Industrial Transformation* (Princeton, NJ: Princeton University Press, 1995), 57. Stephan Haggard, *Pathways from the Periphery: The Politics of Growth in the Newly Industrializing Countries*, Cornell Studies in Political Economy (Ithaca, NY: Cornell University Press, 1990), 89; Robert Wade, *Governing the Market: Economic Theory and the Role of Government in East Asian Industrialization* (Princeton, NJ: Princeton University Press, 1990), 222.

9. K. Y. Yin, *Wo dui Taiwan jingjide kanfa [My Views on the Taiwan Economy]* (Taipei: U.S. Aid to Taiwan Committee, 1963).

10. Yongping Wu, *A Political Explanation of Economic Growth: State Survival, Bureaucratic Politics, and Private Enterprises in the Making of Taiwan's Economy, 1950–1985* (Cambridge, MA: Harvard University Asia Center, 2005), 67.

11. Hoyt Cleveland Tillman, "Translator's Introduction," in *Business as a Vocation: The Autobiography of Wu Ho-Su*, ed. Chin-Shing Huang and Hoyt Cleveland Tillman, xix–xxxvi (Cambridge, MA: Harvard University Press, 2002), xxiii.

12. Huang and Tillman, *Business as a Vocation: The Autobiography of Wu Ho-Su*, 182.

13. Robert Wade, "State Intervention in 'Outward-Looking' Development: Neoclassical Theory and Taiwanese Practice," in *Developmental States in East Asia*, ed. Gordon White, 30–67 (New York: St. Martin's Press, 1988), 40.

14. Tak-Wing Ngo, "The Political Bases of Episodic Agency in the Taiwan State," in *Asian States: Beyond the Developmental Perspective*, ed. Richard Boyd and Tak-Wing Ngo, 83–109 (London; New York: RoutledgeCurzon, 2005), 92.

15. Akira Suehiro and Tom Gill, *Catch-Up Industrialization: The Trajectory and Prospects of East Asian Economies* (Honolulu: University of Hawaii Press, 2008). See also Oyebanji Oyelaran-Oyeyinka and Rajah Rasiah, *Uneven Paths of Development: Innovation and Learning in Asia and Africa* (Cheltenham: Edward Elgar, 2009).

16. Wade, "State Intervention in 'Outward-Looking' Development: Neoclassical Theory and Taiwanese Practice," 60.

17. Thomas B. Gold, *State and Society in the Taiwan Miracle* (Armonk, NY: M. E. Sharpe, 1986), 124.

18. Atul Kohli, *State-Directed Development: Political Power and Industrialization in the Global Periphery* (New York: Cambridge University Press, 2004).

19. Ngo, "The Political Bases of Episodic Agency in the Taiwan State," 89–90.

20. W. van Warmelo, *The Development of Small Enterprises in Taiwan, Republic of China* (Tokyo: Asian Productivity Organization, 1968), 15, 3.

21. Ngo, "The Political Bases of Episodic Agency in the Taiwan State," 105.

22. Guiheux, *Les grands entrepreneurs privés à Taiwan: La main visible de la prospérité*, 51.

23. Wu, *A Political Explanation of Economic Growth: State Survival, Bureaucratic Politics, and Private Enterprises in the Making of Taiwan's Economy, 1950–1985*, 226, tab. 6.13.

24. Guiheux, *Les grands entrepreneurs privés à Taiwan: La main visible de la prospérité*, 137; Jonathan Brookfield, "The Network Structure of Big Business in Taiwan," *Asia Pacific Journal of Management* 27, no. 2 (2010): 257–79.

25. Peter Ferdinand, *Governance in Pacific Asia Political Economy and Development from Japan to Burma* (London: Continuum, 2011); Jeffrey Henderson, *East Asian Transformation: On the Political Economy of Dynamism, Governance and Crisis* (London: Routledge, 2011).

26. Richard Boyd and Tak-Wing Ngo, "Preface," in *Asian States: Beyond the Developmental Perspective*, ed. Boyd and Ngo, xiii–xv, xiii.

27. David Goldblatt, "Politics and Governance in Asia-Pacific: Historical and Thematic Overview," in *Governance in the Asia-Pacific*, ed. R. A. Maidment, David Goldblatt, and Jeremy Mitchell, 1–28 (London: Routledge, 1998), 22.

28. Benjamin Schwartz, "The Primacy of Political Order in East Asian Societies," in *China and Other Matters*, 114–24 (Cambridge, MA: Harvard University Press, 1996), 119.

29. United Nations Economic Commission for Asia and the Far East, *Economic Bulletin for Asia and the Far East: 1949*, Economic Bulletin for Asia and the Far East (New York: United Nations Publications, 1950), xiv, xvii.

30. Hla Myint, "The 'Classical Theory' of International Trade and the Underdeveloped Countries," *Economic Journal* 68, no. 270 (1958): 317–37, 336.

31. Peter Bennet Stone, *Japan Surges Ahead: The Story of an Economic Miracle* (New York: Praeger, 1969), xi.

32. Xing-Hu Kuo, *Free China: Asian Economic Miracle* (Stuttgart: Seewald, 1984); Thomas Stern, *The Korean Economic "Miracle" – Yesterday, Today, and Tomorrow* (Washington, D.C.: Korea Economic Institute of America, 1983); Crocker National Bank, *Indonesia: The Inevitable Miracle* (San Francisco: Crocker National Bank, 1973).

33. World Bank, *The East Asian Miracle: Economic Growth and Public Policy*, A World Bank Policy Research Report (New York: Oxford University Press, 1993).

34. Angus Maddison, *The World Economy: A Millennial Perspective*, Development Centre Studies (Paris: OECD, 2001).
35. IMF World Economic Outlook Database.
36. International Labour Organization, *Key Indicators of the Labour Market*, various years, http://kilm.ilo.org/kilmnet/, tab. 7a.
37. Paul Krugman, "The Myth of Asia's Miracle," *Foreign Affairs* 73, no. 6 (1994): 62–78.
38. Michael B. Devereux, "Real Exchange Rate Trends and Growth: A Model of East Asia," *Review of International Economics* 7, no. 3 (1999): 509–21.
39. Pham Hoang Van, Ghunsu Park, and Dong Soo Ha, "Missing a Miracle: How Aggregate TFP Accounting Overlooks Sectoral Efficiency Gains," *Journal of the Korean Economy* 4, no. 1 (2003): 1–28.
40. Edward Chen, "The Total Factor Productivity Debate: Determinants of Economic Growth in East Asia," *Asian-Pacific Economic Literature* 11, no. 1 (1997): 18–38.
41. World Bank, *East Asia and Pacific Data Monitor* (October 2012), fig. 14.
42. Peter Debaere and Ufuk Demiroglu, "Factor Accumulation without Diminishing Returns: The Case of East Asia," *Review of International Economics* 14, no. 1 (2006): 16–29.
43. Jagdish N. Bhagwati, "The 'Miracle' That Did Happen: Understanding East Asia in Comparative Perspective," in *The Wind of the Hundred Days: How Washington Mismanaged Globalization*, 27–49 (Cambridge, MA: MIT Press, 2000).
44. A. B. Susanto and Patricia Susanto, *The Dragon Network: Inside Stories of the Most Successful Chinese Family Businesses* (New York: Wiley/Bloomberg Press, 2013).
45. Peter Gray, "Culture and Economic Performance: Policy as an Intervening Variable," *Journal of Comparative Economics* 23, no. 3 (1996): 278–91, 288.
46. F. Gerard Adams and Heidi Vernon, "Evaluating the 'Asian Culture/Asian Success' Hypothesis," *Journal of Asia-Pacific Business* 8, no. 4 (2007): 5–20.
47. Gray, "Culture and Economic Performance: Policy as an Intervening Variable," 284.
48. Stone, *Japan Surges Ahead: The Story of an Economic Miracle*, 183.
49. Kyung-sup Chang, "Developmental Citizenship in Perspective: The South Korean Case and Beyond," in *Contested Citizenship in East Asia*, ed. Kyung-sup Chang and Bryan S. Turner, 182–202 (New York: Routledge, 2012), 187.
50. Kazuhiko Shimizu, "Head-to-Head in Shanghai: Ping an Insurance," *Institutional Investor*, June 1, 2000.
51. Richard Butwell, *Southeast Asia: A Political Introduction* (New York: Praeger, 1975), 109.
52. "Leaving Asia's Shade," *The Economist*, July 24, 2010.
53. *World Values Survey*, Wave 4 (2005–2008). Based on questions V69 (High economic growth is the first aim of our country), V121 (Wealth is positive sum), V158 (Democracy means the economy is prospering), and Y001 (Materialism index).

54. James Raphael and Thomas Rohlen, "How Many Models of Japanese Growth Do We Want or Need?," in *Behind East Asian Growth: The Political and Social Foundations of Prosperity*, ed. Henry S. Rowen, 265–96 (New York: Routledge, 1998), 276.

55. Minxin Pei, "Constructing the Political Foundations of an Economic Miracle," in *Behind East Asian Growth: The Political and Social Foundations of Prosperity*, ed. Rowen, 39–59, 53; Etel Solingen, "Pax Asiatica Versus Bella Levantina: The Foundations of War and Peace in East Asia and the Middle East," *American Political Science Review* 101, no. 4 (2007): 757–80.

56. Mark Clifford, *Troubled Tiger: Businessmen, Bureaucrats, and Generals in South Korea* (Armonk: M. E. Sharpe, 1994), 102.

57. Xiaoming Huang, *The Rise and Fall of the East Asian Growth System, 1951–2000: Institutional Competitiveness and Rapid Economic Growth* (London: RoutledgeCurzon, 2005).

58. Cristóbal Kay, "Why East Asia Overtook Latin America: Agrarian Reform, Industrialisation and Development," *Third World Quarterly* 23, no. 6 (2002): 1073–102.

59. Adam Fforde, "Economics, History, and the Origins of Vietnam's Post-War Economic Success," *Asian Survey* 49, no. 3 (2009): 484–504.

60. David C. Kang, *Crony Capitalism: Corruption and Development in South Korea and the Philippines* (New York: Cambridge University Press, 2002).

61. Adrian Leftwich, *States of Development: On the Primacy of Politics in Development* (Oxford: Polity, 2000), 124.

62. Geoffrey Underhill and Zhang Xiaoke, "The State-Market Condominium Approach," in *Asian States: Beyond the Developmental Perspective*, ed. Boyd and Ngo, 43–66, 46.

63. Stephan Haggard, *The Political Economy of the Asian Financial Crisis* (Washington, DC: Institute for International Economics, 2000), 231.

64. Stone, *Japan Surges Ahead: The Story of an Economic Miracle*, 183.

65. Henderson, *East Asian Transformation: On the Political Economy of Dynamism, Governance and Crisis*, 57.

66. David Friedman, *The Misunderstood Miracle: Industrial Development and Political Change in Japan*, Cornell Studies in Political Economy (Ithaca, NY: Cornell University Press, 1988).

67. Suehiro and Gill, *Catch-Up Industrialization: The Trajectory and Prospects of East Asian Economies*, 122.

68. Kui Wai Li, *Capitalist Development and Economism in East Asia: The Rise of Hong Kong, Singapore, Taiwan, and South Korea* (London: Routledge, 2002).

69. Yung-chol Park, *Economic Liberalization and Integration in East Asia: A Post-Crisis Paradigm* (Oxford: Oxford University Press, 2006), 28–29.

70. Gordon White and Robert Wade, "Developmental States and Markets in East Asia: An Introduction," in *Developmental States in East Asia*, ed. Gordon White and Jack Gray, 1–29 (New York: St. Martin's Press, 1988), 10.

71. Daron Acemoglu and James Robinson, *The Role of Institutions in Growth and Development* (Washington, DC: Commission on Growth and Development, 2008), 19.

72. Thomas Markussen, "Property Rights, Productivity, and Common Property Resources: Insights from Rural Cambodia," *World Development* 36, no. 11 (2008): 2277–296.

73. World Bank, *Cambodia – More Efficient Government Spending for Strong and Inclusive Growth:* Integrated Fiduciary Assessment and Public Expenditure Review (Washington, DC: World Bank, 2011).

74. Tae-Woo Lee and Matthew Flynn, "Charting a New Paradigm of Container Hub Port Development Policy: The Asian Doctrine," *Transport Reviews* 31, no. 6 (2011): 791–806.

75. Ibid., 795.

76. Ibid., 802.

77. Qiao Liu, Paul Lejot, and Douglas A. Arner, *Finance in Asia: Institutions, Regulation and Policy* (New York: Routledge, 2013); Gerald Paul McAlinn and Caslav Pejovic, *Law and Development in Asia* (New York: Routledge, 2011).

78. Ricardo Chica, Oscar Guevara, Diana Lopez, and Daniel Osorio, "Growth Determinants in Latin America and East Asia: Has Globalization Changed the Engines of Growth?," *Coyuntura Economica: Investigacion Economica y Social* 42, no. 1 (2012): 161–203.

79. Leftwich, *States of Development: On the Primacy of Politics in Development,* 155; Shigeko Hayashi, "The Developmental State in the Era of Globalization: Beyond the Northeast Asian Model of Political Economy," *Pacific Review* 23, no. 1 (2010): 45–69, 47.

80. Stone, *Japan Surges Ahead: The Story of an Economic Miracle,* 74–75.

81. Mark Beeson and Hung Hung Pham, "Developmentalism with Vietnamese Characteristics: The Persistence of State-Led Development in East Asia," *Journal of Contemporary Asia* 42, no. 4 (2012): 539–59.

82. K. S. Jomo and Yün-chung Chen, *Southeast Asia's Misunderstood Miracle: Industrial Policy and Economic Development in Thailand, Malaysia and Indonesia* (Boulder, CO: Westview Press, 1997).

83. Amar Bhattacharya and Mari Pangestu, "Indonesia: Development Transformation and the Role of Public Policy," in *Lessons from East Asia,* ed. Danny M. Leipziger, 387–442 (Ann Arbor: University of Michigan Press, 1997).

84. Gitte Heij, "The 1981–83 Indonesian Income Tax Reform Process: Who Pulled the Strings?," *Bulletin of Indonesian Economic Studies* 37, no. 2 (2001): 233–51.

85. Nancy Lee Peluso, Suraya Afiff, and Noer Fauzi Rachman, "Claiming the Grounds for Reform: Agrarian and Environmental Movements in Indonesia," *Journal of Agrarian Change* 8, no. 2 (2008): 377–408, 394.

86. Bernard S. Silberman, *Cages of Reason: The Rise of the Rational State in France, Japan, the United States, and Great Britain* (Chicago: University of Chicago Press, 1993).

87. K. Lee, "Can Korea Be a Role Model for Development? A 'Capability-Based View' of Korea," Paper Presented at *UNU-WIDER Conference on Country Role Models for Development Success,* Helsinki, 13–14 June 2008, 13.

88. James V. Jesudason, *Ethnicity and the Economy: The State, Chinese Business, and Multinationals in Malaysia* (New York: Oxford University Press, 1989).

89. Jeffrey Henderson and Richard Phillips, "Unintended Consequences: Social Policy, State Institutions and the 'Stalling' of the Malaysian Industrialization Project," *Economy and Society* 36, no. 1 (2007): 78–102.

90. Rajah Rasiah, "Clusters and Regional Industrial Synergies: The Electronics Industry in Penang and Jalisco," in *Development on the Ground: Clusters, Networks and Regions in Emerging Economies*, ed. Allen John Scott and Gioacchino Garofoli, 223–250 (London; New York: Routledge, 2007); Prema-chandra Athukorala, "Growing with Global Production Sharing: The Tale of Penang Export Hub," *Australian National University, Arndt-Corden Department of Economics, Departmental Working Papers* (2011); Rajah Rasiah, "Innovation and Institutions: Moving towards the Technological Frontier in the Electronics Industry in Malaysia," *Journal of Industry Studies* 3, no. 2 (1996): 79–102.

91. Jonathan A. Batten, "Financial Sector Reform and Regulation in the Asia-Pacific Region: A Perspective," *Journal of the Asia Pacific Economy* 16, no. 3 (2011): 285–93

92. Anne Booth, "Rethinking the Role of Agriculture in The 'East Asian' Model: Why Is Southeast Asia Different from Northeast Asia?," *ASEAN Economic Bulletin* 19, no. 1 (2002): 40–51.

93. Katharina Pistor, Philip Wellons, and Jeffrey Sachs, *The Role of Law and Legal Institutions in Asian Economic Development: 1960–1995* (New York: Oxford University Press, 1999).

94. Mushtaq H. Khan, "Rents, Efficiency, and Growth; Rent-Seeking as Process," in *Rents, Rent-Seeking and Economic Development: Theory and Evidence in Asia*, ed. Mushtaq H. Khan and K. S. Jomo, 21–144 (Cambridge: Cambridge University Press, 2000).

95. Reuven Glick and Ramon Moreno, "Government Intervention and the East Asian Miracle," *FRBSF Economic Letter* 97, no. 20 (1997): 1–4.

96. Joseph E. Stiglitz and Shahid Yusuf, *Rethinking the East Asia Miracle* (Washington, DC: World Bank, 2001).

97. "Proton Bomb," *The Economist*, May 8, 2004.

98. Yun-han Chu, "The State and the Development of the Automobile Industry in South Korea and Taiwan," in *The Role of the State in Taiwan's Development*, ed. Joel D. Aberbach, David Dollar, and Kenneth Lee Sokoloff, 125–69 (Armonk, NY: M. E. Sharpe, 1994).

99. Ann Markusen and Sam Ock Park, "The State as Industrial Locator and District Builder: The Case of Changwon, South Korea," *Economic Geography* 69, no. 2 (1993): 157–81.

100. Peter Petri, "Common Foundations of East Asian Success," in *Lessons from East Asia*, ed. Leipziger, 541–67.

101. José Edgardo L. Campos and Hilton L. Root, *The Key to the Asian Miracle: Making Shared Growth Credible* (Washington, DC: Brookings Institution, 1996), 7.

102. Steve Chan and Cal Clark, *Flexibility, Foresight, and Fortuna in Taiwan's Development: Navigating between Scylla and Charybdis* (London: Routledge, 1992), 107.

103. Minxin Pei, "Constructing the Political Foundations of an Economic Miracle," 40.

104. Stephan Haggard, "Institutions and Growth in East Asia," *Studies in Comparative International Development* 38, no. 4 (2004): 53–81, 56.

105. Joyce Low, Shao Wei Lam, and Loon Ching Tang, "Assessment of Hub Status among Asian Ports from a Network Perspective," *Transportation Research Part A: Policy & Practice* 43, no. 6 (2009): 593–606.

106. Dong-Wook Song, "Port Reform and Privatisation in Korea," in *Port Privatisation: The Asia-Pacific Experience*, ed. James Reveley and Malcolm T. Tull, 138–51 (Cheltenham: Edward Elgar, 2008).

107. Sung-Woo Lee and Geun-Sub Kim, "Port Challenge in Northeast Asia: Korea's Two-Port Hub Strategy," in *Ports in Proximity: Competition and Coordination among Adjacent Seaports*, ed. Theo Notteboom, César Ducruet, and Peter W. de Langen, 247–60 (Burlington, VT: Ashgate, 2009).

108. Dong-Ho Shin, "Governing Interregional Conflicts: The Planning Approach to Managing Spillovers of Extended Metropolitan Pusan, Korea," *Environment & Planning* 32, no. 3 (2000): 507–19, 514.

109. "Exporters Protest Busan City's Tax Extension," *The Korea Herald*, November 5, 2001.

110. "South Korea Maritime Workers Vote to Strike – Report," *Reuters News*, August 16, 2004.

111. Kim Joon-sool, "Town Slighted by New Port Name," *Joonai*, December 19, 2005.

112. Dong-keun Ryoo and Yun-su Hur, "Busan: The Future Logistics Hub of Northeast Asia," in *Asian Container Ports: Development, Competition and Co-Operation*, ed. Kevin Cullinane and Dong-Wook Song, 34–61 (New York: Palgrave Macmillan, 2007), 50.

113. Song, "Port Reform and Privatisation in Korea," 148.

114. Gregory W. Noble, *Collective Action in East Asia: How Ruling Parties Shape Industrial Policy*, Cornell Studies in Political Economy (Ithaca, NY: Cornell University Press, 1998).

115. Martin Andersson and Christer Gunnarsson, "Beyond Policy Explanations," in *Development and Structural Change in Asia-Pacific: Globalising Miracles or End of a Model?*, ed. Martin Andersson and Christer Gunnarsson, 127–47 (London: RoutledgeCurzon, 2003), 128.

116. Stephan Haggard, "Business, Politics, and Policy in East and Southeast Asia," in *Behind East Asian Growth: The Political and Social Foundations of Prosperity*, ed. Rowen, 78–104, 83.

117. Campos and Root, *The Key to the Asian Miracle: Making Shared Growth Credible*, 102–3.

118. Kang, *Crony Capitalism: Corruption and Development in South Korea and the Philippines*.

119. Mitsuo Hosen, "Accelerating Economic Reform in Japan: The Role of the Council on Economic and Fiscal Policy," in *Institutions for Economic Reform in Asia*, ed. Philippa S. Dee, 53–62 (London: Routledge, 2010).

120. David Martin Jones, "The Politics of Economic Governance," in *Governance in the Asia-Pacific*, ed. Maidment, Goldblatt, and Mitchell, 172–94, 175.

121. O. Fiona Yap, *Citizen Power, Politics, and the 'Asian Miracle': Reassessing the Dynamics* (Boulder, CO: L. Rienner Publishers, 2005).

122. Robert Garran, *Tigers Tamed: The End of the Asian Miracle* (Honolulu: University of Hawaii Press, 1998).

123. Martin Andersson and Christer Gunnarsson, *Development and Structural Change in Asia-Pacific: Globalising Miracles or End of a Model?*, RoutledgeCurzon Studies in the Growth Economies of Asia (London; New York: RoutledgeCurzon, 2003); Vedi R. Hadiz, *Empire and Neoliberalism in Asia*, Routledge Politics in Asia Series (New York: Routledge, 2006); Iain Pirie, *The Korean Developmental State: From Dirigisme to Neo-Liberalism* (London: Routledge, 2008).

124. Richard Robinson, Gary Roddan, and Kevin Hewison, "Transplanting the Neoliberal State in Southeast Asia," in *Asian States: Beyond the Developmental Perspective*, ed. Boyd and Ngo, 172–98, 177.

125. Su-Hsing Hung and Ming-Jang Weng, "Did the IMF Put out the Fire or Start One when the Financial Crisis Struck Asia?," *International Research Journal of Finance and Economics* 40, no. 2 (2010): 174–85; Medhi Krongkaew, "The IMF in the Thai Crisis: Villain or Savior?," in *Development and Structural Change in Asia-Pacific: Globalising Miracles or End of a Model?*, ed. Andersson and Gunnarsson, 93–107.

126. Andrea Boltho and Maria Weber, "Did China Follow the East Asian Development Model?," *European Journal of Comparative Economics* 6, no. 2 (2009): 267–86.

127. Ben Kiernan, "The Demography of Genocide in Southeast Asia," *Critical Asian Studies* 35, no. 4 (2003): 585–97.

128. Thomas Spoorenberg and Daniel Schwekendiek, "Demographic Changes in North Korea: 1993–2008," *Population & Development Review* 38, no. 1 (2012): 133–58.

129. Gary Hawes, *The Philippine State and the Marcos Regime: The Politics of Export*, Cornell Studies in Political Economy (Ithaca, NY: Cornell University Press, 1987).

130. Carl H. Landé, *Leaders, Factions, and Parties: The Structure of Philippine Politics* (New Haven, CT: Yale University Press, 1965).

131. Jonathan Fast and Jim Richardson, *Roots of Dependency: Political and Economic Revolution in 19th Century Philippines* (Quezon City: Foundation for Nationalist Studies, 1979); Walden F. Bello, Marissa De Guzman, Mary Lou Malig, and Herbert Docena, *The Anti-Development State: The Political Economy of Permanent Crisis in the Philippines* (London: Zed, 2005).

132. William N. Holden and R. Daniel Jacobson, "Ecclesial Opposition to Nonferrous Metals Mining in the Philippines: Neoliberalism Encounters Liberation Theology," *Asian Studies Review* 31, no. 2 (2007): 133–54; Robert L. Youngblood, *Marcos against the Church: Economic Development*

and Political Repression in the Philippines (Ithaca, NY: Cornell University Press, 1990).

133. Homi Kharas, "The Philippines: Three Decades of Lost Opportunities," in *Lessons from East Asia*, ed. Leipziger, 443–79, 456.

134. Willa Boots J. Tolo, "The Determinants of Economic Growth in the Philippines: A New Look," *IMF Working Papers* (2011).

135. Gilberto Llanto, "The Policy Development Process and the Agenda for Effective Institutions in the Philippines," in *Institutions for Economic Reform in Asia*, ed. Dee, 88–105, 91.

136. Jude Esguerra and Enrique Villanueva, "Pathways out of Patronage Politics: New Roles for Communities, New Rules for Politics in the Philippines," *IDS Bulletin* 40, no. 6 (2009): 13–21.

137. Sean Turnell, "Fundamentals of Myanmar's Macroeconomy: A Political Economy Perspective," *Asian Economic Policy Review* 6, no. 2 (2011): 136–53.

138. Masahiro Hori and Yu Ching Wong, "Efficiency Costs of Myanmar's Multiple Exchange Rate Regime," *IMF Working Papers* (2008).

139. Sai Khaing Myo Tun, "A Comparative Study of State-Led Development in Myanmar (1988–2010) and Suharto's Indonesia: An Approach from the Developmental State Theory," *Journal of Current Southeast Asian Affairs* 30, no. 1 (2011): 69–94.

4. Democracy

1. Damien Kingsbury, *The Politics of Indonesia*, 3rd ed. (Melbourne: Oxford University Press, 2005), 29.

2. Nippon Eigasha, *Indonesia Raya [Motion Picture]* (Japan, 1946), 11 min. sd. b&w. 16 mm.

3. Li Narangoa and R. B. Cribb, *Imperial Japan and National Identities in Asia, 1895–1945* (London: Routledge, 2003); Yohanna Johns, "The Japanese as Educators in Indonesia," in *Japan in Asia, 1942–1945*, ed. William Henry Newell (Singapore: Singapore University Press, 1981).

4. Herbert Feith, *The Decline of Constitutional Democracy in Indonesia* (Ithaca, NY: Cornell University Press, 1962).

5. J. D. Legge, *Sukarno: A Political Biography* (London: Allen Lane, 1972), 4.

6. Ibid., 271.

7. Ethan Mark, "Suharto's New Order Remembers Japan's New Order," in *Representing the Japanese Occupation of Indonesia*, ed. R. Raben, 72–85 (Amsterdam: Netherlands Institute for War Documentation, 1999).

8. Feith, *The Decline of Constitutional Democracy in Indonesia*; Richard Robinson, "Indonesia: Tensions in State and Regime," in *Southeast Asia in the 1990s: Authoritarianism, Democracy and Capitalism*, ed. Kevin Hewison, Richard Robison, and Garry Rodan, 23–54 (St. Leonards, NSW, Australia: Allen & Unwin, 1993); Herbert Feith and Lance Castles, *Indonesian Political Thinking, 1945–1965* (Ithaca, NY: Cornell University Press, 1970).

9. David Martin Jones, *Political Development in Pacific Asia* (Cambridge: Polity Press, 1997), 152.

10. Mark R. Thompson, "The Limits of Democratisation in ASEAN," *Third World Quarterly* 14, no. 3 (1993): 469–84, 476, 482.

11. Edward Aspinall, *Opposing Suharto: Compromise, Resistance, and Regime Change in Indonesia* (Stanford, CA: Stanford University Press, 2005), 209, 244.

12. Kingsbury, *The Politics of Indonesia*, 68; World Bank, "Industrial Licensing," in *Indonesia – Selected Issues of Industrial Development and Strategy* (Washington, DC: World Bank, 1981).

13. World Bank, *Indonesia – Strategy for Growth and Structural Change* (Washington, DC: World Bank, 1989), 58.

14. Aspinall, *Opposing Suharto: Compromise, Resistance, and Regime Change in Indonesia*, 87.

15. Anders Uhlin, *Indonesia and the "Third Wave of Democratization": The Indonesian Pro-Democracy Movement in a Changing World* (New York: St. Martin's Press, 1997), 155.

16. Jeremy Wallach, "Underground Rock Music and Democratization in Indonesia," *World Literature Today* 79, no. 3/4 (2005): 16–20, 19.

17. Uhlin, *Indonesia and the "Third Wave of Democratization": The Indonesian Pro-Democracy Movement in a Changing World*, ch. 9.

18. Aspinall, *Opposing Suharto: Compromise, Resistance, and Regime Change in Indonesia*, 35; Uhlin, *Indonesia and the "Third Wave of Democratization": The Indonesian Pro-Democracy Movement in a Changing World*, 160.

19. R. William Liddle, "Indonesia: Suharto's Tightening Grip," *Journal of Democracy* 7, no. 4 (1996): 58–73, 59.

20. "Kim's 'Close Friend' Megawati Expresses Condolences, Praises Leadership," *Kyodo News*, December 19, 2011.

21. Edward Aspinall, Geert Arend van Klinken, and Herbert Feith, *The Last Days of President Suharto* (Clayton, Australia: Monash Assia Institute, 1999), 20.

22. Arief Budiman, quoted in Edward Aspinall, "Indonesia: Moral Force Politics and the Struggle against Authoritarianism," in *Student Activism in Asia: Between Protest and Powerlessness*, ed. Meredith L. Weiss and Edward Aspinall, 153–79 (Minneapolis: University of Minnesota Press, 2012), 167.

23. Stefan Eklöf, *Indonesian Politics in Crisis: The Long Fall of Suharto, 1996–1998*, Studies in Contemporary Asia Series (Copenhagen: Nordic Institute of Asian Studies, 1999), 197; Bilveer Singh, *Succession Politics in Indonesia: The 1998 Presidential Elections and the Fall of Suharto* (New York: St. Martin's Press, 1999), 24.

24. Singh, *Succession Politics in Indonesia: The 1998 Presidential Elections and the Fall of Suharto*, 85.

25. Patrick Ziegenhain, *The Indonesian Parliament and Democratization* (Singapore: Institute of Southeast Asian Studies, 2008), 68.

26. Eklöf, *Indonesian Politics in Crisis: The Long Fall of Suharto, 1996–1998*, 203.

27. Ibid., 212.

28. Ibid., 131.

29. Aspinall, *Opposing Suharto: Compromise, Resistance, and Regime Change in Indonesia*, 217–18.
30. Singh, *Succession Politics in Indonesia: The 1998 Presidential Elections and the Fall of Suharto*, 82.
31. Eklöf, *Indonesian Politics in Crisis: The Long Fall of Suharto, 1996–1998*, 198–99; Singh, *Succession Politics in Indonesia: The 1998 Presidential Elections and the Fall of Suharto*, 116–44.
32. Singh, *Succession Politics in Indonesia: The 1998 Presidential Elections and the Fall of Suharto*, 128.
33. Aspinall, *Opposing Suharto: Compromise, Resistance, and Regime Change in Indonesia*, 182; Singh, *Succession Politics in Indonesia: The 1998 Presidential Elections and the Fall of Suharto*, 123.
34. Singh, *Succession Politics in Indonesia: The 1998 Presidential Elections and the Fall of Suharto*, 87.
35. Ibid., 92.
36. Aspinall, van Klinken, and Feith, *The Last Days of President Suharto*, 92.
37. Ibid., 183.
38. Rizal Sukma, "Political Transition and Democratic Resilience in Indonesia," in *Political Change, Democratic Transitions and Security in Southeast Asia*, ed. Mely Caballero Anthony, 16–33 (London: Routledge, 2010), 21.
39. Aspinall, *Opposing Suharto: Compromise, Resistance, and Regime Change in Indonesia*, 270.
40. Jamie S. Davidson, "Dilemmas of Democratic Consolidation in Indonesia," *Pacific Review* 22, no. 3 (2009): 293–310, 297.
41. Ibid., 294.
42. David Bourchier, *Illiberal Democracy in Indonesia* (New York: Routledge, 2014).
43. David Beetham, "Defining and Justifying Democracy," in *Democracy and Human Rights*, 1–29 (Cambridge: Polity Press, 1999).
44. Bernard S. Silberman, "The Political Theory and Program of Yoshino Sakuzō," *Journal of Modern History* 31, no. 4 (1959): 310–24; Jung-Sun Han, "Envisioning a Liberal Empire in East Asia: Yoshino Sakuzō in Taisho Japan," *Journal of Japanese Studies* 33, no. 2 (2007): 357–82; Brett McCormick, "When the Medium Is the Message: The Ideological Role of Yoshino Sakuzo's Minponshugi in Mobilising the Japanese Public," *European Journal of East Asian Studies* 6, no. 2 (2007): 185–215.
45. Tunku Abdul Rahman, "Malaysia: Key Area in Southeast Asia," *Foreign Affairs* 43, no. 4 (1965): 659–70, 668.
46. Steven J. Hood, "The Myth of Asian-Style Democracy," *Asian Survey* 38, no. 9 (1998): 853–66.
47. Leah Gilbert and Payam Mohseni, "Beyond Authoritarianism: The Conceptualization of Hybrid Regimes," *Studies in Comparative International Development* 46, no. 3 (2011): 270–97.
48. Jones, *Political Development in Pacific Asia*, ch. 3.
49. Sukarno, February 21, 1957, quoted in George McTurnan Kahin and Harold C. Hinton, *Major Governments of Asia* (Ithaca, NY: Cornell University Press, 1958), 566.

50. Samuel P Huntington, "Will More Countries Become Democratic?," *Political Science Quarterly* 99, no. 2 (1984): 193–218, 216.

51. Lucian W. Pye, *Asian Power and Politics: The Cultural Dimensions of Authority* (Cambridge, MA: Belknap Press, 1985), 339, 341.

52. Kanishka Jayasuriya, "Understanding 'Asian Values' as a Form of Reactionary Modernization," *Contemporary Politics* 4, no. 1 (1998): 77–93; Joakim Öjendal and Hans Antlöv, "Asian Values and Its Political Consequences," *Pacific Review* 11, no. 4 (1998): 525–40.

53. Ethan Scheiner, *Democracy without Competition in Japan: Opposition Failure in a One-Party Dominant State* (Cambridge; New York: Cambridge University Press, 2006); Roger W. Bowen, *Japan's Dysfunctional Democracy: The Liberal Democratic Party and Structural Corruption* (Armonk, NY: M. E. Sharpe, 2003).

54. R. E. Bedeski, "The Concept of the State: Sun Yat-Sen and Mao Tse-Tung," *China Quarterly* 70, no. 3 (1977): 338–54.

55. Sakuzo Yoshino, *Minponshugiron: Yoshino Sakuzo Hakushi minshushugi ronshu [Yoshino Sakuzo's Collected Essays on Democracy]* (Tokyo: Shin Kingensha, 1948), 59–60.

56. McCormick, "When the Medium Is the Message: The Ideological Role of Yoshino Sakuzo's Minponshugi in Mobilising the Japanese Public," 212.

57. Doh Chull Shin, *Confucianism and Democratization in East Asia* (New York: Cambridge University Press, 2012), 128, tab. 4.1. Recalculated using total responses.

58. Karl-Friedrich Walling, *Republican Empire: Alexander Hamilton on War and Free Government*, American Political Thought (Lawrence: University Press of Kansas, 1999).

59. Alexander Hamilton, James Madison, and John Jay, *The Federalist Papers* (New York: Penguin Books, 1987), 89, no. 1.

60. Ibid., 402, no. 70.

61. Kunal Mukherjee, "Is There a Distinct Style of Asian Democracy?," *Journal of Asian & African Studies* 45, no. 6 (2010): 684–94.

62. Robert W. Compton, *East Asian Democratization: Impact of Globalization, Culture, and Economy* (Westport, CT: Praeger, 2000).

63. Jones, *Political Development in Pacific Asia*, 200.

64. Mark Thompson, "Pacific Asia after 'Asian Values': Authoritarianism, Democracy, and 'Good Governance,'" *Third World Quarterly* 25, no. 6 (2004): 1079–95.

65. David Martin Jones, "The Southeast Asian Development Model: Non-Liberal Democracy with Market Accountability," *Southeast Asian Affairs* (2007): 59–76, 74.

66. Samuel P. Huntington, *The Third Wave: Democratization in the Late Twentieth Century*, The Julian J. Rothbaum Distinguished Lecture Series (Norman: University of Oklahoma Press, 1991).

67. Yung-myung Kim, "Understanding East Asian Political Systems," *Sungkyun Journal of East Asian Studies* 3, no. 1 (2003): 45–78.

68. Seymour Martin Lipset, "Some Social Requisites of Democracy: Economic Development and Political Legitimacy," *American Political Science Review* 53, no. 1 (1959): 69–100.

69. James William Morley and Harold Crouch, "The Dynamics of Political Change," in *Driven by Growth: Political Change in the Asia-Pacific Region*, ed. James William Morley, 313–54 (Armonk, NY: M. E. Sharpe, 1999).

70. Edward Friedman, "Introduction," in *The Politics of Democratization: Generalizing East Asian Experiences*, ed. Edward Friedman, 1–16 (Boulder, CO: Westview Press, 1994), 6.

71. Kheang Un, "Cambodia: Moving away from Democracy?," *International Political Science Review* 32, no. 5 (2011): 546–62, 560.

72. Carlos Lo, "Deng Xiaoping's Ideas on Law," *Asian Survey* 32, no. 7 (1992): 649–66, 652; Merle Goldman, *Sowing the Seeds of Democracy in China: Political Reform in the Deng Xiaoping Era* (Cambridge, MA: Harvard University Press, 1994).

73. Samantha Fay Ravich, *Marketization and Democracy: East Asian Experiences*, Rand Studies in Policy Analysis (Cambridge; New York: Cambridge University Press, 2000); Russell J. Dalton and To-chol Sin, *Citizens, Democracy, and Markets around the Pacific Rim: Congruence Theory and Political Culture* (Oxford: Oxford University Press, 2006).

74. Beverly Crawford, *Markets, States, and Democracy: The Political Economy of Post-Communist Transformation* (Boulder, CO: Westview Press, 1995).

75. Philip Oxhorn and Pamela K. Starr, *Markets & Democracy in Latin America: Conflict or Convergence?* (Boulder, CO: Lynne Rienner Publishers, 1999).

76. Francis Fukuyama, *The End of History and the Last Man* (New York: Free Press, 1992); Beth A. Simmons, Frank Dobbin, and Geoffrey Garrett, *The Global Diffusion of Markets and Democracy* (Cambridge; New York: Cambridge University Press, 2008); Michael Mandelbaum, *The Ideas That Conquered the World: Peace, Democracy, and Free Markets in the Twenty-First Century*, 1st ed. (New York: Public Affairs, 2002); Samuel Bowles, Herbert Gintis, and Bo Gustafsson, *Markets and Democracy: Participation, Accountability, and Efficiency* (Cambridge; New York: Cambridge University Press, 1993).

77. Milan Svolik, "Authoritarian Reversals and Democratic Consolidation," *American Political Science Review* 102, no. 2 (2008): 153–68.

78. Thompson, "Pacific Asia after 'Asian Values': Authoritarianism, Democracy, and 'Good Governance.'"

79. Alan Chong, "Singapore's Political Economy, 1997–2007: Strategizing Economic Assurance for Globalization," *Asian Survey* 47, no. 6 (2007): 952–76, 954.

80. Anita Doraisami, "The Political Economy of Capital Flows and Capital Controls in Malaysia," *Journal of Contemporary Asia* 35, no. 2 (2005): 249–63.

81. Simon Johnson and Todd Mitton, "Cronyism and Capital Controls: Evidence from Malaysia," *Journal of Financial Economics* 67, no. 2 (2003): 351–82, 371.

82. S. M. Ali Abbas and Raphael Espinoza, "Evaluating the Success of Malaysia's Exchange Controls (1998–99)," *Oxford Development Studies* 34, no. 2 (2006): 151–91, 182.

83. Helen Nesadurai, "In Defence of National Economic Autonomy? Malaysia's Response to the Financial Crisis," *Pacific Review* 13, no. 1 (2000): 73–113.

84. Jianjun Zhang, *Marketization and Democracy in China* (New York: Routledge, 2008).

85. Kellee S. Tsai, *Capitalism without Democracy: The Private Sector in Contemporary China* (Ithaca, NY: Cornell University Press, 2007).

86. Garry Rodan and Kanishka Jayasuriya, "Capitalist Development, Regime Transitions, and New Forms of Authoritarianism in Asia," *Pacific Review* 22, no. 1 (2009): 23–47, 27.

87. Lipset, "Some Social Requisites of Democracy: Economic Development and Political Legitimacy," 72.

88. Jones, *Political Development in Pacific Asia*, 140, 141.

89. Reinhard Bendix, *Kings or People: Power and the Mandate to Rule* (Berkeley: University of California Press, 1978).

90. David Martin Jones, "Democratization, Civil Society, and Illiberal Middle Class Culture in Pacific Asia," *Comparative Politics* 30, no. 2 (1998): 147–69.

91. Seth Mydans, "Aquino Might Bypass Governmental Structure," *The New York Times*, February 28, 1986.

92. Meredith L. Weiss, Edward Aspinall, and Mark Thompson, "Introduction," in *Student Activism in Asia: Between Protest and Powerlessness*, ed. Weiss and Aspinall, 1–32, 9, 20.

93. Adrian Karatnycky and Peter Ackerman, *How Freedom Is Won: From Civic Resistance to Durable Democracy* (New York: Freedom House, 2005). I have added data for post-2004 transitions in Afghanistan, Iraq, Pakistan, Egypt, Tunisia, Libya, Haiti, Lebanon, and Liberia.

94. Ian Marsh, *Democratisation, Governance, and Regionalism in East and Southeast Asia: A Comparative Study* (New York: Routledge, 2006).

95. Dan Slater and Joseph Wong, "The Strength to Concede: Ruling Parties and Democratization in Developmental Asia," *Perspectives on Politics* 11, no. 3 (2013): 717–33.

96. Sunhyuk Kim, *The Politics of Democratization in Korea: The Role of Civil Society* (Pittsburgh, PA: University of Pittsburgh Press, 2000).

97. Ibid., 92.

98. Sungsoo Kim, *The Role of the Middle Class in Korea Democratization* (Seoul: Jimoondang, 2008), 149, italics added.

99. Paul Freston, "Evangelical Protestantism and Democratization in Contemporary Latin America and Asia," *Democratization* 11, no. 4 (2004): 21–41; David Halloran Lumsdaine, *Evangelical Christianity and Democracy in Asia* (Oxford; New York: Oxford University Press, 2009); Tun-jen Cheng and Deborah A. Brown, *Religious Organizations and Democratization: Case Studies from Contemporary Asia* (Armonk, NY: M. E. Sharpe, 2006).

100. Kim, *The Role of the Middle Class in Korea Democratization*.

101. Jones, "Democratization, Civil Society, and Illiberal Middle Class Culture in Pacific Asia," 159–60.

102. Fred Hiatt, "Korean Farmers See Roh Protecting Their Gains; 'What We Really Want Is Stability,'" *Washington Post Foreign Service*, December 15, 1987.

103. Mi Park, "South Korea: Passion, Patriotism, and Student Radicalism," in *Student Activism in Asia: Between Protest and Powerlessness*, ed. Weiss and Aspinall, 125–51, 148.
104. Kim, *The Politics of Democratization in Korea: The Role of Civil Society*, 96.
105. "Protest over Korean Vote Irks Some Bystanders," *St. Petersburg Times*, December 24, 1987.
106. Robert E. Bedeski, *The Transformation of South Korea: Reform and Reconstitution in the Sixth Republic under Roh Tae Woo, 1987–1992* (London; New York: Routledge, 1994).
107. Hamish McDonald, "A Tour of Duty for Democracy," *Sun Herald* (Australia), April 1, 2012.
108. Svolik, "Authoritarian Reversals and Democratic Consolidation."
109. Felix Heiduk, "From Guardians to Democrats? Attempts to Explain Change and Continuity in the Civil-Military Relations of Post-Authoritarian Indonesia, Thailand and the Philippines," *Pacific Review* 24, no. 2 (2011): 249–71, 253.
110. Søren Ivarsson and Lotte Isager, *Saying the Unsayable: Monarchy and Democracy in Thailand* (Copenhagen: Nordic Institute of Asian Studies, 2010).
111. John Minns, *The Politics of Developmentalism: The Midas States of Mexico, South Korea, and Taiwan* (New York: Palgrave Macmillan, 2006), 233.
112. Duncan McCargo, "Network Monarchy and Legitimacy Crises in Thailand," *Pacific Review* 18, no. 4 (2005): 499–519, 501.
113. United Nations Public Administrative Network, "Administrative Reform Efforts in Thailand: Current Experiences and Successes" (1998), unpublished.
114. Nicholas Farrelly, "Why Democracy Struggles: Thailand's Elite Coup Culture," *Australian Journal of International Affairs* 67, no. 3 (2013): 281–96.
115. Robert B. Albritton and Thawilwadee Bureekul, "Consolidating Democracy in Thailand: The First Four Years of Democracy under the Constitution of 1997," *Asian Journal of Political Science* 16, no. 1 (2008): 41–63.
116. Michael Joseph Oakeshott, *On Human Conduct* (Oxford: Clarendon Press, 1975).
117. Leonardo Morlino, Björn Dressel, and Riccardo Pelizzo, "The Quality of Democracy in Asia-Pacific: Issues and Findings," *International Political Science Review* 32, no. 5 (2011): 491–511, 500.
118. Benjamin Reilly, "Democratization and Electoral Reform in the Asia-Pacific Region," *Comparative Political Studies* 40, no. 11 (2007): 1350–371.
119. Brian Woodall, "The Politics of Reform in Japan's Lower House Electoral System," in *Elections in Japan, Korea, and Taiwan under the Single Non-Transferable Vote: The Comparative Study of an Embedded Institution*, ed. Bernard Grofman, 23–50 (Ann Arbor: University of Michigan Press, 1999).
120. Dirk Tomsa, "The Indonesian Party System after the 2009 Elections: Towards Stability?," in *Problems of Democratisation in Indonesia: Elections,*

Institutions, and Society, ed. Edward Aspinall and Marcus Mietzner, 141–58 (Singapore: Institute of Southeast Asian Studies, 2010).

121. Jungug Choi, "District Magnitude, Social Diversity, and Indonesia's Parliamentary Party System from 1999 to 2009," *Asian Survey* 50, no. 4 (2010): 663–83.

122. Sunny Tanuwidjaja, "Indonesia's Electoral System: Finetuning the Reforms," January 6, 2011, http://www.eastasiaforum.org/2011/01/06/indonesias-electoral-system-finetuning-the-reforms/.

123. Hanta Yuda A. R., "The Problem of Presidential-Multiparty System" *The Jakarta Post*, August, 3, 2010.

124. Reilly, "Democratization and Electoral Reform in the Asia-Pacific Region," 1367.

125. "Chairman of National Reform Committee Comments on Ways to Achieve Reform," *Thai News Service*, August 5, 2010.

126. Jungug Choi, *Votes, Party Systems and Democracy in Asia* (New York: Routledge, 2012), 132.

127. Robert Dahl, *A Preface to Democratic Theory* (Chicago: University of Chicago Press, 1956), 146.

128. Tatsuo Inoue, "Legitimacy, Justice and Critical Democracy," in *Legitimacy in East Asia*, ed. Joseph Chan and Melissa Williams (Cambridge: Cambridge University Press, 2013).

129. Aurel Croissant, "Electoral Reform and Party Systems in East Asian Democracies: A Comparative Analysis with Implications for Thailand," in *Occasional Papers* (Bangkok: Friedrich Ebert Stiftung, 2007), 21.

130. Reilly, "Democratization and Electoral Reform in the Asia-Pacific Region," 1368.

131. T. J. Pempel, *Uncommon Democracies: The One-Party Dominant Regimes* (Ithaca, NY: Cornell University Press, 1990).

132. Hae Yung Song, "Democracy against Labour: The Dialectic of Democratisation and De-Democratisation in Korea," *Journal of Contemporary Asia* 43, no. 2 (2013): 338–62.

133. Willy Jou, "The Heuristic Value of the Left-Right Schema in East Asia," *International Political Science Review* 31, no. 3 (2010): 366–94, 373; Emile Sheng, "Partisanship in East Asia," *Journal of East Asian Studies* 7, no. 2 (2007): 275–93, 284.

134. Russell J. Dalton, To-chol Sin, and Yun-han Chu, *Party Politics in East Asia: Citizens, Elections, and Democratic Development* (Boulder, CO: Lynne Rienner Publishers, 2008); Andreas Ufen, "Party Systems, Critical Junctures, and Cleavages in Southeast Asia," *Asian Survey* 52, no. 3 (2012): 441–64.

135. Allen Hicken and Erik Martinez Kuhonta, "Shadows from the Past: Party System Institutionalization in Asia," *Comparative Political Studies* 44, no. 5 (2011): 572–97.

136. Choi, *Votes, Party Systems and Democracy in Asia*.

137. Ibid., 131.

138. Ceren Lord, "The Persistence of Turkey's Majoritarian System of Government," *Government and Opposition* 47, no. 2 (2012): 285–55.

139. R. E. Elson, "Two Failed Attempts to Islamize the Indonesian Constitution," *Sojourn: Journal of Social Issues in Southeast Asia* 28, no. 3 (2013): 379–437.

140. "Dr M: Respect Rights of Majority," *New Straits Times*, November 11, 2011.

141. Timothy Meisburger, "Getting Majoritarianism Right," *Journal of Democracy* 23, no. 1 (2012): 155–63.

142. Hicken and Martinez Kuhonta, "Shadows from the Past: Party System Institutionalization in Asia," 587.

143. Nizam U. Ahmed and Philip Norton, *Parliaments in Asia* (Portland: Frank Cass, 1999).

144. Kun-oh Kim, "Fiscal Consolidation and Budget Reform in Korea: The Role of the National Assembly," *RAND Center for Asia Pacific Policy Occasional Papers* (2012), 9.

145. USAID-Cambodia, (2008) *Political Competitiveness and Civil Society Assessment* (2008), 39.

146. Patrick Hein, "Strengthening the Legitimacy of Representative Democracy: Public Participation, Bipartisan Floor Bills and Plenary Deliberations in the Japanese Diet," *East Asia: An International Quarterly* 27, no. 3 (2010): 289–311.

147. Nobuo Ishihara, *Kengen no Daiido [The Major Transfer of Authority]* (Tokyo: Kanki Shuppan, 2001), 85.

148. Sherry L. Martin and Gill Steel, *Democratic Reform in Japan: Assessing the Impact* (Boulder, CO: Lynne Rienner Publishers, 2008).

149. Parliament of Malaysia, "Standing Orders" (2008), sec. 23, article C.

150. Rainer Heufers, "The Politics of Democracy in Malaysia," *Asien* 85, no. 10 (2002): 39–60.

151. Wan Azhar Wan Ahmad, "The Legislative, the Role and Functions of Parliament," in *Governing Malaysia*, ed. Baginda Abdul Razak Abdullah, 165–81 (Kuala Lumpur: Malaysian Strategic Research Centre, 2009), 178.

152. Gordon P. Means, *Malaysian Politics* (London: University of London Press, 1970), 354.

153. Raja Noriza Raja Ariffin and Norma Mansor, "The Cabinet: Highest Decision Maker in the Land," in *Governing Malaysia*, ed. Baginda, 113–39, 135.

154. Tippawan Lorsuwannarat and Ponlapat Buracom, "Performance Management Reforms in Thailand," in *Public Administration in Southeast Asia: Thailand, Philippines, Malaysia, Hong Kong and Macao*, ed. Evan M. Berman, 95–112 (Boca Raton, FL: CRC Press, 2010).

155. Stephen Sherlock, "The Parliament in Indonesia's Decade of Democracy: People's Forum or Chamber of Cronies?," in *Problems of Democratisation in Indonesia: Elections, Institutions, and Society*, ed. Aspinall and Mietzner, 160–78, 168.

156. "Rules of the House of Representatives of the Republic of Indonesia," http://www.dpr.go.id/id/tentang-dpr/tata-tertib. See ch. 17, articles 272–73; ch. 15, article 212; ch. 14, sec. 203.

157. Hans David Tampubolon, "Legislators Divided over 'Aspiration Home,'" *The Jakarta Post*, August 4, 2010.

158. Andreas Ufen, "Political Parties and Democratization in Indonesia," in *Democratization in Post-Suharto Indonesia*, ed. Marco Bünte and Andreas Ufen, 153–75 (London: Routledge, 2009), 167.

159. Stephen Sherlock, "Made by Committee and Consensus: Parties and Policy in the Indonesian Parliament," *South East Asia Research* 20, no. 4 (2012): 551–68.

160. Linda Yulisman, "House Set to Pass Long-Awaited Land Acquisition Bill This Week," *The Jakarta Post*, December 12, 2011.

161. "Analysts Urge Lawmakers to Work as 'Professionals,'" *The Jakarta Post*, March 11, 2010.

162. "Reform Capability Questioned," *The Jakarta Post*, March 29, 2010.

163. Patrick Ziegenhain, "The Indonesian Legislature and Its Impact on Democratic Consolidation," in *Democratization in Post-Suharto Indonesia*, ed. Bünte and Ufen, 33–52, 44.

164. Kuan Yew Lee, "What Price Democracy? (1962)," in *Lee Kuan Yew: The Man and His Ideas*, ed. Fook Kwang Han, Warren Fernandez, and Sumiko Tan, 365–67 (Singapore: Singapore Press Holding, 1998).

165. Michael D. Barr, "Lee Kuan Yew and the 'Asian Values' Debate," *Asian Studies Review* 24, no. 3 (2000): 309–35.

166. Kuan Yew Lee, "Democracy, Human Rights, and the Realities," *Ministerial Speeches: A Monthly Collection of Ministerial Speeches (Government of Singapore)* 16, no. 6 (1992): 20–37.

167. Morton H. Halperin, Joseph T. Siegle, and Michael M. Weinstein, *The Democracy Advantage: How Democracies Promote Prosperity and Peace* (New York: Routledge, 2005).

168. Pye, *Asian Power and Politics: The Cultural Dimensions of Authority*, 32–39, 339.

169. Clifford Geertz, *The Interpretation of Cultures: Selected Essays* (New York: Basic Books, 1973), 420.

170. Dan Slater, "Can Leviathan Be Democratic? Competitive Elections, Robust Mass Politics, and State Infrastructural Power," *Studies in Comparative International Development* 43, no. 3/4 (2008): 252–72; Dan Slater, *Ordering Power: Contentious Politics and Authoritarian Leviathans in Southeast Asia* (Cambridge: Cambridge University Press, 2011).

171. Yung-Myung Kim, "'Asian-Style Democracy': A Critique from East Asia," *Asian Survey* 37, no. 12 (1997): 1119–134, 1124.

172. Dan Slater, "Strong State Democratization in Malaysia and Singapore," *Journal of Democracy* 23, no. 2 (2012): 19–33.

173. Friedman, "Introduction," 7.

174. Pauline Baker, "The Dilemma of Democratization in Fragile States," *UN Chronicle* 48, no. 4 (2011): 34–36, 35.

175. Conor O'Dwyer, *Runaway State-Building: Patronage Politics and Democratic Development* (Baltimore: Johns Hopkins University Press, 2006).

176. Amy Blitz, "The Philippines: The Contested State," in *Nation Building, State Building, and Economic Development: Case Studies and Comparisons*, ed. S. C. M. Paine (New York: M. E. Sharpe, 2010).

177. Reinhard Bendix, *Nation-Building and Citizenship: Studies of Our Changing Social Order* (Berkeley: University of California Press, 1977).
178. Mark Robinson and Gordon White, *The Democratic Developmental State: Politics and Institutional Design* (New York: Oxford University Press, 1998).
179. Tat Yan Kong, "From Relative Autonomy to Consensual Development: The Case of South Korea," *Political Studies* 43, no. 4 (1995): 630–44; see also Hyug Baeg Im, "Better Democracy, Better Economic Growth? South Korea," *International Political Science Review* 32, no. 5 (2011): 579–97.
180. Gordon White, "Towards a Democratic Developmental State," *IDS Bulletin* 37, no. 4 (1995 [2006]): 60–70.
181. Carl Henrik Knutsen, "Investigating the Lee Thesis: How Bad Is Democracy for Asian Economies?," *European Political Science Review* 2, no. 3 (2010): 451–73.
182. Jing Chen, "Democratization and Government Education Provision in East Asia," *Journal of East Asian Studies* 8, no. 2 (2008): 175–97.
183. Michael T. Rock, "Has Democracy Slowed Growth in Asia?," *World Development* 37, no. 5 (2009): 941–52; Michael T. Rock, "East Asia's Democratic Developmental States and Economic Growth," *Journal of East Asian Studies* 13, no. 1 (2013): 1–34.
184. Michael T. Rock, "Has Democracy Slowed Growth in Asia?," 949.
185. Morlino, Dressel, and Pelizzo, "The Quality of Democracy in Asia-Pacific: Issues and Findings," 504–5.
186. James C. Scott, *Political Ideology in Malaysia: Reality and the Beliefs of an Elite* (New Haven, CT: Yale University Press, 1968).
187. Thomas W. D. Davis and Brian Galligan, *Human Rights in Asia* (Cheltenham: Edward Elgar, 2011).
188. Bernard Crick, *In Defence of Politics* (Chicago: University of Chicago Press, 1962), 98.
189. Larisa M. Efimova, "Stalin and the Revival of the Communist Party of Indonesia," *Cold War History* 5, no. 1 (2005): 107–20.
190. Zhengxu Wang, *Democratization in Confucian East Asia: Citizen Politics in China, Japan, Singapore, South Korea, Taiwan, and Vietnam* (Youngstown, NY: Cambria Press, 2008), 198–202.
191. Andrew Nathan, "Authoritarian Resilience," *Journal of Democracy* 14, no. 1 (2003): 6–17.
192. Bruce Gilley, "Legitimacy and Institutional Change: The Case of China," *Comparative Political Studies* 41, no. 3 (2008): 259–84.

5. Governance

1. Feng Li, *Bureaucracy and the State in Early China: Governing the Western Zhou* (Cambridge: Cambridge University Press, 2008).
2. Hans Bielenstein, *The Bureaucracy of Han Times* (Cambridge: Cambridge University Press, 1980).
3. S. E. Finer, *The History of Government from the Earliest Times* (Oxford: Oxford University Press, 1997).

4. Richard J. Miller, *Japan's First Bureaucracy: A Study of Eighth-Century Government* (Ithaca, NY: China-Japan Program, Cornell University, 1978).

5. Kiri Paramore, "The Nationalization of Confucianism: Academism, Examinations, and Bureaucratic Governance in the Late Tokugawa State," *Journal of Japanese Studies* 38, no. 1 (2012): 25–53.

6. Bidhya Bowornwathana, "History and Political Context of Public Administration in Thailand," in *Public Administration in Southeast Asia: Thailand, Philippines, Malaysia, Hong Kong and Macao*, ed. Evan M. Berman, 29–52 (Boca Raton, FL: CRC Press, Taylor & Francis, 2010), 32.

7. Roger H. Brown, "Shepherds of the People: Yasuoka Masahiro and the New Bureaucrats in Early Showa Japan," *Journal of Japanese Studies* 35, no. 2 (2009): 285–319.

8. Ibid., 294.

9. W. D. Reeve, *Public Administration in Siam* (London: Royal Institute of International Affairs, 1951), 35–36.

10. Anthony Cheung, "Government Reinvention in Taiwan: Administrative Modernisation and Regime Transition," in *Governance and Public Sector Reform in Asia: Paradigm Shifts or Business as Usual?*, ed. Anthony Cheung and Ian Scott, 90–116 (New York: RoutledgeCurzon, 2003).

11. Harry Harding, *Organizing China: The Problem of Bureaucracy, 1949–1976* (Stanford, CA: Stanford University Press, 1981).

12. Max Weber, *The Religion of China: Confucianism and Taoism* (Glencoe, IL: Free Press, 1951), 61–2.

13. Evan M. Berman, "Public Administration in East Asia: Common Roots, Ways, and Tasks," in *Public Administration in East Asia: Japan, South Korea, Chinese Mainland and Taiwan*, ed. Evan M. Berman, 1–29 (Boca Raton, FL: Taylor & Francis, 2010), 9.

14. U. Myint Thein, "Myanmar: Initiating Administrative Reform," in *Re-Thinking Administrative Reforms in Southeast Asia*, ed. Khai Leong Ho, 195–223 (Singapore: Marshall Cavendish Academic, 2006).

15. Alex Brillantes, Jr., and Maricel Fernandez, "Is There a Philippine Public Administration? Or Better Still, for Whom Is Philippine Public Administration?," paper presented at the conference *Is There a Philippine Public Administration: A Timeless Issue*, Manila, 2008, 16, tab. 5.

16. Fred Warren Riggs, *Thailand; the Modernization of a Bureaucratic Polity* (Honolulu, HI: East-West Center Press, 1966).

17. Bernard S. Silberman, *Ministers of Modernization; Elite Mobility in the Meiji Restoration, 1868–1873* (Tucson: University of Arizona Press, 1964).

18. James Chin, "History and Context of Public Administration in Malaysia," in *Public Administration in Southeast Asia: Thailand, Philippines, Malaysia, Hong Kong and Macao*, ed. Berman, 141–54, 144–45.

19. David Osborne and Ted Gaebler, *Reinventing Government: How the Entrepreneurial Spirit Is Transforming the Public Sector* (New York: Plume, 1992); David Osborne and Peter Plastrik, *Banishing Bureaucracy: The Five Strategies for Reinventing Government* (Reading, MA: Addison Wesley Pub. Co., 1997).

20. Anthony Cheung and Ian Scott, "Governance and Public Sector Reform in Asia: Paradigms, Paradoxes, and Dilemmas," in *Governance and Public Sector Reform in Asia: Paradigm Shifts or Business as Usual?*, ed. Cheung and Scott, 1–24, 7.

21. Anthony B. Cheung, "The Politics of Administrative Reforms in Asia: Paradigms and Legacies, Paths and Diversities," *Governance* 18, no. 2 (2005): 257–82, 276, 273.

22. Martin Painter, "Transforming the Administrative State: Reform in Hong Kong and the Future of the Developmental State," *Public Administration Review* 65, no. 3 (2005): 335–46, 342.

23. Mark Turner, "Choosing Items from the Menu: New Public Management in Southeast Asia," *International Journal of Public Administration* 25, no. 12 (2002): 1493–512.

24. Bowornwathana, "History and Political Context of Public Administration in Thailand," 34.

25. Martin Painter, "The Politics of Administrative Reform in East and Southeast Asia: From Gridlock to Continuous Self-Improvement?," *Governance* 17, no. 3 (2004): 361–86, 368.

26. Chin, "History and Context of Public Administration in Malaysia."

27. Hong-hai Lim, "Improving Administrative Performance in Malaysia," in *Transforming Asian Governance: Rethinking Assumptions, Challenging Practices*, ed. M. Ramesh and Scott Fritzen, 19–41 (London; New York: Routledge, 2009).

28. Lucian W. Pye, *Asian Power and Politics: The Cultural Dimensions of Authority* (Cambridge, MA: Belknap Press, 1985), 263.

29. Osborne and Gaebler, *Reinventing Government: How the Entrepreneurial Spirit Is Transforming the Public Sector*, 93, 233.

30. Masao Kikuchi, "Public Policy Processes and Citizen Participation in Japan," in *Public Administration in East Asia: Japan, South Korea, Chinese Mainland and Taiwan*, ed. Berman, 213–32, 219.

31. Akira Nakamura, "Reforming Government and Changing Styles of Japanese Governance: Public Administration at the Crossroads," in *Handbook of Comparative Public Administration in the Asia-Pacific Basin*, ed. Hoi-kwok Wong and Hon S. Chan, 123–40 (New York: M. Dekker, 1999), 131.

32. Yang Sung-jin, "Park Won-Shik Reserved for BOK Senior Deputy Governor," *The Korea Herald*, February 21, 2012.

33. In-Soo Nam, "New Attitudes on Age Rattle Korean Hierarchies," *The Wall Street Journal*, October 18, 2012.

34. Chun-Oh Park and Jaehyun Joo, "Re-Control over the Korean Bureaucracy: A Review of the NPM Civil Service Reforms under the Roh Moo-Hyun Government," *Review of Public Personnel Administration* 30, no. 2 (2010): 189–210, 197, 204.

35. Ibid., 204.

36. "Rationale for PS21: Why Is It Important to Have a Public Service Change Movement?" http://www.ps21.gov.sg/rationale.html.

37. Bidhya Bowornwathana, "Thaksin's Model of Government Reform: Prime Ministerialisation through 'A Country Is My Company' Approach," *Asian Journal of Political Science* 12, no. 1 (2004): 135–53.

38. Anthony Cheung, "One Country, Two Experiences: Administrative Reforms in China and Hong Kong," *International Review of Administrative Sciences* 78, no. 2 (2012): 261–83, 275.

39. Bing Hu, "Xingzheng sanfenzhi: Zhidu beijing fenxi [Administrative Trifurcation: A Background Analysis]," *Hubei Shehui Kexue (Hubei Social Sciences)*, no. 7 (2004): 14–17; Liuning Yu, "Woguo xingzheng tizhi gaigede xin tujing – Xingzheng sanfen zhi [Administrative Trifurcation: A New Breakthrough in Administrative Reforms in China]," *Qiye Daobao (Enterprise Herald)*, no. 5 (2012): 19–20.

40. Cheung, "One Country, Two Experiences: Administrative Reforms in China and Hong Kong," 276.

41. Christoph Knill, "Explaining Cross-National Variance in Administrative Reform," *Journal of Public Policy* 19, no. 2 (1999): 113–39; Myung-Jae Moon and Patrician Ingraham, "Shaping Administrative Reform and Governance: An Examination of the Political Nexus Triads in Three Asian Countries," *Governance* 11, no. 1 (1998): 77–100.

42. Painter, "The Politics of Administrative Reform in East and Southeast Asia: From Gridlock to Continuous Self-Improvement?"

43. Ezra F. Vogel, "A Little Dragon Tamed," in *Management of Success: The Moulding of Modern Singapore*, ed. Kernial Singh Sandhu and Paul Wheatley, 1049–67 (Singapore: Institute of Southeast Asian Studies, 1989), 1049.

44. Jon S. T. Quah, *Public Administration Singapore Style* (Singapore: Talisman Pub., 2010).

45. UNDESA and UNDP, *Report On Key Findings Of The Regional Forum On Reinventing Government In East And Southeast Asia* (August 21–23, 2004), 20, http://unpan1.un.org/intradoc/groups/public/documents/un/unpan020550.pdf.

46. Heungsuk Choi, "E-Government in South Korea," in *Public Administration in East Asia: Japan, South Korea, Chinese Mainland and Taiwan*, ed. Berman, 473–93.

47. Mark Beeson, "Japan's Reluctant Reformers and the Legacy of the Developmental State," in *Governance and Public Sector Reform in Asia: Paradigm Shifts or Business as Usual?*, ed. Cheung and Scott, 25–43, 25.

48. Jorrit de Jong and Arre Zuurmond, "The Hara Factor: Some Lessons from Innovations in Governance in Japan," in *Transforming Asian Governance: Rethinking Assumptions, Challenging Practices*, ed. Ramesh and Fritzen, 97–115.

49. See http://www.navi.go.jp/.

50. Amelia P. Varela, *Administrative Culture and Political Change*, 1st ed. (Diliman, Quezon City: College of Public Administration, University of the Philippines, 1996).

51. Frances F. Korten and Robert Y. Siy, *Transforming a Bureaucracy: The Experience of the Philippine National Irrigation Administration* (Quezon City: Ateneo de Manila University Press, 1989).

52. Open Budget Initiative, Open Budget Index, 2011.

53. Michael T. Rock and Heidi Bonnett, "The Comparative Politics of Corruption: Accounting for the East Asian Paradox in Empirical Studies of

Corruption, Growth and Investment," *World Development* 32, no. 6 (2004): 999–1007.

54. Jon S. T. Quah, *Curbing Corruption in Asia: A Comparative Study of Six Countries* (Singapore: Eastern Universities Press, 2003); Ting Gong and Stephen K. Ma, *Preventing Corruption in Asia: Institutional Design and Policy Capacity* (London: Routledge, 2009).

55. Mushtaq H. Khan, "Rents, Efficiency, and Growth; Rent-Seeking as Process," in *Rents, Rent-Seeking and Economic Development: Theory and Evidence in Asia*, ed. Mushtaq H. Khan and K. S. Jomo, 21–144 (Cambridge: Cambridge University Press, 2000).

56. Tsuyoshi Tsuru, "Union Participation in the Local Public Sector – Evidence from the Membership Survey of a Japanese Public Sector Union in the Tokyo and Kanagawa Areas," *Keizai Kenkyu (Economic Review)* 46, no. 4 (1995): 323–33.

57. Youngmo Yoon, "A Comparative Study on Industrial Relations and Collective Bargaining in East Asian Countries " *ILO Working Papers* 8(2009), 23.

58. Ibid.

59. Chung-yang Kim, *The Korean Civil Service System* (Seoul: Bubwoosa, 2006), 267.

60. Martin Painter, "Bureaucratic Autonomy and Administrative Reform Capacity in East and Southeast Asia," in *Public Service Reform in East Asia: Reform Issues and Challenges in Japan, Korea, Singapore and Hong Kong*, ed. Anthony Cheung, 231–54 (Hong Kong: Chinese University Press, 2005), 235.

61. Leonardo Morlino, Björn Dressel, and Riccardo Pelizzo, "The Quality of Democracy in Asia-Pacific: Issues and Findings," *International Political Science Review* 32, no. 4 (2011): 491–511, 503.

62. Martin Painter, "Bureaucratic Performance, Policy Capacity and Administrative Reform," in *Democratisation, Governance and Regionalism in East and South East Asia: A Comparative Study*, ed. Ian Marsh and Jean Blondel, 123–51 (London: Routledge, 2006), 134.

63. Bidhya Bowornwathana, "Administrative Reform and the Politician-Bureaucrat Perspective: Visions, Processes, and Support for Reform," in *Handbook of Comparative Public Administration in the Asia-Pacific Basin*, ed. Wong and Chan, 69–78, 69.

64. Jeeyang Rhee Baum, *Responsive Democracy: Increasing State Accountability in East Asia* (Ann Arbor: University of Michigan Press, 2011), 2.

65. Martin Painter, "Thaksinisation or Managerialism? Reforming the Thai Bureaucracy," *Journal of Contemporary Asia* 36, no. 1 (2006): 26–47, 34.

66. Tippawan Lorsuwannarat and Ponlapat Buracom, "Performance Management Reforms in Thailand," in *Public Administration in Southeast Asia: Thailand, Philippines, Malaysia, Hong Kong and Macao*, ed. Berman, 95–112.

67. Chaiwatt Mansrisuk, "Decentralisation in Thailand and the Limits of the Functionalist Perspective of Institutional Reform," *European Journal of East Asian Studies* 11, no. 1 (2012): 71–97, 87.

68. Kikuchi, "Public Policy Processes and Citizen Participation in Japan," 217.

69. Tomohito Shinoda, *Leading Japan: The Role of the Prime Minister* (Westport, CT: Praeger, 2000), xvi. See also Kenji Hayao, *The Japanese Prime Minister and Public Policy* (Pittsburgh: University of Pittsburgh Press, 1993). For an updated statement of bureaucratic power, see: Brian Woodall, *Growing Democracy in Japan: The Parliamentary Cabinet System since 1868* (Lexington: University Press of Kentucky, 2014).

70. Gene Park, "The Politics of Budgeting in Japan: How Much Do Institutions Matter?," *Asian Survey* 50, no. 5 (2010): 965–89.

71. Masao Kikuchi, "Performance Management Reforms in Japan," in *Public Administration in East Asia: Japan, South Korea, Chinese Mainland and Taiwan*, ed. Berman, 273–90, 281.

72. John M. Maki, "The Prime Minister's Office and Executive Power in Japan," *Far Eastern Survey* 24, no. 5 (1955): 71–75, 71.

73. Brown, "Shepherds of the People: Yasuoka Masahiro and the New Bureaucrats in Early Showa Japan," 289.

74. Anthony Cheung, "Rebureaucratization of Politics in Hong Kong," *Asian Survey* 37, no. 8 (1997): 720–38.

75. James Ockey, "State, Bureaucracy and Polity in Modern Thai Politics," *Journal of Contemporary Asia* 34, no. 2 (2004): 143–62.

76. World Bank, *Philippines Growth with Equity: The Remaining Agenda*, report no. 20066-PH (2000), vi, 100, 98.

77. Diane Claire Jiao, "Task Force to Monitor Activities of Gov't Agencies, Says DBM," *BusinessWorld* (Manila), January 6, 2012.

78. Hiroyuki Mori, "Innovation for Constrained Municipalities in Japan," in *Innovative Trends in Public Governance in Asia*, ed. Ari-Veikko Anttiroiko, S. J. Bailey, and Pekka Valkama, 48–58 (Amsterdam: IOS Press, 2011).

79. OECD, Government at a Glance 2011, tab. 22.2. Change in the Percentage of Government Staff Employed at the Central Level (2000 and 2008).

80. Shun-ichiro Bessho, "Implementation of Public Works and Intergovernmental Relationships in Japan," *Public Policy Review* 6, no. 1 (2010): 167–98.

81. Takashi Tsukamoto, "Neoliberalization of the Developmental State: Tokyo's Bottom-up Politics and State Rescaling in Japan," *International Journal of Urban and Regional Research* 36, no. 1 (2012): 71–89.

82. Ministry of Strategy and Finance, Digital Budget and Accounting System, http://www.digitalbrain.go.kr.

83. Charles Conteh, "Governance of Private Sector Development Policy Implementation in Singapore," *Asian Journal of Political Science* 17, no. 1 (2009): 71–88.

84. Khai Leong Ho, "Bureaucratic Accountability in Malaysia: Control Mechanisms and Critical Concerns," in *Handbook of Comparative Public Administration in the Asia-Pacific Basin*, ed. Wong and Chan, 23–46, 40.

85. Hiroaki Richard Watanabe, "Why and How Did Japan Finally Change Its Ways? The Politics of Japanese Labour-Market Deregulation since the 1990s," *Japan Forum* 24, no. 1 (2012): 23–50.

86. Hiroshi Itoh, *The Impact of Globalization on Japan's Public Policy: How the Government Is Reshaping Japan's Role in the World* (Lewiston: Edwin Mellen Press, 2008).

87. Tong-yi Huang and Wenming Tu, "Public Policy Processes and Citizen Participation in Taiwan," in *Public Administration in East Asia: Japan, South Korea, Chinese Mainland and Taiwan*, ed. Berman, 517–31, 522.

88. Yi Jiang and Xiaoting Zheng, "Private Sector Participation and Performance of Urban Water Utilities in the People's Republic of China," *ADB Economics Working Papers*, no. 237 (2010), 10.

89. Mark Dumol, *The Manila Water Concession: A Key Government Official's Diary of the World's Largest Water Privatization* (Washington, DC: World Bank, 2000).

90. Bidhya Bowornwathana, "Thailand," in *Government Agencies: Practices and Lessons from 30 Countries*, ed. Koen Verhoest Sandra Van Thiel, Geert Bouckaert, and Per Laegreid, 381–92 (New York: Palgrave, 2012).

91. John Owen Haley, *Authority without Power: Law and the Japanese Paradox*, Studies on Law and Social Control (New York: Oxford University Press, 1991).

92. Veronica Taylor, "Globalization and Japanese Regulation: A Commercial Dispute Case Study," in *Regulation in Asia: Pushing Back on Globalization*, ed. John Gillespie and Randall Peerenboom, 213–37 (London: Routledge, 2009).

93. Andrew Walter, "From Developmental to Regulatory State? Japan's New Financial Regulatory System," *Pacific Review* 19, no. 4 (2006): 405–28, 407, 419.

94. Shiu-fai Wong and Martin Painter, "Varieties of the Regulatory State? Government-Business Relations and Telecommunications Reforms in Malaysia and Thailand," *Policy and Society* 24, no. 3 (2005): 27–52, 44.

95. OECD Government at a Glance 2011, sec. 47. Evaluating Regulatory Performance.

96. Jeeyang Rhee Baum and Kathleen Bawn, "Slowing at Sunset: Administrative Procedures and the Pace of Reform in Korea," *Journal of East Asian Studies* 11, no. 2 (2011): 197–221.

97. "Background." http://www.prokhas.com.my.

98. Aishah Bidin, "Law Reform and Corporate Governance in Malaysia," in *Regulation in Asia: Pushing Back on Globalization*, ed. Gillespie and Peerenboom, 296–317, 312.

99. Henry Wai-chung Yeung, "From National Development to Economic Diplomacy? Governing Singapore's Sovereign Wealth Funds," *Pacific Review* 24, no. 5 (2011): 625–52.

100. Jolene Lin, "The Judicialization of Governance: The Case of Singapore," in *Administrative Law and Governance in Asia: Comparative Perspectives*, ed. Tom Ginsburg and Hongyi Chen, 287–312 (New York: Routledge, 2008), 288, 306.

101. Roselyn Hsueh, *China's Regulatory State: A New Strategy for Globalization* (Ithaca, NY: Cornell University Press, 2011).

102. Mark Beeson, "Globalization, Governance, and the Political-Economy of Public Policy Reform in East Asia," *Governance* 14, no. 4 (2011): 481–503.

103. Darryl Jarvis, "The Regulatory State in Developing Countries: Can It Exist and Do We Want It? The Case of the Indonesian Power Sector," *Journal of Contemporary Asia* 42, no. 3 (2012): 464–92.

104. Patricia Hodgson, "The Rise and Rise of the Regulatory State," *Political Quarterly* 77, no. 2 (2006): 247–54.
105. Patrick Hassenteufel, Marc Smyrl, William Genieys, and Francisco Javier Moreno-Fuentes, "Programmatic Actors and the Transformation of European Health Care States," *Journal of Health Politics, Policy, and Law* 35, no. 4 (2010): 517–38.
106. R. P. Peerenboom, "Varieties of Rule of Law: An Introduction and Provisional Conclusion," in *Asian Discourses of Rule of Law: Theories and Implementation of Rule of Law in Twelve Asian Countries, France, and the U.S.*, ed. R. P. Peerenboom, 1–55 (New York: Routledge, 2004), 27.
107. John Henry Merryman, David Scott Clark, and John Owen Haley, *Comparative Law: Historical Development of the Civil Law Tradition in Europe, Latin America, and East Asia* (New Providence, NJ: LexisNexis, 2009), 548.
108. David Martin Jones, *Political Development in Pacific Asia* (Cambridge: Polity Press, 1997), 56.
109. Haig Patapan, "Leadership, Law and Legitimacy: Reflections on the Changing Nature of Judicial Politics in Asia," in *The Judicialization of Politics in Asia*, ed. Björn Dressel, 219–33 (New York: Routledge, 2012), 231.
110. Sungmoon Kim, "Confucian Constitutionalism: Mencius and Xunzi on Virtue, Ritual, and Royal Transmission," *Review of Politics* 73, no. 3 (2011): 371–99; Tom Ginsburg, "Confucian Constitutionalism? The Emergence of Constitutional Review in Korea and Taiwan," *Law & Social Inquiry* 27, no. 4 (2002): 763–99.
111. Stewart Fenwick, "Law and Judicial Review in Indonesia," in *Administrative Law and Governance in Asia: Comparative Perspectives*, ed. Ginsburg and Chen, 329–58, 331–2.
112. Jolene Lin, "The Judicialization of Governance: The Case of Singapore," in *Administrative Law and Governance in Asia: Comparative Perspectives*, ed. Ginsburg and Chen, 287–312, 296.
113. Ernst Fraenkel, *The Dual State: A Contribution to the Theory of Dictatorship* (New York: Oxford University Press, 1941).
114. Kanishka Jayasuriya, *Law, Capitalism and Power in Asia: The Rule of Law and Legal Institutions*, Asian Capitalisms (London: Routledge, 1999).
115. Richard Sakwa, *The Crisis of Russian Democracy: The Dual State, Factionalism, and the Medvedev Succession* (Cambridge: Cambridge University Press, 2012).
116. Victor Vridar Ramraj and Arun K. Thiruvengadam, *Emergency Powers in Asia: Exploring the Limits of Legality* (Cambridge: Cambridge University Press, 2009); David Streckfuss, *Truth on Trial in Thailand: Defamation, Treason, and Lèse-Majesté* (New York: Routledge, 2011).
117. Li-ann Thio, "Soft Constitutional Law in Nonliberal Asian Constitutional Democracies," *International Journal of Constitutional Law* 8, no. 4 (2010): 766–99.
118. Hitoshi Ushijima, "Administrative Law and Judicialized Governance in Japan," in *Administrative Law and Governance in Asia: Comparative Perspectives*, ed. Ginsburg and Chen, 81–100.

119. Jiunn-rong Yeh, "Democracy-Driven Transformation to Regulatory State," in *Administrative Law and Governance in Asia: Comparative Perspectives*, ed. Ginsburg and Chen, 127–42, 138.

120. Tae-Ung Baik, "Public Interest Litigation in South Korea," in *Public Interest Litigation in Asia*, ed. Po Jen Yap and Holning Lau, 115–35 (London: Routledge, 2011), 126.

121. Chris Lydgate, *Lee's Law: How Singapore Crushes Dissent* (Melbourne: Scribe, 2004), 38.

122. Makoto Ibusuki, "'Quo Vadis': First Year Inspection to Japanese Mixed Jury Trial," *Asian-Pacific Law and Policy Journal* 12, no. 1 (2010): 25–58.

123. Lawrence Ward Beer, *Constitutional Systems in Late Twentieth Century Asia*, Asian Law Series (Seattle: University of Washington Press, 1992).

124. Kanishka Jayasuriya, "Riding the Accountability Wave? Accountability Communities and New Modes of Governance," in *Administrative Law and Governance in Asia: Comparative Perspectives*, ed. Ginsburg and Chen, 59–79, 60, 61.

125. John Owen Haley, *The Spirit of Japanese Law* (Athens: University of Georgia Press, 1998).

126. Frank K. Upham, "Political Lackeys or Faithful Public Servants? Two Views of the Japanese Judiciary," *Law & Social Inquiry* 30, no. 2 (2005): 421–55, 449.

127. Gan Ching Chuan, "Administrative Law and Judicialized Governance in Malaysia: The Indian Connection," in *Administrative Law and Governance in Asia: Comparative Perspectives*, ed. Ginsburg and Chen, 257–86, 270.

128. Japan Federation of Bar Associations, "Urgent Recommendations on Policies for the Number of Legal Professionals," March 27, 2011.

129. Bjorn Dressel, "Judicialization of Politics or Politicization of the Judiciary? Considerations from Recent Events in Thailand," *Pacific Review* 23, no. 5 (2010): 671–91.

130. Peter Leyland, "Genealogy of the Administrative Courts and the Consolidation of Administrative Justice in Thailand," in *New Courts in Asia*, ed. Andrew Harding and Penelope Nicholson, 231–50 (London; New York: Routledge, 2010).

131. Annual Report 2010, http://www.admincourt.go.th/00_web/08_service/report/annual_report53.pdf.

132. Tom Ginsburg, "The Constitutional Court and the Judicialization of Korean Politics," in *New Courts in Asia*, ed. Harding and Nicholson, 145–57.

133. Jayasuriya, *Law, Capitalism and Power in Asia: The Rule of Law and Legal Institutions*, xii.

134. Lin, "The Judicialization of Governance: The Case of Singapore," 298.

135. Mark Thompson, "Moore Meets Gramsci and Burke in Southeast Asia: New Democracies And 'Civil' Societies," in *The Crisis of Democratic Governance in Southeast Asia*, ed. Aurel Croissant and Marco Bünte, 57–74 (New York: Palgrave Macmillan, 2011).

136. Berman, "Public Administration in East Asia: Common Roots, Ways, and Tasks," 23.

137. Moon and Ingraham, "Shaping Administrative Reform and Governance: An Examination of the Political Nexus Triads in Three Asian Countries."

138. R. Common, "Administrative Change in the Asia Pacific: Applying the Political Nexus Triad," *International Public Management Journal* 7, no. 3 (2004): 347–64, 359.

139. Jennifer S. Oh, "Strong State and Strong Civil Society in Contemporary South Korea," *Asian Survey* 52, no. 3 (2012): 528–49.

140. Julia Lai Po-Wah Tao, *Governance for Harmony in Asia and Beyond* (New York: Routledge, 2011).

141. Bryan S. Turner, "Nation and Social Citizenship: Some Structural and Cultural Problems with Modern Citizenship," in *Contested Citizenship in East Asia*, ed. Kyung-sup Chang and Bryan S. Turner, 15–42 (New York: Routledge, 2012), 30.

142. Johan Olsen, "Change and Continuity: An Institutional Approach to Institutions of Democratic Government," in *Comparative Administrative Change and Reform*, ed. Patricia W. Ingraham, Jon Pierre, and B. Guy Peters, 15–47 (Montreal: McGill-Queen's University Press, 2010).

143. Jacob Torfing, "Harmony through Network Governance?," in *Governance for Harmony in Asia and Beyond*, ed. Julia Lai Po-Wah Tao, 243–64 (New York: Routledge, 2011).

144. Turner, "Nation and Social Citizenship: Some Structural and Cultural Problems with Modern Citizenship," 22.

145. Cheung and Scott, "Governance and Public Sector Reform in Asia: Paradigms, Paradoxes, and Dilemmas," 3.

146. Pan Suk Kim, "Government Reform in Korea," in *Handbook of Comparative Public Administration in the Asia-Pacific Basin*, ed. Wong and Chan, 163–78, 176.

147. Daeyong Choi, "A Radical Approach to Regulatory Reform in Korea," paper presented at the Annual Conference of the American Society for Public Administration, Rutgers University, March 2001.

148. Joan Leung, "State Capacity and Public Sector Reforms in Post-Crisis Korea," in *Governance and Public Sector Reform in Asia: Paradigm Shifts or Business as Usual?*, ed. Cheung and Scott, 44–66, 44.

149. Jongcheol Kim, "Government Reform, Judicialization, and the Development of Public Law in the Republic of Korea," in *Administrative Law and Governance in Asia: Comparative Perspectives*, ed. Ginsburg and Chen, 101–26, 112.

150. Euiyoung Kim, "The Limits of Ngo-Government Relations in South Korea," *Asian Survey* 49, no. 5 (2009): 873–94.

151. Sheldon M. Garon, *Molding Japanese Minds: The State in Everyday Life* (Princeton, NJ: Princeton University Press, 1997), 6, 19.

152. Gesine Foljanty-Jost, "Bringing the Citizen Back In: Democratic Dimensions of Local Reforms in Germany and Japan," *East Asia: An International Quarterly* 28, no. 4 (2011): 313–28, 320.

153. Yasuo Takao, "Co-Governance by Local Government and Civil Society Groups in Japan: Balancing Equity and Efficiency for Trust in Public

Institutions," *Asia Pacific Journal of Public Administration* 28, no. 2 (2006): 171–99.

154. Laothamatas Anek, *Business Associations and the New Political Economy of Thailand: From Bureaucratic Polity to Liberal Corporatism* (Boulder, CO: Westview Press, 1992).

155. Bidhya Bowornwathana, "Bureaucrats, Politicians, and the Transfer of Administrative Reform in Thailand," in *Comparative Administrative Change and Reform: Lessons Learned*, ed. Ingraham, Pierre, and Peters, 207–30, 214.

156. Mark Turner, "How to Win Friends and Influence People: Civic Engagement in the Philippines," *Public Administration and Development* 31 (2011): 91–101.

157. Garry Rodan and Kanishka Jayasuriya, "The Technocratic Politics of Administrative Participation: Case Studies of Singapore and Vietnam," *Democratization* 14, no. 5 (2007): 795–815, 800.

158. Kamaludeen Mohamed Nasir and Bryan Turner, "Governing as Gardening: Reflections on Soft Authoritarianism in Singapore," *Citizenship Studies* 17, no. 3/4 (2013): 339–52.

159. "Decision on Casino 'Will Take Time,'" *Straits Times*, December 30, 2004.

160. Statement By Prime Minister Lee Hsien Loong on Proposal to Develop Integrated Resorts, Parliament House, April 18, 2005, http://www.mti.gov. sg/MTIInsights/Documents/Ministerial%20Statement%20-%20PM%20 18apro5.pdf.

161. Edmund Burke, "Speech to the Electors of Bristol," in *The Works of the Right Honourable Edmund Burke*, 446–48 (London: H. G. Bohn, 1774 [1854]).

6. Public Policy

1. "What Is BFR Really?" http://www.pemandu.gov.my/gtp/Big_Fast_Result-@-Big_Fast_Results.aspx.

2. Anthony Cheung, "Interpreting East Asian Social Policy Development," in *Changing Governance and Public Policy in East Asia*, ed. Ka-Ho Mok and Ray Forrest, 38–46 (London: Routledge, 2009), 38.

3. The World Bank, "Government Expense as % GDP, Cluster and Country Averages," *Country Indicators* (mostly 2009 to 2011), http://data.worldbank. org/indicator/GC.XPN.TOTL.GD.ZS.

4. Byung-In Lim and Jin Kwon Hyun, "What Makes the Income Tax System So Progressive? – The Case of Korea," *Applied Economics Letters* 16, nos. 7–9 (2009): 683–87.

5. Konstantinos Angelopoulos, Apostolis Philippopoulos, and Efthymios Tsionas, "Does Public Sector Efficiency Matter? Revisiting the Relation between Fiscal Size and Economic Growth in a World Sample," *Public Choice* 137, nos. 1–2 (2008): 245–78.

6. Eric C. Wang and Eskander Alvi, "Relative Efficiency of Government Spending and Its Determinants: Evidence from East Asian Countries," *Eurasian Economic Review* 1, no. 1 (2011): 3–28.

7. Chandran Govindaraju, Ramesh Rao, and Sajid Anwar, "Economic Growth and Government Spending in Malaysia," *Economic Change and Restructuring* 44, no. 3 (2011): 203–19.

8. Young Jun Choi, "End of the Era of Productivist Welfare Capitalism? Diverging Welfare Regimes in East Asia," *Asian Journal of Social Science* 40, no. 3 (2012): 275–94.

9. "New Cradles to Graves," *The Economist*, September 8, 2012.

10. Gregory James Kasza, *One World of Welfare: Japan in Comparative Perspective*, Cornell Studies in Political Economy (Ithaca, NY: Cornell University Press, 2006), 133–34.

11. Ian Holliday, "Productivist Welfare Capitalism: Social Policy in East Asia," *Political Studies* 48, no. 4 (2000): 706–23.

12. Christian Aspalter, "The East Asian Welfare Model," *International Journal of Social Welfare* 15, no. 4 (2006): 290–301, 292, 297.

13. Wayne Vroman and Vera Brusentsev, "Unemployment Compensation throughout the World: A Comparative Analysis," *W. E. Upjohn Institute for Employment Research* (2005).

14. Mari Miura, *Welfare through Work: Conservative Ideas, Partisan Dynamics, and Social Protection in Japan* (Ithaca, NY: Cornell University Press, 2012).

15. Chak Kwan Chan, "Workfare in East Asia: Development and Characteristics," in *Welfare Reform in East Asia: Towards Workfare?*, ed. Chak Kwan Chan and King Lun Ngok, 151–66 (New York: Routledge, 2011), 164.

16. Agus Mohd. Razali, J. F. Doling, and Dong-Sung Lee, *Housing Policy Systems in South and East Asia* (New York: Palgrave Macmillan, 2002).

17. Rick Groves, Alan Murie, and C. J. Watson, *Housing and the New Welfare State: Perspectives from East Asia and Europe* (Aldershot: Ashgate, 2007).

18. Richard Ronald and John Doling, "Shifting East Asian Approaches to Home Ownership and the Housing Welfare Pillar," *International Journal of Housing Policy* 10, no. 3 (2010): 233–54, 237.

19. Gordon White and Roger Goodman, "Welfare Orientalism and the Search for an East Asian Welfare Model," in *The East Asian Welfare Model: Welfare Orientalism and the State*, ed. Roger Goodman, Gordon White, and Huck-ju Kwon, 3–24 (London: Routledge, 1998), 15.

20. Ito Peng and Joseph Wong, "Institutions and Institutional Purpose: Continuity and Change in East Asian Social Policy," *Politics & Society* 36, no. 1 (2008): 61–88, 79–82.

21. James Lee, James Midgley, and Yapeng Zhu, *Social Policy and Change in East Asia* (Lanham, MD: Lexington Books, 2013).

22. White and Goodman, "Welfare Orientalism and the Search for an East Asian Welfare Model."

23. Ezra F. Vogel, *Japan as Number One: Lessons for America* (Cambridge, MA: Harvard University Press, 1979).

24. Misa Izuhara and Ray Forrest, "'Active Families': Familization, Housing and Welfare across Generations in East Asia," *Social Policy & Administration* 47, no. 5 (2013): 520–41.

25. Sarah Conly, *Against Autonomy: Justifying Coercive Paternalism* (Cambridge: Cambridge University Press, 2013).

26. Douglas H. Brooks, *Infrastructure's Role in Lowering Asia's Trade Costs* (Manila: Asian Development Bank Institute, 2009); Kalpana Seethepalli, Maria Caterina Bramati, and David Veredas, "How Relevant Is Infrastructure to Growth in East Asia?," *World Bank Policy Research Working Paper Series,* no. 4597 (2008).

27. Martin Painter, "Governance for Harmony: Challenges for Public Service Delivery Reform in China and Vietnam," in *Governance for Harmony in Asia and Beyond,* ed. Julia Lai Po-Wah Tao, 138–58 (New York: Routledge, 2011).

28. Tsuyoshi Kotaka and David L. Callies, *Taking Land: Compulsory Purchase and Regulation in Asian-Pacific Countries* (Honolulu: University of Hawaii Press, 2002).

29. Tsuyoshi Kotaka, David Callies, and Heidi Guth, "Taking Land: Compulsory Purchase and the Regulation of Land in Asia-Pacific Countries," *Asia Pacific Law Review* 9, no. 2 (2001): 103–32, 127.

30. Adrienne La Grange and Hee Nam Jung, "The Commodification of Land and Housing: The Case of South Korea," *Housing Studies* 19, no. 4 (2004): 557–80, 566.

31. Kevin J. O'Brien and Lianjiang Li, *Rightful Resistance in Rural China* (Cambridge: Cambridge University Press, 2006).

32. David E. Apter and Nagayo Sawa, *Against the State: Politics and Social Protest in Japan* (Cambridge, MA: Harvard University Press, 1984), 216, 200.

33. Tom Gillespie, "Runway Run-In," *Mother Jones* 16, no. 1 (January/February 1991): 24–26, 24.

34. "Black Day at Narita Airport: Farmers and Students Thwart an Embarrassed Government," *Time Magazine,* April 10, 1978.

35. Apter and Sawa, *Against the State: Politics and Social Protest in Japan,* 231, 239, 209, 204.

36. International Energy Agency, *World Energy Outlook, Electricity Consumption Series* (various years).

37. Lorenzo Kristov, "The Price of Electricity in Indonesia," *Bulletin of Indonesian Economic Studies* 31, no. 3 (1995): 73–101.

38. Fabby Tumiwa, *The Electricity Governance Initiative: The Case of Indonesia* (Washington, DC: World Resources Institute, 2005). See also Fabby Tumiwa, "Switch On/Switch Off: Lessons Learned from the Reform of the Indonesia Power Sector," paper presented at the International Conference on "Establishing a Dialogue on Fuel and Energy Sector Transparency Initiative," Bishkek, September 26–27, 2011.

39. Darryl Jarvis, "The Regulatory State in Developing Countries: Can It Exist and Do We Want It? The Case of the Indonesian Power Sector," *Journal of Contemporary Asia* 42, no. 3 (2012): 464–92, 485, 486.

40. Mika M. Purra, "The Indonesian Electricity Sector: Institutional Transition, Regulatory Capacity and Outcomes," *Centre on Asia and Globalization, Lee Kuan Yew School of Public Policy, National University of Singapore* (2010).

41. Ibid.

42. Thilde Bruun, Andreas Neergaard, Deborah Lawrence, and Alan Ziegler., "Environmental Consequences of the Demise in Swidden Cultivation in

Southeast Asia: Carbon Storage and Soil Quality," *Human Ecology* 37, no. 3 (2009): 375–88.

43. Anthony T. H. Chin and Joyce M. W. Low, "Port Performance in Asia: Does Production Efficiency Imply Environmental Efficiency?," *Transportation Research: Part D* 15, no. 8 (2010): 483–8.

44. I-Shin Chang, Jing Wu, Yanxia Yang, Mingmin Shi, Xiaochun Li, "Ecological Compensation for Natural Resource Utilisation in China," *Journal of Environmental Planning and Management* 57, no. 2 (2013): 273–96.

45. Corey J. A. Bradshaw, Xingli Giam, and Navjot S. Sodhi, "Evaluating the Relative Environmental Impact of Countries," *PlosOne* 5, no. 5 (2010): 1–23.

46. Hiroyuki Taguchi, "The Environmental Kuznets Curve in Asia: The Case of Sulphur and Carbon Emissions," *Asia-Pacific Development Journal* 19, no. 2 (2012): 77–92; Samsul Alam and Nurul Kabir, "Economic Growth and Environmental Sustainability: Empirical Evidence from East and South-East Asia," *International Journal of Economics and Finance* 5, no. 2 (2013): 86–97.

47. Global Footprint Network, *The Ecological Footprint Atlas* (2010), http://www.footprintnetwork.org/atlas

48. Sajid Anwar and Choon-Yin Sam, "Is Economic Nationalism Good for the Environment? A Case Study of Singapore," *Asian Studies Review* 36, no. 1 (2012): 39–58.

49. Catherine Mei Ling Wong, "The Developmental State in Ecological Modernization and the Politics of Environmental Framings: The Case of Singapore and Implications for East Asia," *Nature & Culture* 7, no. 1 (2012): 95–119, 111.

50. Ibid., 96.

51. Ministry of Environment and Water Resources, *Singapore Green Plan* (2012), x, 9, 13.

52. Mark Beeson, "The Politics of East Asia's Environmental Crisis: The Coming Environmental Authoritarianism," in *Global Warming and Climate Change: Prospects and Policies in Asia and Europe*, ed. Antonio Marquina Barrio, 378–93 (New York: Palgrave Macmillan, 2010).

53. Darius Nassiry, *Partnerships and Cooperation for Inclusive Green Growth: Asian Approaches to Green Growth and Climate Change Mitigation: Experience, Lessons and Opportunities for Cooperation* (Seoul: Global Green Growth Institute, 2013).

54. Tim Winter, "An Uncomfortable Truth: Air-Conditioning and Sustainability in Asia," *Environment and Planning* 45, no. 3 (2013): 517–31.

55. Rachel Chang, "Air-Condition This Nation," *Straits Times*, April 8, 2013.

56. Edward Grumbine and Jianchu Xu, "Creating a 'Conservation with Chinese Characteristics,'" *Biological Conservation* 144, no. 5 (2011): 1347–55, 1352.

57. W. Tu, "The Ecological Turn in New Confucian Humanism: Implications for China and the World," *Daedalus* 130, no. 3 (2001): 243–65.

58. Shahar Hameiri, "Theorising Regions through Changes in Statehood: Rethinking the Theory and Method of Comparative Regionalism," *Review of International Studies* 39, no. 2 (2013): 313–35.

59. Christian Wirth, "Ocean Governance, Maritime Security and the Consequences of Modernity in Northeast Asia," *Pacific Review* 25, no. 2 (2012): 223–45.

60. Sung Won Kim, David Fidler, and Sumit Ganguly, "Eastphalia Rising?: Asian Influence and the Fate of Human Security," *World Policy Journal* 26, no. 2 (2009): 53–64.

61. Henri d'Orléans, *Around Tonkin and Siam* (London: Chapman & Hall, 1894), 426.

62. Jens Stilhoff Sörensen, *Challenging the Aid Paradigm: Western Currents and Asian Alternatives* (New York: Palgrave Macmillan, 2012).

63. Sara Davies, "The Asian Rejection?: International Refugee Law in Asia," *Australian Journal of Politics & History* 52, no. 4 (2006): 562–75.

64. Alex Bellamy and Mark Beeson, "The Responsibility to Protect in Southeast Asia: Can ASEAN Reconcile Humanitarianism and Sovereignty?," *Asian Security* 6, no. 3 (2010): 262–79.

65. Kelly Gerard, "From the ASEAN People's Assembly to the ASEAN Civil Society Conference: The Boundaries of Civil Society Advocacy," *Contemporary Politics* 19, no. 4 (2013): 411–26.

66. Tom Ginsburg, "Eastphalia as the Perfection of Westphalia," *Indiana Journal of Global Legal Studies* 17, no. 1 (2010): 27–45; Haig Patapan, "Triumph of the West? The Politics of Legitimacy in Asia," *Australian Journal of International Affairs* 66, no. 5 (2012): 567–78.

67. Timo Kivimäki, "East Asian Relative Peace and the ASEAN Way," *International Relations of the Asia Pacific* 11, no. 1 (2011): 57–85.

68. S. S. Tan, "America the Indispensable: Singapore's View of the United States' Engagement in the Asia-Pacific," *Asian Affairs: An American Review* 38, 2011, 156–71.

69. Etel Solingen, "Pax Asiatica versus Bella Levantina: The Foundations of War and Peace in East Asia and the Middle East," *American Political Science Review* 101, no. 4 (2007): 757–80; Stein Tønnesson, "How Historians May Explain the 'East Asian Peace,'" paper presented at the International Studies Association Annual Meeting, San Francisco, 2008.

70. Erik Ringmar, "Performing International Systems: Two East-Asian Alternatives to the Westphalian Order," *International Organization* 66, no. 1 (2012): 1–25; Robert E. Kelly, "A 'Confucian Long Peace' in Pre-Western East Asia?," *European Journal of International Relations* 18, no. 3 (2012): 407–30; David Kang, "Hierarchy and Legitimacy in International Systems: The Tribute System in Early Modern East Asia," *Security Studies* 19, no. 4 (2010): 591–622.

71. Amitav Acharya and Barry Buzan, *Non-Western International Relations Theory: Perspectives on and Beyond Asia* (London: Routledge, 2010).

72. Ringmar, "Performing International Systems: Two East-Asian Alternatives to the Westphalian Order."

73. William L. Swan, "Japan's Intentions for Its Greater East Asia Co-Prosperity Sphere as Indicated in Its Policy Plans for Thailand," *Journal of Southeast Asian Studies* 27, no. 1 (1996): 139–49.
74. Mikael Weissmann, *The East Asian Peace* (New York: Palgrave Macmillan, 2012).
75. Giovanni Capannelli, Jong-Wha Lee, and Peter Petri, "Economic Interdependence in Asia: Developing Indicators for Regional Integration and Cooperation," *Singapore Economic Review* 55, no. 1 (2010): 125–61.

Index

Anderson, Benedict, 26, 37
Anderson, Perry, 26
Asia
 centrality of China, 11
 definition, 8–10, 12–13
 diversity, 9
 integration, 11
 theories, 14, 15–16, 18
Asian Financial Crisis, 49, 59, 75, 76,
 82, 83, 94, 108, 109, 167, 180, 200,
 228n63
Asian Governance Model, 15, 16–19,
 27, 32, 51, 56, 58, 70, 71, 86, 99,
 102, 105, 114, 119, 140, 145, 148,
 151, 160, 180, 183, 195, 204, 205,
 206, 208
 economic development, 56
 patrimonialism, 27, 29
Asian Values, 19, 47, 68, 102
 democracy, 134
authoritarianism, 70, 151

Bambang Yudhoyono, 31
Buddhism, 13, 17, 42–45, 49–50, 60, 144
bureaucracy. See public management
Burma. See Myanmar

Cambodia
 decentralization, 31
 democracy, 107
 economic development, 72
 electoral system, 125
Cambodian People's Party (CPP), 31,
 71, 127

capital punishment. See death penalty
Chiang, Ching-kuo, 24, 58
China. See also Asia: centrality of China
 as Asian model, 12
 democracy, 110, 139–41
 emergence of growth alliance, 70
 federalism, 30
 network governance, 183
 public management, 151
 Tiananmen movement 1989, 39, 45, 83
Christianity, 43, 44, 238n99
citizenship, 81
civil society, 22–24, 46–49, 115–16,
 164–65, 178–85
collaborative governance. See public
 management: networks
Confucianism, 13, 47, 49, 143, 144, 172,
 217n14, 220n72, 221n91, 222n95,
 222n96, 222n97, 223n120, 236n57,
 243n190, 244n5, 244n12, 250n110,
 256n57, 257n70
courts. See law

death penalty, 21–25
decentralization, 30–32, 161–63
 See also federalism
democracy, 19
 Asia and West, 104
 breakdowns, 90, 101
 consolidation, 117–21
 death penalty, 24
 diffusion, 93, 94, 101
 electoral systems, 121–27
 legitimacy, 103

Made in the USA
Coppell, TX
29 September 2021

63186115R00154